THE TECHNIQUE
of
THE MOTION PICTURE
CAMERA

THE LIBRARY
OF COMMUNICATION TECHNIQUES

THE TECHNIQUE OF FILM EDITING
Karel Reisz and Gavin Millar

THE TECHNIQUE OF FILM ANIMATION
John Halas and Roger Manvell

THE TECHNIQUE OF FILM MUSIC
John Huntley and Roger Manvell

THE TECHNIQUE OF FILM AND TELEVISION MAKE-UP
Vincent J-R. Kehoe

THE TECHNIQUE OF TELEVISION PRODUCTION
Gerald Millerson

THE TECHNIQUE OF THE SOUND STUDIO
Alec Nisbett

THE TECHNIQUE OF DOCUMENTARY FILM
PRODUCTION
W. Hugh Baddeley

THE TECHNIQUE OF THE TELEVISION CAMERAMAN
Peter Jones

THE TECHNIQUE OF SPECIAL EFFECTS
CINEMATOGRAPHY
Raymond Fielding

THE TECHNIQUE OF TELEVISION ANNOUNCING
Bruce Lewis

THE TECHNIQUE OF THE MOTION PICTURE CAMERA
H. Mario Raimondo Souto

THE TECHNIQUE OF EDITING 16 mm FILM
John Burder

THE TECHNIQUE OF THE

MOTION PICTURE CAMERA

by

H. MARIO RAIMONDO SOUTO

COMMUNICATION ARTS BOOKS
Hastings House, Publishers,
New York

© FOCAL PRESS LIMITED 1969

SBN 8038 7088 4

Manuscript translated by
H. M. Grierson-Rodriguez

First Edition 1967
Second Revised and Enlarged Edition 1969

*Printed and bound in Great Britain
by Page Bros. (Norwich) Ltd.*

CONTENTS

To my Mother

INTRODUCTION TO THE REVISED EDITION

MANY innovations have appeared in world markets on this book's subject matter in the year and a half since the first edition. Besides updating the material, this second edition penetrates deeper both into the camera's design, as well as into its evaluation, application, servicing and related techniques.

Thus, more construction details of the various components are given, the operating principles of others are explained and historical notes are given on their development.

This edition also includes more information on various techniques in which the motion picture camera plays an important role. The basic concepts of equipment for time-lapse cinematography, cineradiology and kinescopic recordings are described in the corresponding sections.

It was also considered useful to provide descriptions of the techniques for inspecting the camera and checking breakdowns and troubles. The best methods developed by manufacturers and scientific institutions are described, as well as some simplified tests which the cinematographer himself can carry out where there are no specialised workshops at hand.

The camera is of course dovetailed with motion picture production and direction. Introductions into those subjects are included, showing how the choice of equipment affects production costs, and giving pointers on film language for the benefit of operators when they are faced with the twofold responsibility of also directing the film.

An attempt is also made to humanize what was previously an exclusively technical description, by adding historical notes on famous items of equipment used for shooting films which are now classics. These notes highlight the relationship between man and instrument, which has been typical of this profession.

Montevideo, Uruguay, Nov. 1968   H. MARIO RAIMONDO SOUTO

INTRODUCTION

OF the many books written on the seventh art, very few deal with the techniques of professional film making, and in these the space devoted specifically to the instrument that made motion pictures possible is very scant indeed.

Most of today's well-established directors of photography, camera operators, assistants, and newsreel cameramen have attained an inside knowledge of their equipment in a manner similar to mediaeval apprenticeship, that is, after mastering each phase in turn, by step-by-step promotions in their scale of responsibilities. Continuous hard work and the instruction of more experienced colleagues eventually give them a thorough familiarity with the more readily available instruments. But even the most highly reputed cameramen are often unacquainted with instruments used by colleagues abroad, or with facilities provided by foreign manufacturers.

Perhaps even more frustrating than this was the fact that there was no concentrated and readily available source of information to the budding cameraman on the instruments he would handle, nor on the best techniques for operating them.

The increasing development of international co-productions requires many cinematographers to travel abroad where they face equipment with which they have had no experience. Moreover, the mushroom growth of low budget and "new wave" production units, incorporating a large proportion of new and young blood into the industry, has increased the number of those interested in learning thoroughly the techniques of this branch of the cinema.

Television, too, has created an enormous demand for filmed material for filling time-gaps and this, in turn, has considerably increased the need for skilled operators. The 16 mm gauge has become professional to such a degree that camera makers have concentrated their attention on this medium and have come out with a succession of new instruments to meet this specific demand.

A specialized source of information on the subject was therefore urgently needed. The author hopes this volume fills the gap. His intention in writing it was to provide readers in the field of TV and motion pictures with a source of information, comprehensive and concise, on the professional cinematographer's main tool— the camera.

For many reasons, specifically scientific instruments have been left out. Their operating principles are generally totally different from standard cameras. They are used only by very few scientific investigators and the mechanisms and characteristics of many are carefully guarded secrets.

This book gathers together widely scattered information and the know-how of experienced cinematographers for the benefit of newcomers to the art, and provides them with a descriptive roster of the cameras most extensively used in Europe and the American continent. It is hoped that this work will help all those interested in becoming acquainted with the "innards" of the instruments, and in obtaining practical hints on their operation and maintenance. The experience of skilled cinematographers, as well as the author's, have been summarized in the technical chapters as well as in the final chapter on shooting techniques.

However, this book is not intended only for cinematographers. The author trusts that other specialists in the film production industry—producers, directors, laboratory workers, specialized camera mechanics, documentary film makers and others, will find useful information to apply to their specific tasks, and that they will thereby derive a wider and more exact comprehension of the industry's basic instrument.

The author takes pleasure in acknowledging the generous contributions from equipment manufacturers mentioned in the text: *Arnold & Richter A.G.; Arriflex Corporation of America*; *Bach Auricon Inc.; Beckman & Whitley Inc.; Bell & Howell Company; Consortium Pathé; Eclair International Diffusion; Etablissements André Debrie, Federal Manufacturing & Engineering Corp.; Houston Fearless Corp.; James A. Sinclair Co.; John M. Wall Inc.; Mitchell Camera Corp.; Producers Sales Corp.; Paillard S.A.; Rank Precision Industries Ltd.; The Animation Equipment Inc.; S.D.S. Aerospace Systems; Technicolor Corporation; Vinten Ltd.*

They have all kindly provided technical information on their products as well as most of the illustrations in this volume. Special acknowledgement must be extended to *Messrs. F & B/ Ceco; Camera Service Center; S.O.S. Photo-Cine-Optics Inc.; Unitalia Film and A.U.R.Y.T.C.;* as well as to *Warner Brothers, Pathé Laboratories Inc.* and *Twentieth Century Fox Studios,* who

11

were kind enough to give the author access to many of their facilities and equipment and to supply all the information that was asked of them.

Thanks are also due to the American Society of Cinematographers for the use of reference material in the *American Cinematographer Manual* and the *American Cinematographer Magazine*.

Finally the author wishes to thank *Mr. Daniel Arijon* for his valuable help in the preparation of several sections, to *Mr. Carlos Cabrera* for cooperation in preparing the art work, and to the translator *Mr. H. M. Grierson-Rodriguez* for his careful work and useful suggestions in drawing up this English language version.

Montevideo, Uruguay, 1967   H. MARIO RAIMONDO SOUTO

1

THE MOTION PICTURE CAMERA

THE motion picture camera employs the basic principles of still photography. The fundamental difference lies in the fact that while the still camera is designed only to print a single image on the film at each exposure, the motion picture camera is built to effect multiple successive exposures, thus accomplishing a photographic breakdown of motion.

To achieve such results, a complicated precision mechanism must be included inside the darkened chamber where the image is formed on the film. This mechanism is placed within a strong and light-tight, but easily accessible, body.

Until 1920, camera bodies were built mostly of wood and the mechanisms of bronze, with the key parts in steel. But the characteristics of these materials greatly impaired performance, since ambient atmospheric conditions and rough and continuous wear and tear reduced their efficiency considerably.

Nowadays, manufacturers have obviated such difficulties by building camera bodies in special pressed steel or aluminium alloy, which provide great strength combined with light weight. Light-excluding problems have been solved by means of sealing strips and special-action hinges and locks. Mechanical wear has been eliminated by making moving parts with special alloy steels or fibre. Moreover, the shape of the camera has been improved, as well as its appearance, by sophisticated finish on outside surfaces.

Mechanical Unit

The mechanical principle of the modern motion picture camera has been developed from that of those earlier models which blazed the trail for today's cinematography. To make its study easier, the complete system can be broken down into two mechanisms, each with an individual task but with a common purpose.

The first mechanism has the task of drawing the unexposed film (or raw stock) from the storage chamber, called a *magazine*, and after exposure, driving it into a similar magazine for exposed film. This mechanism runs continuously.

The other mechanism is an intermittent one whose function is to arrest sections of film, called frames, one at a time, behind an opening or *aperture*, on which the camera lens focuses an image of an object in the outside world. Operating in combination with this intermittent mechanism, a *shutter*, placed in front of the film obscures the light from the lens each time the film is drawn down to the next frame.

Continuous drive

Since the intermittent drive alternately holds the film stationary and moves it rapidly downwards, it would be impossible to feed the film directly into it without snatching and tearing. To avoid this, slack loops of film are formed above and below the intermittent mechanism (often called a *gate*), so that the intermittent and continuous drives can be combined.

The continuous drive of the film is effected by means of sprocket wheels whose teeth penetrate the film perforations, thus causing it to move smoothly and steadily. The steadiness of the film flow is assisted by having an adequate diameter of sprocket wheel, designed so that several teeth simultaneously penetrate the perforations of the film wrapped round it.

Moreover, to cope with the constant and continuous action, in which the teeth penetrate into and withdraw from the perforations at a given angle, the teeth are given a tapered rounded shape so as to avoid damage to the perforation edges. Large sprockets generally have 32 teeth (or even up to 40 for wide-screen film) and run at 180 r.p.m. for 24 frames per second. In cameras provided with more than one sprocket wheel, each wheel may have 8, 12 or 16 teeth and run at much higher working speeds. The size of the sprocket is also determined by the camera design and how the film travels. Most sprocket wheels are provided with a stripper near the edge of the teeth to keep the film from wrapping round the sprocket if the teeth should accidentally hook up the perforations. Specially located rollers guide the films towards the other sections of the mechanism.

14

Fig. 1. Bell & Howell's 32-teeth large sprocket with pressure rollers and strippers.

Adequate penetration of the teeth into the perforations is ensured by pressure rollers, which do not press the film, but merely prevent the perforations from slipping out, or from meshing less teeth than were originally designed. The pressure rollers contact the film only in the area of the perforations and not at the central part where the image is formed, to avoid damaging this surface. Pressure rollers are designed to open up so that the film can be easily threaded. Unless the rollers are replaced in their working position the camera access door cannot be closed. This avoids damage to the film and mechanism if the roller is incorrectly reclosed or if the film is not properly threaded. Some camera manufacturers have introduced devices for opening all pressure rollers simultaneously when working with more than one sprocket, especially in the case of hand held cameras used by newsreel cameramen, for whom fast and sure threading is essential.

Within the camera, film travels from one magazine chamber to the other by one of two methods. The first method, whereby the film travels lengthwise in the same plane all the time, is known as *single plane travel*. This means that the magazine chambers have to be in the same plane, too, but when working with large film loads the magazines must be placed outside the camera body itself, and keeping them in the same plane adds considerably to the bulk of the instrument. Single plane travel is used by most camera manufacturers in America as well as by some in Europe. It simplifies camera construction and allows for easy loading. Continuous drive is effected either with only one combined-action sprocket working simultaneously on top and below or two smaller-diameter sprockets placed for feed and take-up respectively.

The other method is known as *three plane travel* and was first used by the André Debrie company when trying to reduce the size of the camera. To attain this, they placed the magazine chambers within the camera, side by side and thus in two different planes. By this method the film leaves the feed chamber in one plane, passes to another plane on going through the film gate and into a third plane when being drawn to the take-up chamber. Three plane travel was extensively used by European makers (Debrie, Askania, Eclair, Prevost, Vinten, etc) including the Russians (Rodina) because it enables the camera to be made smaller and permits the use of separate magazines. However it complicates the mechanism and makes loading difficult. A simplified form of this method uses coaxial magazines.

Fig. 2. The three-plane travel as in Debrie Parvo cameras. Note the complicated film path from supply to take-up magazine. (1) Supply magazine, (2) supply sprocket, (3) film gate, (4) take-up sprocket, (5) take-up magazine.

Intermittent mechanism

The intermittent drive is the most delicate of all the components in the camera's mechanism. As explained above, its function is to expose frames of film in rapid succession behind the aperture or

16

Fig. 3. Diagram shows the shape of the sprocket teeth which are tapered and rounded to avoid damage to the film perforations.

film gate. This is achieved by means of a series of coordinated motions which can be roughly broken down as follows:

(i)   three-quarter inch downward pull (for 35 mm film) effected by a shuttle with one or more claws which have penetrated the film perforations. This places the film frame behind the aperture;

(ii) retraction of the claws from the perforations. Immediately afterwards the shuttle starts its upward motion, while the film frame is held steady behind the aperture;

Fig. 4. Detail of displacement pattern of two different types of shuttle. (A) Typical 16 mm camera claw shuttle; (B) shuttle and pin registration system; (1) shuttle; (2) film; (3) pilot pin.

17

(iii) after the shuttle's upward displacement is completed, the claws penetrate the film perforations and start the cycle over again.

Synchronized with the intermittent motion of the shuttle, another mechanism completes this operation, ensuring the exact registration of the photographic impression by holding the film steady during the period it remains motionless in order to record the image.

Once the film has been placed in position by the shuttle claws and these are withdrawn to start the cycle over again, one or two *register pins* or *pilot pins* immediately penetrate the perforations close to the aperture. Their purpose is to steady the film completely so that the image is printed on a steady surface, free of jerks or vibrations.

But the pilot or register pin also adjusts the placing of the film in relation to the aperture. In mechanisms where the pilot pin moves towards the perforation, the latter is not always in its exact position. Therefore, in many instruments the pin is cone-shaped. As it completes its travel, the perforation edge bears on the pin's surface and the film shifts to its correct position. The pin's travel is designed so that it remains completely motionless while the film is being exposed. All this is effected at very high speed within the short lapse afforded by the next action of the shuttle and that of another mechanism called the shutter which we shall study further below.

Another system for registration known as the *fixed pilot pin* was introduced in the early 1900s by Arthur Newman, from an idea suggested by one of his mechanics, called Woodhead. It works on the principle of a register pin fixed on the film gate at a side of the aperture; registration is effected when the film seats on the aperture plate and is kept steady by one or two pilot pins penetrating the perforations. This method depends on a special movement of the film instead of the pilot pin(s). The fixed pilot pin was used on all Newman Sinclair cameras and was improved upon by the Bell & Howell Company for their studio cameras. Because of its effective registering and minimum wear, it is still used on many special-effects cameras.

Registration devices may act on both or on only one side of the film. When they work on both sides, horizontal accuracy is attained by the pin on one side while that on the other side effects vertical registration. Pilot pins working on only one side of the film effect vertical registration, while horizontal correction is effected by side pressure devices mounted in the film gate. This method is used on many 35 mm cameras, and is practically standard on 16 mm equipment.

Pilot pin systems are used mainly on studio cameras, owing to their complex mechanism, but they give an image steadiness of 0·001 mm. On comparing this value with the 0·02 mm steadiness obtained by cameras without register pin, we understand why images taken with cameras with register pin show a much better

Fig. 5. Typical characteristics of eccentric in professional standard camera.

relief and definition and can be combined in multiple exposures with no apparent blurring round the edges.

The design of the intermittent mechanism has undergone many modifications since the primitive devices constructed by Lumière and Edison. Most intermittent drives and many moving register pins work on the basis of an eccentric. Figs. 5 and 6 give some idea of the variety of eccentrics in use and the many different ways in which they are made to work and are combined with other mechanical methods.

A study of today's shuttle and register pin movements leads to the conclusion that the design of any such mechanism is very closely connected to the individual personality of each camera manufacturer. Consequently, to identify each system one must refer to the make and model of the camera using it.

MITCHELL CAM AND GEAR MOVEMENT. The intermittent drive designed by the Mitchell Camera Corp. for their Standard, High Speed and 16 mm camera (not SSR 16 model) is based on the properties of the *Trezel* cam to operate within a frame which

19

Fig. 6. *Top.* Action of eccentric pin on a shuttle frame, in a Traid manufactured camera, similar to the Eyemo. (1) Cam, (2) shuttle, (3) shuttle claws, (4) register pin, (5) aperture plate. *Bottom.* Use of a three-sided eccentric working on a similar principle upon the intermittent mechanism of the Filmo camera.

20

makes up the shuttle. The upward or downward movement of the shuttle is achieved by the displacement of a fixed shaft along a groove in the shuttle.

The shaft of the cam is also the shaft of a gear wheel which meshes into another of the same dimensions and in its turn, drives the register pin movements. The object of the latter is to drive the pins into and then withdraw them from the film perforations, under the action of a second cam on a frame which is part of a sliding shaft.

The whole mechanism achieves two objects. First, an intermittent shuttle motion whereby four claws (two on each side) penetrate the film perforations and pull the film down by the height of one frame.

In co-ordination with this, two register pins (one on each side), actuated by the registration mechanism, penetrate the perforations when the film is motionless, and thus ensure its steadiness during the exposure period.

MITCHELL ECCENTRIC MOVEMENT. When sound filming requirements called for a noiseless camera, the Mitchell Corp. engineers had to change their cam and gear mechanism for a less noisy one but working with the same degree of precision. The new design of mechanism was introduced about 1930 in the NC model and incorporated later in the Studio BNC and recently in S35-R (Mark II) and BNCR. The outstanding feature of the new mechanism was that gears were reduced to a minimum thus eliminating a large portion of the noise so that scenes could be shot with direct sound recording, without any danger that the microphone would pick up any camera noise, at least at medium distances.

Figure 7 shows the main shaft of the unit (1), running at a number of revolutions equivalent to the film speed, and provided with an eccentric (2) at one of its ends. The eccentric is provided with a shaft which ends up in a cube shaped block placed inside the frame of the pull down arm (3). The right hand side of the frame is connected to the housing (4) of the eccentric by means of a rod (5). The left hand side end of the housing is provided with a part jutting out which operates in a housing (6) built into the plate of the whole unit.

When the main shaft (1) rotates, the housing (4) of the eccentric is moved, providing an eliptical displacement of the frame (3) by means of the shaft (7). At the opposite end of the frame where

21

Fig. 7. Simplified diagram of the operation of the eccentric mechanism in Mitchell NC, BNC and BNCR cameras. (1) Main shaft, (2) eccentric, (3) pull-down **arm**, (4) eccentric housing, (5) connecting rod, (6) housing, (7) shaft, (8) operating **rod**.

the claws are placed, a magnified elliptical travel is obtained which drives the film down the film gate. The housing (4) also starts the register pin moving by causing an elliptical travel at the bottom end of the rod (8), which is provided with a frame at its top end to drive the long horizontal rod of the register pins to and fro.

This shuttle mechanism ensures maximum registration: in the first place, it is provided with four claws (two on each side) which

Fig. 8. *Left*. Mitchell cam and gear movement. *Right*. Mitchell eccentric movement.

22

give fast and even film travel; two register pins are used, the non-sound track pin fully fits the perforation hole, while the other fits the perforation hole in the vertical plane but is smaller horizontally to allow for film shrinkage.

All parts of this mechanism are machined and lapped to 0·0001 in. accuracy. Register pins are ground lapped and polished to 0·0005 in. accuracy, this being also the tolerance value estimated for the shuttle travel.

BELL & HOWELL SHUTTLE & PILOT PIN MOVEMENTS. The intermittent drive of this American-manufactured camera was created some fifty years ago by *Mr. A. S. Howell.* A special feature of this mechanism is its ingenious fixed pilot pins, that is to say, two small registration pins jutting out from, and forming an integral part of the aperture plate. During its vertical travel, the film is not pressed but is allowed to run freely driven by the shuttle claws. When the shuttle completes its vertical displacement, a pressure plate seats the film onto the aperture plate and the fixed pilot pins penetrate two perforations.

After the frame is exposed the pressure plate is withdrawn and the film is free again to repeat the cycle.

Another characteristic of this mechanism is that shuttle, pilot pins and aperture plate are all contained within a single interchangeable assembly called "Unit I", which is used in all standard B & H Model 2709 cameras. It can run at speeds up to 32 frames per second (f.p.s.), but can be easily interchanged with another, similar unit specially designed for high speeds, thus making the camera capable of operating at a wide range of speeds.

BELL & HOWELL ECCENTRIC MOVEMENTS. For their Filmo and Eyemo cameras, the Bell & Howell Company designed a new drive mechanism located on the same plane as the aperture plate, that is to say, at right angles to the movements studied above. The intermittent motion is obtained by the rotation of a Trezel eccentric within a shuttle frame with sliding shafts. The penetration or withdrawal of the shuttle claws into or from the film perforations, is effected by the rotation of a disc of unequal thickness acting upon the shuttle.

In some special models, this assembly is complemented by a pilot pin fixed at the side of the aperture to provide greater film steadiness.

NOISELESS DRIVE SYSTEM. About 1939/40, Robert Stevens, Charles Miller, D. B. Clark and G. Laube were working on the design for the 20th Century Fox camera. In connection with the intermittent mechanism for it, they successfully carried out research and trials to achieve the elimination of noise at its source. Their investigations were aimed at reducing the weight and size of the parts with a fast shuttling travel in order to adjust speed-increase and decrease values, thus minimizing vibrations which produce most of the noise. These concepts were applied to a movement which operates as follows: an eccentric with a very accurately designed shape is provided with a pin which drives a

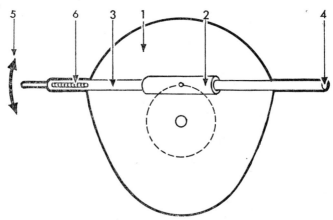

Fig. 9. Noiseless mechanism of the 20th Century Fox camera. (1) Eccentric, (2) sliding sleeve, (3) pull-down arm, (4) pivot, (5) sliding travel, (6) pull-down pin.

sliding sleeve; within this sleeve there is an arm at one end of which the take down pin is held; the pin moves forwards and backwards as it bears on the edge of the eccentric, while the arm, provided with a pivot at its other end, produces the pull down as it slides within the sleeve. At the same time, a scroll cam acts upon two register pins which hold the film steady behind the aperture.

The extremely silent operation of this movement, eliminating noise at its source, made any form of cumbersome and heavy blimping unnecessary; unfortunately, other manufacturers did not adopt this efficient and practical mechanism.

ADJUSTABLE REGISTER PIN SYSTEM. One of the most interesting design improvements of recent years is that achieved by the French engineers *Coutant* and *Mathot*: a device for adjusting

24

the stroke of the register pin. This system was applied to the mechanism of the Eclair Camé 300 Reflex, and it comprises a lever which effects a fractional displacement of the position of the register pin by means of an adjustable bearing. The value of the

Fig. 10. Diagram of Eclair's adjustable register pin system. (1) Calibrated scale; (2) register pin displacement; (3) shuttle; (4) main sprocket; (5) lever; (6) adjusting bearing; (7) oscillating or swivel bearing; (8) film.

displacement can be read on a scale, and it is allowed for by an oscillating bearing. Thus, the distance between the register pin and the shuttle claws is adjusted according to the pitch of the film perforations. Such adjustments bring about not only maximum image steadiness but also minimum movement noise, as well as an appreciable reduction in maintenance.

Early in 1963, The Mitchell Camera Corporation brought out a device for the intermittent mechanism of their NC and BNC cameras, which achieved the same end, although based on a different principle. They called it the "vari-stroke control".

The adjustable register pin is an important contribution towards solving the problem of film steadiness in warm climates where film tends to shrink.

Film gate

This is the part of the camera in which raw stock is placed behind the aperture in order to print the image. On passing through

25

the gate, the film tends to steady its run in order to reach the aperture without vibrations. This steadying is effected by side pressure devices which control the film's travel and help to obtain registration of the take, specially in cameras without register pins.

In different cameras the film gate is built either all straight, or partially curved, or with a curve only at the place where the shuttle claws act. In some instruments the film gate is very long

Fig. 11. Aperture plate of Mitchell Camera. Note bottom curve where shuttle claws operate, as well as two holes below and on both sides of aperture where register pins operate. The part jutting out is a gelatin filter holder.

(up to ten frames) while in others it is half that length. Such differences depend on the shape of the camera and where the continuous drive is located.

The main elements of the film gate are undoubtedly the interior surfaces of two separate parts, the aperture and pressure plates. The aperture plate is of course the one with the aperture in it and on which the emulsion side of the film bears in its travel. For the latter it is essential that this surface should be very carefully polished so as to avoid the least damage to the emulsion. To this end all parts in contact with the film are thickly chrome plated. Moreover, contact at the central (emulsion bearing) section of the film is reduced by building this part with a strip at both edges

26

jutting out slightly so that the film should bear only at the edges. The pressure plate is the other inner face of the gate which presses lightly on the film base (rear face) in order that it should be flat when placed behind the aperture. Although its surface is in contact with the film base and not with the emulsion, manufacturers tried to reduce friction to a minimum here also, using rollers and slides. The pressure plate of some cameras press the film intermittently, only during the period of exposure, thus reducing fricttion appreciably and improving registration.

To facilitate threading and to afford easy access, some film gates are made so that the pressure plate is hinged by a special device to the aperture plate and opens up backwards. Thus the operator can quickly check that the gate is clean and brush off the emulsion deposits frequently built-up there.

To adjust the instrument to requirements of special shooting processes, the aperture of 35 mm cameras must often be changed from standard (sound) to silent, or panoramic, or "scope" apertures. To facilitate this, manufacturers frequently provide for interchanging apertures, either the film gate complete or only the aperture plate.

Many cameras are provided with a slot on the front of the film gate to take filters or masks. This concept has been further refined in cameras like the Mitchell or the Newall by adding, besides the filter slot, a device with masks which can be regulated from the outside and which up to a certain extent controls the size of the aperture, by blocking the image formed on the film plane.

Shutter

The shutter mechanism is synchronized with the intermittent drive, so that each frame of the film, after exposure to the light rays, is obscured from them while it is being pulled down and the next frame is taking its place. A simple shutter takes the form of a rotating disc occupying the minimum space available between the film and the lens. The opening of this disc is so situated that the film is covered while it is in motion. In different cameras this opening is given angles ranging from 120° to 230°, the larger angles corresponding to faster pull-down movements.

Several camera makers have built their instruments with a large diameter shutter with its shaft placed as far away from the aperture as possible, to reduce exposure time, while maintaining a considerably wide shutter opening angle.

There are other shuttering systems besides the rotating disc.

One is the *guillotine*, which consists of a small plate travelling up and down in front of the aperture, under the action of an eccentric co-ordinated with the shuttle mechanism. The disadvantage of this system is that exposure time cannot be regulated. Another type is the "focal plane" shutter used only on the Akeley camera; it consists of a narrow cylinder band running round the camera body, which is also cylinder shaped. Its characteristics allow for very wide openings.

Some cameras provide shutters with openings which can be adjusted by means of a control placed on the outside, from maximum angle to zero. This affords the camera operator a high degree of control of film exposure without utilizing the lens diaphragm, and it facilitates the shooting of fast moving subjects.

The shutter opening control is generally a lever placed either behind or at the side of the camera, sliding over a calibrated scale. Some improved camera models complement the reading on this scale with a miniature reproduction of the shutter which is synchronized to the main shutter mechanism. It reproduces the actual shutter opening and its position relative to the camera aperture, at all times.

As demands for a system of focusing and framing through the taking lens became insistent, manufacturers designed a new type of shutter rotating on an axis at an angle of 45° to the plane of the film and the lens. The side facing the lens is silvered, so that when it is in the closed position, the image formed by the lens is reflected into a magnifying optical system. This allows for framing and focusing through the taking lens itself. Further details of this device, known as a reflex viewfinder, will be found in the section on framing and focusing devices (p. 38).

Recording unit

Cameras designed for simultaneous image and sound recording are provided with a unit for recording the sound track on the film itself, either by the magnetic, the optical process or both. The inclusion of this unit demands the incorporation of means, such as compensating rollers and an inertia flywheel, to counteract the effect of the intermittent movement of the film and thus ensure the steadiness of the film's travel through the sound gate. The recording unit is installed on or very near the flywheel; and may consist of either two magnetic heads (one for recording and the other for reproduction) or, in the case of optical recording, a device to project the modulated beam produced by the galvano-

meter. The recording head must be placed so that the standard distance from image and sound is maintained between the aperture and the point where sound recording is effected.

Motor

In most professional-type motion picture cameras the mechanism is driven by an electric motor. Some portable cameras are spring driven, with a capacity of about fifty feet of film in 35 mm cameras, and about twenty-two feet in 16 mm cameras, each time the spring is wound.

As the electric motor is the principal source of power for the film camera, its design has been developed so that it will operate the mechanism at a very constant rate, with the minimum effort. Such steady running is essential in order to maintain the exposure of the film with a high degree of constancy. Other vital characteristics are:

(i)   instantaneous start-up at rated speed,

(ii) capacity for running without excessive heating,

(iii) capacity for continuous and constant operation.

Such characteristics vary according to the type of motor. There are three types of motor widely used for camera drive:

Fig. 12. Kinotechnique motor for Cameflex with transistorized speed regulation. This is typical of the light weight and precision provided by modern techniques.

Fig. 13. Mitchell variable speed motor which is detachable from the camera and incorporates its own speed regulator in the form of a rheostat.

(i)   the synchronous motor,
(ii) the interlocked motor,
(iii) the variable speed motor.

Synchronous and interlock motors are generally provided with a soundproof covering to make them completely noiseless. Their main characteristics are:

(i)   constant speed,
(ii) noiseless running,
(iii) capability of precise synchronization with similar motors driving sound recorders or background projectors.

The speed of synchronous motors is necessarily in direct ratio to the frequency of the alternating current fed to it. They are generally bulky and consequently heavy and are usually employed when direct sound recording must be effected while shooting. Their capacity for synchronizing with other equipment driven by the same power source results from their design and construction characteristics; the induction coil of such motors produces a

30

magnetic field in the armature; thus if two motors are adequately connected their armatures will rotate synchronized with such magnetic field, just the same as if their shafts were mechanically coupled.

Normally, synchronous motors work with 3-phase, 220 v. 50 or 60 cycles per second (c.p.s.), AC. However, there are single-phase, 110 v. models. When shooting at the studio, the power source is obtained directly from public utility line, or own generating plant, but when this is not available, from portable generators. In the latter event, it is essential that the frequency of the AC generated should be perfectly constant in order to keep the camera speed steady.

Interlock and synchronous motors have similar characteristics. At present the former are used only for back projection shots and for focus remote control.

Induction motors are also used by some camera makers. Their speed is constant but they are not synchronized to the frequency of the AC feeding them. Their drive power is quite high in relation to their size. Generally they are designed to run at 24 f.p.s. only, and they are used with many cameras for direct sound recording.

The variable speed motor is noisier, since it is not provided with sound proofing protection, and it is used for shooting without sound recording. It incorporates a special rheostat which regulates the operating speed from a minimum of four frames per second, to fifty or more f.p.s.

Certain models also include a tachometer to indicate the speed at which the camera is running.

Special models have recently been marketed, utilizing transistor systems in order to ensure that speed is maintained constant to a high degree. These motors are combined with others incorporating signal generators inserted in their circuits, and are employed in new methods for synchronizing image and sound.

Motors are separate units from the camera and can be easily mounted on it, and easily interchanged. They generally incorporate the starting switch, as well as a socket for the feed cable. They run with either single, two-, or three-phase, AC, or DC, at voltages varying according to make and model, ranging from 8, 12, 16 or 24 volts for DC from battery source, or 90, 110 or 220/230 v. with AC for studio running.

SPRING DRIVE. Spring (or mechanical) motors work on similar principles to the drive of gramophones early this century. They are generally built into the camera body and operate under a spring (or two in some cameras) held in tension by a complex gear set. Speed is regulated by a special governor working by centrifugal force. The governor can be adjusted from the outside by means of a dial, in order to select the most convenient speed, and its

Fig. 14. Method of fitting the spring drive in the Bell & Howell Filmo. Note how the shape of the camera is governed by the design of the various mechanisms.

action on the mechanism does not allow speed variations greater than 4 per cent of the pre-set working speed.

The spring is wound by turning a handle, which can be quite long in some cameras, or a collapsible, non-rotating winding key. In some instruments like the Cameraflex and the Kohbac Automat, the spring drive is an easily installed separate unit. Nowadays, spring drive tends to be discontinued because of its excessive weight and bulk, as against modern lightweight, midget electric motors.

Camera controls

The camera controls and indicating instruments are the elements which enable the camera to be operated, and they provide information on how it is running. These components are located either behind or at the side of the camera, and they are of great help in handling the camera properly while it is operating. The main controls are:

Starting switch

The starting switch is installed either on the motor itself or on the feed cable. In general it consists of an adequately dimensioned

32

toggle switch, with protection devices to avoid accidents while handling the camera. Spring-driven cameras are started by pressing on a push-button which releases the mechanism lock.

External focusing control

In most studio cameras, focusing is effected by means of controls geared to the lens focus ring. Such controls are calibrated to a high degree of accuracy, and they are located for easy use by the assistant camera operator.

External iris control

Besides the external focusing control, some European cameras are provided with a similar device to adjust the diaphragm without touching the lens. This control uses interchangeable plates and can be applied to any type of lens.

Variable shutter control

As explained above, the shutter opening control is effected by means of a lever sliding over a scale which can be calibrated each ten degrees from maximum to minimum openings (as in the Mitchell and Newall cameras) or with special calibration (Debrie cameras).

Automatic dissolve control

This is an additional feature provided on the most up-to-date studio cameras. It comprises two push-buttons which close or open the shutter automatically thus producing a dissolve or fade effect at the beginning or at the end of a take, over a length of film of about five feet.

Footage and exposed-frame counters

These are small counters connected to the main movements, which indicate the amount of exposed film. The frame counter is used for special work requiring such information. In some cameras the footage counter is of a simpler type connected to a lever inside the film storage magazine, which bears on the roll of film.

In some studio cameras the counters have their own light source to facilitate readings when the lighting level is low. Counters are provided with a knob to turn them to zero when changing the film magazine.

33

B

Built-in telemeter (range-finder)

This is an accessory to the focusing control whereby the camera assistant can obtain exact focusing without using a measuring tape.

Magazine footage counter

This is a dial indicator showing the amount of exposed film and the amount remaining in the feed magazine chamber. It is very useful since it allows immediate readings of raw stock and exposed film, data which the camera assistant must fill in on his photographic report sheets.

Exposure speed indicator

The working speed of the camera is controlled by the electric motor itself (if it is a variable-speed motor), and is indicated by the rheostat markings, as well as by a detachable speed indicator. In some cameras, this speed indicator or tachometer is built in, while in others it is coupled to the motor. Their scales are calibrated in frames per second.

Automatic safety switch

Many cameras designed for direct sound recording, run so noiselessly that if any mishap should occur inside (oversize loop, film running off the track) the operator will not realise it. Therefore an automatic device is provided whereby the slight pressure of the miscarried film acts upon an adequately placed plate which stops the camera automatically. In some cameras, this is complemented by a warning light on the outside. The automatic safety switch is used in the best studio cameras or sound-on-film cameras.

Spirit level

This small item is of great use to the operator when mounting the camera. Since the camera's position must be changed frequently for shooting from different angles, the adjustment of the tripod or mounting element must be modified, and consequently it is essential to check the level of the camera. These instruments are located either in front of or behind the camera, and they can be either spirit-levels or oil-filled levels.

Viewing system

The viewfinder is an optical system working in combination with the camera lenses and providing the operator with an exact view of the image being recorded on the film. Many years hard work have been put into the search for a viewing system which would show an image of the field as framed by the aperture and taken by the shooting lens.

The first such cameras were built in France. Framing was obtained through the thickness of the film or by withdrawing it from the camera aperture and substituting a piece of translucent material. When camera manufacturing crossed the Atlantic, American manufacturers introduced the camera side-framing viewfinder working independently of the taking lens. Thus the camera was for the first time able to move, and could be panned and travelled. This improvement was soon widely accepted by all cinematographers, and Europeans immediately started to manufacture their cameras with a side viewfinder, since the new system saved time and made for far greater convenience with all types of framing. The main European viewfinder conceived on these lines was the Orthoviseur developed by Debrie for their Parvo T and Super Parvo cameras. With the progress of research, the viewing and focusing system of the modern camera has become more and more elaborate. The systems most widely used at present are the following.

Side viewfinder

This is the type used in some portable camera models. It is fixed to the side of the camera and is carefully centred in relation to the camera aperture. It affords an image obtained through an optical system of small lenses, which is a replica of the taking lens. Some cameras have these viewing lenses mounted on a small turret so that, by displacing the tube's eyepiece along a calibrated scale, the operator can correct for parallax, which is the angle formed by the different viewing positions of the tube and the taking lens.

Monitoring viewfinder

This viewfinder is known as a monitor since its work is complementary to a focusing and framing device through the taking lens. It is also placed at the side of the camera and produces an upright image correct from left to right. The size of the image is $1\frac{7}{8} \times 3\frac{5}{16}$ in. (47×84 mm) which allows more than one person to look at it at the same time.

The image obtained is projected by a short focal length optical system (consisting of a large lens and a porro prism) upon a

35

ground glass. The size of this image is controlled by means of separate masks which are inserted in a slot, or by four masking (or graticule) lines which are adjusted externally by means of knobs, so as to reproduce the field actually taken by the camera lens. The graticule system also allows the operator to see what is happening just outside the effective field, so that he can prevent unwanted objects appearing in the picture.

Fig. 15. Mitchell monitoring viewfinder. The two knobs are calibrated and control the variable frame lines which reproduce the exact field covered by the camera lens.

Other characteristics of the monitor viewfinder are automatic focusing control, and easy panning while keeping the operator's head away from the camera and with both eyes open, as well as checking the field covered by the various lenses. These range in focal length from 25 to 152 mm in the 35 mm gauge camera, and from 13 to 75 mm (approx) in the 16 mm gauge model.

Among well known monitor viewfinders are those made by the Mitchell Corp., as described above. Messrs. Bach-Auricon, Maurer, Bell & Howell, and Maier-Hancock have also produced monitor viewfinder models, devised specially for 16 mm cameras.

Viewfinder through taking lens

The operator requires the image framed in the viewfinder to be exactly the same as the one being recorded on the film, and this necessitates a focusing and framing device free from the parallax problems encountered with side viewfinders. The search for these qualities led to the development of a mechanical device for framing and focusing, which displaces the film from behind the taking lens and places a ground glass in its stead, on which the image is projected.

Two important manufacturers adopted this system: the Mitchell Camera Corp. in the U.S.A. for all their early models, and Ets. André Debrie in France for their Parvo and Super Parvo cameras.

The Mitchell Corp. used a method developed by John E. Leonard and subsequently improved. Basically, it consists in displacing the camera body to one side so that a special lens focusing system may be placed behind the camera taking lens; the image projected on the lens can be magnified from 5 to 10 times, thus obtaining good focus control. This displacement

Fig. 16. (S) Front view of rackover type camera in shooting position; (F) the same camera in focusing position.

(often called *rackover*) is achieved by building the camera in two parts. The *camera base* is fixed to the tripod and the taking lenses are mounted on it. The *camera body* comprises the film drive mechanism, the magazines and the viewfinder, and it is displaced over slides on the base by means of a rackover handle. By displacing the camera body so that the viewfinder is placed behind the lens, the framing obtained is perfect, since it is effected through the taking lens and the aperture through which the film is exposed.

The method adopted by the Debrie company was developed from a principle introduced by the Russell camera and was based on the sideways rotation of the aperture together with the film, simultaneously placing an identical aperture with a ground glass behind the lens. A permanent optical system affords a magnified upright image correct from left to right, either through the film itself or through the ground glass. The aperture switchover mechanism is simply and instantly operated by means of a knob behind the camera (or on top of it in the Parvo 120).

When this system was developed, framing and focusing through the film was common practice. To facilitate the work of the operator and to prevent his being momentarily dazzled, a thick black cloth was used around the optical tube, in the fashion of old-time photographers. When emulsions became more sensitive, necessitating an appreciable closing of the lens diaphragm, and with the advent of colour film with its black anti-halo coating, focusing and framing through the film became increasingly difficult.

Reflex viewing

Viewfinding by displacing the film and substituting a ground glass does indeed provide an accurate image devoid of parallax, but it is not practical when shooting a moving subject. We have seen that when framing by this method, the camera cannot be operating, and if panning or travelling has to be effected, the operator must use the monitor viewfinder as a guide.

To obviate this problem, August Arnold, engineer of the German company Arnold & Richter, developed in 1931 the ingenious reflex viewfinder system. Reflex viewing signifies the viewing of an image as reflected by a shutter whose blades are silvered on their front surfaces, and which rotates at a 45° angle to the

Fig. 17. Reflex shutter. (1) Mirrored shutter blade; (2) taking lens; (3) prism; (4) viewfinder tube prism; (5) film; (6) eyepiece.

plane of the lens and of the film. This reflected image enters an optical system which magnifies it and turns it upright. The image is transmitted to the operator's eye by the shutter blades only during the short period the shutter is closed, but it is maintained at constant brightness.

The reflex viewfinder was first incorporated into the Arriflex camera, and its appearance on the market was very widely welcomed by all cinematographers. As this system was evidently superior to other types of viewfinder, most camera manufacturers in Europe, and subsequently some in America, have included reflex viewing systems in their cameras. They eliminate parallax, and the elements needed to correct it, thus simplifying a great many problems of design.

The positioning of the reflex shutter was improved upon by some other manufacturers. For example: Debrie and Eclair have placed the shaft of the shutter beneath the lens, so that the blades blank out the frame from side to side, which facilitates quick panning by reducing the stroboscopic effect. This layout also permits reflection of the image from the wide side of the aperture, instead of from the narrow side as in the Arriflex. This method of mirroring allows for the use of extremely wide angle lenses and permits the design of more convenient camera shapes.

Fig. 18. Method of operation of a reflex system with mirror at 45°. (1) Semi-reflecting mirror, (2) shutter, (3) plane of the film, (4) prism.

A different type of reflex viewing system has been adopted on some cameras, such as the Pathé, Bolex, and others. It consists of inserting a semi-reflecting mirror between the lens and the aperture, at an angle of 45° to the optical axis. This mirror splits the light rays forming the image, some of which are diverted to the reflex viewing system, while the rest continue straight through the aperture.

39

The semireflecting mirror may be either a thin specially-treated crystal foil or the face of a specially conditioned prism. By both methods 8% of the light is reflected. The foil system, as compared to the prism, has the disadvantage of producing a double image on the magnifying viewing glass. The secondary image is produced by the other face of the foil, but as it represents only 15% of the primary image, it gives little trouble. The loss of light through this mirror is so small that there is no need to compensate for it by increasing the diaphragm opening. Moreover, sufficiently bright images are obtained through the viewfinder, images which are also free of flicker, this being the typical defect of reflex viewing by a silvered shutter.

A variation to the rotating reflex shutter has been introduced in the Japanese Doiflex Camera. It makes use of a focal plane disc shutter, together with a reciprocating balanced reflex mirror. Close to the external side of the shutter a prism is located in such a way that when the shutter blocks the film aperture, the prism comes down into place completing a reflex viewing optical system. As the shutter opens, the prism is elevated, interrupting the reflex vision, and the film aperture is revealed to expose the film frame behind.

A useful auxiliary device for the reflex viewing and focusing system is the periscopic viewer, which allows for swivelling in all directions and thus for viewing from any position. Some makers, (e.g. Eclair) have built this device into the camera itself, while others such as Arnold & Richter supply it as an accessory for their Arriflex cameras. A highly novel device has been designed and built in the U.S.S.R. which consists of a flexible cable connected to a special viewing mask for the operator, The operator can view from any position in relation to the camera by means of this cable, which makes use of the principle of coherent fibre optics.

Reflex TV monitor

The gradual growth of reflex viewing systems has been the result of continuous efforts made to obtain a sharp image, exactly framed and with freedom of vision for the operator. A new step in this process has been to apply electronics to optical cinema equipment by adding a closed-circuit TV camera to the reflex optical viewing systems of some film instruments.

This allows the scene being shot to be viewed remotely from the camera itself on TV monitors placed in a part of the set away from the main event being covered. This in turn facilitates a constant view of the scene as it is being recorded on film. The film director and the director of photography can therefore watch the scene simultaneously through the taking camera, and as these TV signals can be recorded on video tape, the whole scene can be played back immediately to decide the corrections to the camera movement or the action of the players that both may want to introduce. This in certain conditions provides more economical production of a film. It also permits both technicians to operate several cameras at the same time, with precise viewing of what all of them are taking, even to the point of starting and stopping the cameras from the central console where viewing is effected.

Film production using these methods is just beginning, and opens the way to innumerable possibilities for a more dynamic and efficient use of the cine camera.

At present, this electronic system is used in "System 35" manufactured by the Mitchell Camera Corp., incorporating inside a special blimp a Mark II film camera and the electronic TV viewing circuit. Another system created by Gordon Enterprises is known as "Instant Dailies" and has also been applied to studio film cameras. Arnold and Richter have designed a similar system for use with their cameras known as the electronic cam.

Detachable camera parts

Film supply system

The chambers or the compartments where the raw stock and the exposed film are stored are known as magazines. Early in the history of motion pictures, the magazines were housed inside the camera body, and largely governed its shape. Three main systems were evolved: one, introduced by Debrie in 1908 in the Parvo camera, another used by most of the makers in the United Kingdom, and a third adopted by Duval, the French mechanic who developed the Pathé camera.

The Debrie system was the most compact of the three: the two magazines were placed vertically and parallel within the camera box and turning on the same shaft. The size of the camera was thus greatly reduced and it gave the instrument a box shape similar to the still photo camera which the Eastman Kodak Company was making so popular at the time in their specific market. Today's Debrie cameras still maintain this arrangement, which has also been adopted by some makers in Italy, Britain and the Soviet Union.

In the first instruments produced by British makers, the magazines were placed one on top of the other, inside the camera body, which thus became very bulky. Famous instruments like the Moy, the Williamson, the Darling and the Newman Sinclair were good examples of this system which has now been discontinued.

Fig. 19. Typical arrangement of a motion picture camera. Standard double compartment magazine opened, and classical arrangement for threading the film.

When, in 1905, the Pathé Fréres Company launched into the market the camera which made them famous, one of its features was the magazine position, which was totally different from previous systems. Two separate magazines were mounted on top of the camera body and this was so widely accepted by cinematographers, that some years later Bell & Howell Company in America adopted and improved on this system for their new all-metal camera: a double chamber magazine placed on top of the body, which nowadays has been adopted by most camera manufacturers. This system is driven by belt transmission to the take-up chamber. The film comes out and goes into the two chambers through slots provided with plush rollers to avoid light leaking in and also to protect the emulsion. Some models are provided with a device which closes these slots automatically when the magazine is detached from the camera body.

42

Another special type of film storage is known as the magazine-camera; it is used mostly with lightweight cameras and houses the continuous drive in the magazine. One of the first cameras to adopt this system was the Akeley, designed for scientific explorers and news cameramen. The outstanding characteristic of this system is that all the threading is done in the magazine beforehand and thus the loading onto the camera takes only a few seconds. This is a great advantage to newsreel men who must often reload while the events they have to cover are occurring. Instruments of the magazine-camera system are very popular nowadays, and in some the magazines can be interchanged in less than five seconds while the camera keeps running. Most of the magazines incorporate a footage counter.

Finally, another film storage system is the spool, used on hand held cameras and with capacities from 100 to 200 ft. As spools are supplied with black protective leaders they can be loaded into the camera or interchanged in daylight.

Camera Lenses

The lens is an optical device with the function of imaging the subjects within its field of view in a controlled or regulated manner in the plane of the film at the aperture.

The size of the image produced by the camera lens is regulated by its *focal length.* This is the distance from a point within the lens when focused at infinity, to a plane perpendicular to its axis where a clear image is produced.

A lens produces a circular image and the rectangle of the aperture fits the circle. In still photography, lenses are classified as *normal, wide angle* or *telephoto,* when their focal lengths are, respectively, about the same, smaller or greater than the diagonal of the aperture covered by the image. In motion picture photography, however, such classifications are applied with focal length values twice those of still photography. In the six gauges used nowadays in cinematography, the following are normal lenses:

Film gauge	8 mm	9·5 mm	16 mm	35 mm	65/70 mm
Focal length:	13 mm	20 mm	25 mm	50 mm	85/100 mm

Normal lenses cover a medium field and the images produced are similar in their proportions in respect to the frame, to those produced by human sight. Wide angle lenses cover an ample field of view, which appreciably reduces the proportions of the elements making up the image. On the other hand, telephoto lenses cover a limited field but magnify the elements in the image considerably.

Important progress has been achieved in the last few years, in the quality of image produced by still photography and motion picture lenses. These improvements are the result of new and very complex mathematical formulae made possible by the use of electronic computers, the production of new types of glass, the application of anti-reflective coatings on the faces of the lens elements (which improves image contrast), and the combination of glasses to improve colour rendition (apochromatic lenses).

Lenses for cinematography are made in several countries. The best known makes are: Astro, Schneider, Kilfitt, and Zeiss in the German Federal Republic; Eastman, Bausch & Lomb, Century, Elgeet, Panavision, and Wollensak in the U.S.A.; Kern-Paillard in Switzerland; Angenieux, Berthiot and Kinoptic in France; Dallmeyer, Ross and Taylor-Hobson in Britain; Canon, Nikon, Prominar, Sun and Komura in Japan; and Foton in the Soviet Union.

Lens mount

The individual lenses making up the optical unit are installed in a special metal holder called the lens mount. Its task is to house the complete lens and provide an adequate means to effect micro-

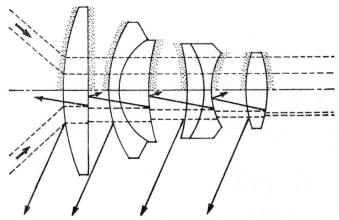

Fig. 20. Lengthwise section of lens showing path of light rays through crystal elements and internal reflections. Shaded parts on elements denote their anti-halo treatment.

44

Fig. 21. Lens for motion picture camera in its mount, with focusing ring and diaphragm (iris) ring.

metric displacements of the various elements along the same axis. The mounts are built with a series of specially connected brass or duralumin cylinders.

A lens for cinematography is generally provided with two rings: one regulates the displacement of the various optical elements in relation to each other (focus ring), while the other controls the passage of light rays by means of an internal iris (diaphragm ring). The focusing ring acts upon a section of the mount which is connected to the rest of the unit by means of a helical pitch thread; this ring is marked all round with a scale of values corresponding to distances between the plane of the film and the subject; the calibrations may be in feet, or in metres or both. In lenses of a short focal length these values start off from very short range (a few inches) and infinity is reached with only a short turn. On the other hand, lenses of long focal length start off from a minimum of more than six feet and the ring must be turned a long way to reach the other end of the scale.

The diaphragm or iris ring is calibrated in "f" or "T" values. The "f" values correspond to a mathematical determination of the capacity of the lens to admit light rays, and are obtained by dividing the focal length by the diameter of the image-forming light beam. "T" values allow for light losses in the lens caused by absorption, reflection, etc. and are therefore more accurate than "f" values and are very useful when working with lenses comprising a large number of elements e.g.: zoom lenses.

Filters and lens hoods (sunshades) are generally installed at the front end of lenses where the barrel is provided with a screw-in thread. The other end of the lens barrel fits into the camera. There are several methods of attaching the lens. Some 16 mm cameras allow for the installation of lightweight lenses with "C" type thread, but this method is not effective with heavier items. Each

45

manufacturer has conceived individual mounting methods, according to the characteristics of each model. Many 35 mm cameras use the bayonet principle, while others use the helical thread system or guides and retaining devices. Sometimes lenses can be interchanged among cameras from the same maker but more often this is only possible with the aid of adaptors sold by camera accessory dealers.

Mounting the camera lenses

The mounting of lenses on the 35 mm camera is effected by either of two methods. One method is single mounting, and is used with only one lens. The other consists of mounting several lenses on a rotating disc called a lens turret.

The single mount system is used on heavy studio cameras, to meet sound-proofing and remote-control-focusing requirements. It is also used on portable cameras requiring simplified lens positioning and light weight.

Some cameras have a single zoom or vari-focal lens which cannot be interchanged. Part of this long lens is built into the camera body so as to afford a better balance of the instrument and also achieve a more functional shape. The application of these concepts to semi-professional 16 mm cameras is a consequence of their many advantages proved over years in amateur 8 mm instruments.

The lens turret method is more frequently used on standard cameras. The turret usually carries three or four lenses which are placed in position by means of clips which fit into grooves in the turret.

Some turrets are star shaped and the lens sockets have been designed with the lens axes divergent, so that they do not interfere with each other's fields.

Sunshade and matte box

This assembly is an essential accessory to the camera. It is intended mainly to protect the lens from reflections, while it also allows for the insertion of filters and masks.

The assembly generally comprises a boom and adjustable bellows, with accessories for its extension and retraction. Some of these sunshades are built so that they can only be used with lenses of medium angle, and must be interchanged with a more open type when using wide angle lenses.

46

Fig. 22. Mitchell matte box and sunshade which can also be used as a filter holder. The adjustable bellows allows the hood to shield lenses of differing viewing angle.

Camera accessories

Besides the camera, the shooting of a film requires a number of accessory elements, which widen its possibilities considerably.

The tripod

THE TRIPOD LEGS. In order to provide a firm and portable base to mount the camera on, early cinematographers adopted the well-known photographic tripod, and to this they subsequently added a head with certain mechanical characteristics. The tripod still keeps its original design, but is now stronger; it must be at the same time durable, stable and easily adjusted.

The tripod comprises three legs of wood or metal. Wood is more commonly used. Wooden legs are made of specially treated beech or maple, because of their strength, light weight, and flexibility. Each leg is tipped with aluminium shoes provided with a spur and steel point to avoid sliding.

The overall length of the legs varies with the model, and the tripod height is adjusted by extending or retracting the legs. The most common tripod heights are 7 ft. 3 in. (220 cms.) fully extended, and 4 ft. 3 in. (130 cms.) with retracted (collapsed) legs. Besides the standard height tripod, there is a specially low model, known as the "baby", whose legs are about half the length of the standard ones, for very low level shots ("worm's eye" views).

THE TRIPOD HEAD. One of the most important parts of the tripod is the head, onto which the camera is mounted, and from

47

which it should be capable of swivelling in all planes. There is a large variety of tripod head designs, amongst which four are widely used.

(i)   the friction head,
(ii) the gyroscopic head,
(iii) the gear head,
(iv) the fluid head.

All four are easily disassembled and interchanged.

The friction head is the commonest, since it is easy to operate, light in weight, and affords smooth movements. As indicated by its name, it is provided with friction surfaces treated with special grease to provide the smoothest possible movement.

The gyroscopic or gyro head is more elaborate and of heavier build. Its outstanding feature is the easy operation for panning, especially on fast moving subjects, liable to alter their direction.

Fig. 23. Friction tripod head. Note the female dovetail for mounting the camera, typical of French cameras.

Its mechanism consists of a gear system which turns a flywheel, damping out irregularities in the panning motion. Another feature is its adaptability to any tripod position, which allows the camera to be set level without having to adjust the length of tripod legs. This feature is so much of a help that it has been adopted on other types of head.

48

The gear heads are the bulkiest. They are used with studio cameras and are provided with a large number of improvements which make them very easy to operate. Their design is based on the action of a mechanism controlled by hand-operated wheels, which drive the horizontal panning and vertical tilting actions through racks and gears. They are built to give a very smooth and easy panning action.

Fig. 24. Heavier studio camera gear head. Horizontal and vertical movements are by rotating the handwheels.

The tripod head known as the fluid head has only recently appeared on the market. It consists of two factory-sealed units containing a special fluid. One of the units is for panning while the other is for tilting. They afford great ease of action and smooth operation, with similar results to the gyro head.

Rolling tripod or camera pedestal

The camera position must be changed continually while shooting a film. In a studio the rolling tripod or camera pedestal is very often used, as it permits repositioning of the camera without dismounting it.

The rolling tripod is very similar to the standard tripod, but it is provided with a three-wheel rolling attachment, allowing the unit to be moved along.

The camera pedestal or rolling support is a much heavier and more elaborate device. It consists of a metal column provided with a device for raising the camera, and has a specially designed wheel assembly, control lever, position fixing device, etc. Camera pedestals are widely used in European cinema and TV studios. The best known manufacturers are Houston Fearless in the United States, Eclair International Diffusion and André Debrie in France, and Vinten Ltd. in the U.K.

49

Gimbal tripod

When shooting on board ship, this tripod is used to keep the head level and steady, no matter what the direction of rolling. The steadying and levelling effect is produced by a device based on the Cardan principle. It is of rugged construction and is immediately identified by the heavy weight suspended between the tripod legs.

Spider

This is a very simple device which ensures the stability of the tripod. It consists of three metal or wooden arms which open up to form a star or "Y". Each arm has notches along its length, into which the points of the tripod legs are inserted. The spider is very useful for shooting in the studio or on locations with smooth floors where tripod legs tend to slide. Another device for the same purpose is the triangle. It is less compact than a spider and not so convenient to move about. Both, however, are widely used.

Suction cups

These are sometimes installed on the ends of tripod legs, to prevent them sliding on highly polished floors. They are made of special anti-slide material, and have the shape of common suction cups.

Hi-Hat

Very often while shooting a film it is necessary to take shots almost from floor level or with the camera placed where one cannot install a tripod. On such occasions the camera with a tripod

Fig. 25. Hi-hat with its three legs for standing on the floor and provision for a tripod head, it allows limited tilt but full pan movement.

50

head is mounted on a hi-hat. This is a metal device of about 8 in. (20 cm.) overall height, with three legs which are provided with holes or slots for fixing it to the base or floor where the camera is to be installed (car, aeroplane, travelling truck or dolly, etc.)

Camera wedge

As its name indicates, this accessory allows for the inclination of the camera at greater angles than those allowed for by normal tilting with the tripod head. It is mounted on the tripod head and the camera is then installed on it at an angle to the horizontal. There are different models with fixed and adjustable angles.

Barney

The Barney is a flexible cover for the camera, to dampen noise and to protect it from extreme high or low temperatures. It is made from several layers of insulating materials, such as kapok, fibreglass, aluminium foil, etc. The outside cover is generally of heat-reflecting white leather. Heating elements are provided inside the cover which allow the instrument to run with outside temperatures as low as − 60° F. The heaters work at 110 v., with power ranging from 55 to 225 watts.

Barneys are easily installed and are made fast by means of zip-fasteners. Allowance is made for operation of camera controls.

Blimp or soundproof cover

Normally the speech of feature films is recorded while the scene is being shot. Early in the era of sound filming, one of the many problems the cinematographers were faced with was the noise made by the camera mechanism which, if audible to the microphone, ruined the recording. This brought about the appearance of the soundproof booth, popular in Hollywood in the early thirties. Although this solved the problem at the time, it was not very practical, as the operator and crew had to be shut up with their camera in the booth.

At the insistent request of studio technicians, several manufacturers substantially modified the mechanical movements of their cameras to make them less noisy. Though such modifications did not totally eliminate noise, they made it possible for cameras to be used more freely on the set when protected with noise dampening covers. These later pioneered the way for to-day's soundproofing systems, of which the best known is the blimp.

51

The blimp is manufactured as an accessory to cameras which are specially designed to shoot while recording speech and sound directly. They consist of bodies of aluminium or magnesium alloy (light and highly resistant materials), lined with several layers of rubber foam combined with plastic foam and/or glass wool. All doors are generally lined with the same layers and they close hermetically, so that the camera is practically floating inside the blimp. The blimp design allows for a number of operations to be carried out from outside. These are

    (i)   lens diaphragm and focus changes,
    (ii) starting switch and speed changes,
    (iii) shutter opening control,
    (iv) direct framing and focusing, etc.

of course, these characteristics vary with each camera and model and the way it is operated.

In most cases the blimp door needs to be opened only for changing the magazine and threading the film. As for sound-proofing, a well built blimp will not allow noise seepage at any recording levels, even when using a highly sensitive microphone directly in front of it.

Fig. 26. Arriflex blimp with all doors open showing construction characteristics and connections of outside controls.

Camera slate

At the beginning of each take a *slate* or clapper board marked with pertinent data is placed in front of the camera to record such information as:

(i) number of the scene, and take,
(ii) whether it is an interior or exterior,
(iii) date,
(iv) number of sound recording,
(v) name of film,
(vi) director, and
(vii) director of photography.

On top of or under this slate there is a hinged section, which can be opened, and closed suddenly to produce a loud crack. This serves as a reference mark to synchronize the sound track with the images.

The numbering is often done by interchangeable hanging slabs.

However, some cameras are provided with built-in automatic slates, with self-illuminating placards, and which are operated from behind. The sound is produced by a special buzzer. The best-known makes of automatic slates are NCE and Kinevox. The Fox camera was one of the first to adopt automatic slating. The makers of the Kinevox describe the operation of their product as follows:

"As the camera is coming up to speed, an optical arm is raised into position before the lens. A trip button is manually operated, sounding a buzzer at the same time as a marking line appears alongside the picture of the slate. These simultaneous operations establish optical and sound sync markings. The slater arm then instantly drops clear of the lens and shooting begins."

Changing bag

This accessory is used for loading magazines, an operation which can be carried out anywhere, even in direct sunlight. The changing bag is essential when shooting far away from a darkroom, and has been used since the very early days of photography. It is a close-mesh, black fabric bag, satin lined. At one end it is provided with two sleeves with elastic cuffs. At the opposite end, an opening allows the magazine and film to be placed inside, and a double zipper makes a light-tight seal.

Changing bags vary in dimensions from the small size, 27 × 25 in., to a large model, 34 × 44 in.

Cameraman's tape

A roll of special adhesive tape is the cameraman's standby. It will seal film cans, fix or fasten cables, secure the photographic report to the can sent to the laboratory, mark references on the floor for the actor's movements, indicate on the magazine cover the type of film loaded in it, and so on. It is made in different colours and dimensions.

Measuring tape

This is a common measuring tape used by the camera assistant to determine the distance from camera to subject in order to make correct focus adjustment. It is usually calibrated in feet and inches.

Ditty bag

This name is applied to a leather bag hanging under the tripod head between its legs. It is a safe and handy place to keep items which are being used continuously, such as light meters, measuring tape, tools, and so on.

Mobile supports

Travelling truck

The travelling truck is one of the most important accessories available to the cinematographer. Modern production techniques demand that the camera be moved during shots and for smooth flowing results a special mobile platform is required.

With the travelling method the camera is propelled along a straight line at any angle to the subject. For this purpose it is mounted on a solidly constructed truck with four or more wheels, and this vehicle runs on parallel guides.

The design of the truck, wheels and guides varies considerably with the maker and model, but the whole assembly should have a high degree of stability and steadiness, smooth rolling and facilities for mounting heavy camera equipment and carrying one operator.

Travelling trucks in use at present are built according to two systems, one adopted in Hollywood and the other in Europe. The Hollywood travelling truck is provided with pneumatic

Fig. 27. Typical lightweight travelling truck with a platform large enough for camera, operator and focus puller.

tyres, sometimes used at very low pressures to seat better on the guides, rolling on wooden parallel guides with a flange.

The other type of truck is widely used in France and Italy. This features ball-bearing-mounted steel tyre wheels, with a groove along the tyre. The wheels roll on a rail system with $1\frac{1}{2}$ in. piping,

Fig. 28. A popular European system for travelling shots using grooved steel tyres running on an easily assembled piping track.

Fig. 29. Another view of the rail system. Note the method of mounting the hi-hat and the bar used by the pusher.

in two-metre lengths, one end of which fits tightly into the open end of the next length.

The platform of a travelling truck must be heavily constructed in order to make it steady, and it must be fitted out to mount lights, hi-hat, etc.

Dolly

This is a special and more elaborate truck for travelling shots, allowing a very wide variety of camera movements. It is provided with an hydraulic mechanism (sometimes a spring and gear mechanism) which operates a boom at the end of which the

Fig. 30. A more elaborate light travelling truck or dolly with pneumatic tyres and steering for crab movements.

camera is installed, thus raising or lowering it, and pivoting it at different angles. The boom can be manually controlled, and the vehicle must be of heavy and solid construction. It usually has five wheels.

Among the different types of dolly the most elaborate

Fig. 31. N.T.C. Hydrolly. The arm is operated by hydraulic pressure and carries the camera and operator.

Fig. 32. Moviola Crab-Dolly with rubber tyres, steering and seat for the operator mounted on the arm.

is the well known crab-dolly. This vehicle is provided with hydraulic controls, usually placed at the rear, allowing for movements of any kind as all wheels can be steered in any direction. Thus the operator can combine diagonal movements, turns round curves, turns at right angles, etc.

Some widely used dollies and crab-dollies are

(i) Houston Fearless Panoram Dolly,
(ii) N.T.C. Hydrolly,
(iii) Moviola Crab-Dolly,
(iv) J. G. McAlister Crab-Dolly,
(v) Vinten Pathfinder Type 1,
(vi) Edmonton Camera Dolly.
(vii) Colortran Crab Dolly
(viii) Elemack Spyder Dolly

The compact Elemack dolly is manufactured in Italy and has been widely accepted, not only in that country, but elsewhere in Europe and in the U.S.A. Its design allows for placing its four double wheels in twelve possible combinations, carrying two operators on it, and it is capable of going through doors and other narrow openings. The Elemack Dolly accepts the Jonathan Jib Arm Assembly, an accessory to convert the unit to a medium size crane.

Crane

The crane used in film studios is a complex item of equipment which affords the camera and the operator an enormous facility of movement. Its dimensions and characteristics vary considerably since it is generally made to order.

Fig. 33. A crane with special wheels adapted for use on rail system. It has a counterweight and parallelogram arm system to maintain a level platform.

The base of the crane is a very heavy vehicle, to which is attached a long boom, which is the crane's main feature. At the end of the boom there is a platform that always remains level, whatever the position of the boom.

On this platform facilities are provided for installing the camera and three seats: one for the director, one for the camera operator and another for the camera assistant.

The crane movements are obtained by means of electric motors driving an elaborate mechanical and hydraulic system. Balance is maintained by counter-balance weights at the other end of the boom.

Some models have total automatic control, allowing the camera operator to raise, lower or swivel the crane from his seat on the platform.

This item of equipment is very much in use for spectacular films where the camera equipment must move over large sets, or for very complex outdoor location takes.

Among crane manufacturers are:

(i) Houston Fearless Corp.;
(ii) Chapman Studio Equipment, and others in the U.S.A.;
(iii) Newall Baby Crane in the U.K.
(iv) A.T.C. Gina Crab-Dolly in Italy.

Fig. 34. Chapman Titan Crane: largest American-made crane. Note the six-wheeled truck.

REFERENCES

[1] Alvar, M. F., *Tecnica Cinematográfica Moderna*, J. M. Yagües, Madrid.
[2] Gregory, C. L., *Motion Picture Photography*, 2nd ed., Falk Publishing Company, New York (1927).
[3] Newman, A. S., Camera Mechanics Ancient and Modern, *Journal of the Society of Motion Picture Engineers*, No. 5, p. 534 (1930).
[4] Spottiswoode, R., *Film and its Techniques*, University of California Press, Los Angeles (1951).
[5] Valera, J. A., *Arte y Tecnica Cinematográfica y Television*, Editorial Albatros, Bs. Aires (1944).
[6] Weisse, Harold, Die Kinematographische Kamera, Springer Verlag, Vienna, (1955).
[7] McKay, H. C., *The Handbook of Motion Picture Photography*, Falk Publishing Company, New York (1927).

2

SURVEY OF 35 MM CAMERAS

Studio cameras

NC and BNC model Mitchell cameras

MODEL NC and BNC Mitchell Cameras have been standard equipment in the film industry for over thirty years. The first Mitchell camera in the American market in 1920 brought out the new "rack-over" system conceived by John E. Leonard, a cinematographer. Soon its excellent construction and improved design gradually established an outstanding reputation in the motion picture industry. As time went by, improvements were added to the original model: a better intermittent mechanism drive (by means of eccentrics and new materials) when sound films cropped up, which led to the semi-noiseless NC model; the BNC model in 1934, with its compact noise dampening devices built into the instrument. The BNC also comprised all the latest refinements of a studio camera at that date, but it was sold extensively only in 1938 when one of the large Hollywood studios (Warner Bros.) bought a considerable number. The first two important films in which the BNC was used, were "Wuthering Heights" in 1939 and "Citizen Kane", in 1941, both photographed by Gregg Toland.

The excellent reputation and renowned high quality of the Mitchell camera are maintained by manufacturing processes with exacting accuracy control. They have achieved a high degree of accuracy in registration for the intermittent movement in their equipment.

Both models are designed to run at any selected speed between one and 24 frames per second. Both use the same driving mechanism, and their wide variety of attached accessories allows them a great adaptability for all types of work. The BNC differs from the NC in that it is supplied with a sound insulated outer case, it has only one lens mounting and is provided with automatic correction of the monitoring viewfinder, automatic dissolve control, and several focusing controls.

GENERAL DESCRIPTION. Most of the Mitchell 35 mm camera models (the Mark II is the exception) are built in two parts: the camera base and the camera body. The base comprises the adjustable matte system, the lens turret (or lens mount in the case of the BNC), and the rack-over mechanism for displacing the body sideways. The camera body comprises the complete mechanism driving the film, the controls, drive motor, focusing system and monitor viewfinder placed at the side. The magazine is attached to the top of this body. The camera body can be displaced sideways to the right so that the focusing tube is placed behind the taking lens; but before shooting the body must be moved back to its normal position on the left-hand side. This sideways displacement is effected by a rack-over mechanism controlled by a handle with a release push button which fixes the body firmly in either of its two positions. The handle is placed at the back of the camera, and the action can be done with only one hand and is instantaneous.

Fig. 1. Mitchell BNC camera with double compartment type soundproof magazines.

The monitor viewfinder is installed on a special mounting on the left hand side of the camera body. A special accessory is provided to correct for the parallax of this viewfinder; in the BNC this parallax correction is effected automatically, as it is connected to the lens focusing control.

As stated above, all controls are placed at the back of the camera body. They are:

(i)   footage counter,
(ii)   magazine footage counter dial,
(iii) frame counter,
(iv) shutter control knob,
(v)   automatic dissolve control (BNC),
(vi) focusing remote control (BNC),
(vii) eyepiece of focusing tube with magnification control,
(viii) miniature reproduction of shutter opening,
(ix) power supply cable to motor, with starting switch,
(x)   hand-wheel for moving motor manually,
(xi) counter zero-reset knob,
(xii) spirit level.

In front of the lens, the camera front, which is part of the base, holds a matte box and sunshade which slides on two horizontal rods attached to the base. This accessory allows for the insertion

Fig. 2. Mitchell NC model showing turret with four lenses and matte box and sunshade attached.

in front of the taking lens of several items for special effects while shooting.

Also for special effects, Mitchell cameras are provided with a revolving disc for mounting filters, and a special adjustable device for matting the image being photographed.

The controls for the 4-way mattes are located on top and on the right hand side of the vertical section of the camera base, and the placing of mattes has been designed to avoid any possibility of catching parasitic reflections. It also provides an independent control to allow horizontal and vertical masking of the aperture.

FOCUSING TUBE. The focusing tube is used to obtain precision focusing and framing through the taking lens itself. The ground glass in the focusing tube moves into the position that was occupied by the film before the camera was racked over. Now the scene can be framed through the taking lens, and the latter adjusted in order to obtain as sharp an image as possible.

On returning the camera to the operating position, the lens adjustment does not vary, and the previously set focus will be the one used on the film.

A knob on the focusing tube eyepiece adjusts for individual eyesight. The image seen on the tube is upright and correct from left to right. Normally this image is magnified five times in relation to the frame size. However, the image can be magnified ten times for focusing purposes, in which case only the central part of the scene is visible through the focusing tube. The magnifying control is located under the focusing tube. Two filters, green and amber, are incorporated in the focusing tube; two buttons control their insertion or withdrawal from the field. The image seen through the amber filter corresponds to panchromatic film, and the one through the green filter to orthochromatic film.

Besides the ground glass where the image to be focused is formed, there is on the front part of the focusing tube a matte slot for inserting masks when special process or matted shots must be taken. Access to this slot is afforded by a sliding door which also allows for cleaning the ground glass.

INTERMITTENT MOVEMENT. This movement consists of a shuttle and register pin mechanism driven by an eccentric, the film being pulled down by means of two pins penetrating the perforations at either side of the film. After the film has travelled the height of one frame and stopped, register pins penetrate one perforation at each side, steadying the film during the exposure period.

A pressure plate presses the film firmly against the aperture, and the 0·0015 in. clearance between pressure and aperture plates allows for the travel of two films at a time for bipack systems, or of a single film allowing for splices. Aperture plates with different size apertures can be interchanged; the standard aperture is 0·868 in. × 0·631 in.

MOTOR TRIP SWITCH. Should the film break on being taken up after exposure, or should there be faulty threading, or any other form of failure in take-up, an oversize loop will be formed in the back of the camera body. This presses against a plate, tripping a switch which opens the motor circuit and stops the camera. This avoids damage to the delicate precision movements of the intermittent drive and tells the operator that the camera is not working properly.

Fig. 3. Rear view of Mitchell NC model. (I) Viewfinder screen; (2) focusing tube eyepiece; (3) variable shutter knob; (4) shutter aperture indicator; (5) synchronous motor; (6) viewfinder parallax control; (7) rackover handle; (8) footage and frame counter; (9) magazine footage dial counter.

VARIABLE-OPENING SHUTTER. This is made up of two blades on a single shaft. Its maximum opening is 175°, and it can be closed in calibrations of 10° each by means of a swivel-handle knob sliding over a scale on the back of the camera. Just below this knob and scale, a miniature shutter reveals at a glance the shutter opening and the relative position of the shutter with respect to the aperture. In the BNC the shutter opening is of the

65

C

automatic dissolving type, allowing fade-ins and fade-outs by pressing one of two buttons.

LENSES AND LENS MOUNTS. In the Mitchell camera lenses are held in position by bayonet type lens locks. They are provided with rings for external focus control.

The NC model has a four-lens turret, which can be quickly and easily rotated and locked in position for each lens by means of a conveniently placed locking or indexing pin. The BNC model takes only one lens at a time. The lenses carry special markings which on mounting must be made to correspond with determined positions, so as to synchronize for parallax and focus.

MOTOR. Mitchell NC & BNC cameras are driven by inter-changeable motors attached on the right hand side by means of two screws and a retaining latch, thus motors can be interchanged very quickly.

The motor is positioned with its shaft in a horizontal position and parallel to the axis of the camera. The transmission is by means of a reduction gear at right angles to the shaft and camera axis. A switch is provided so that it will be acted upon by the oversize loop buckle-trip. All motors are provided with sockets for connecting the leads from the power source, to facilitate a quick change-over of motors when necessary.

COUNTERS. An exposed footage counter and an exposed frame counter are built into the back of the camera, with a zero reset knob on the camera's left-hand side. A magazine footage dial counter, with zero-reset button in the centre, is placed on the lower right side angle of the camera back.

REFLEX ATTACHMENT. The well known American firm F. & B. Ceco has designed a revolutionary device which provides Mitchell NC, BNC and Standard cameras with reflex viewing.

Fundamentally it consists of a beam-splitter prism placed between lens and shutter affording a continuous view through the taking lens even when the camera is shooting. The 'bleed off' of light at the prism face to the viewing optical system results in a loss of only a quarter of a stop with colour film. As with all reflex systems, this device eliminates the sideways displacement of the camera for focusing and framing, and makes the camera quicker to use.

This attachment requires a modification of the system for inserting filters and an adapted viewing eyepiece, but neither the intermittent mechanism nor the sprocket are altered. Moreover, the Mitchell camera's typical monitoring viewfinder is also left untouched, and can be used at any moment at the operator's discretion.

The image appearing through these reflex viewers is bright and does not flicker, the latter being the typical defect of reflex viewing with the shutter reflex system.

MITCHELL BNCR MODEL. The Mitchell Camera Corp. have produced an improved BNC model incorporating reflex viewing and known as the BNCR. The reflex viewing method is totally different from the Ceco system. It consists of a stainless steel shutter with mirrored blades, reflecting 93% of the light passing through the lens. The shutter rotates at 720 r.p.m. and is exactly synchronised with the rotation of the camera's standard shutter (1440 r.p.m.). A very bright image is thus obtained through the viewer, which can magnify it up to 10 times.

The manufacturers took this opportunity to improve the camera's design, specially as regards to noise dampening. Thus a reduction was obtained of about 30% of the noise made by the BNC, bringing it to a level below the capacity of the human ear.

Fig. 4. The Mitchell BNCR, an inproved BNC with reflex viewing.

Furthermore, a new section was built on at the front with treated glasses and self illumination. The rack-over sideways camera-box displacement is eliminated, but otherwise the rest of the instrument is identical to the BNC.

Debrie Super Parvo Model V and AN cameras

The reputation of the Parvo cameras goes back to 1908 when Joseph Debrie with the co-operation of his son André put their first motion picture camera on the market. Thirteen years later, under the name of Etablissements André Debrie, this company started the commercial production of various types of equipment to cover the requirements of motion picture studios and laboratories. Their products were readily and widely accepted in world markets because of their excellent quality and advanced design.

Fig. 5. Debrie Super Parvo Color camera on a rolling pedestal.

The Super Parvo camera appeared in 1932, equipped with a noiseless movement conceived specially for shooting sound films. This camera immediately outdated all previous cameras with sound padding covers, since it is almost noiseless but of compact size, being one of the smallest and most easily handled cameras taking 1000 foot magazines. It is interesting to point out that the Super Parvo was an elaboration of the then well-known Parvo 120, brought about by the requirements of a larger film capacity to compensate for the new filming speed of 24 frames per second, needed for sound filming. The ancester of the Super Parvo was the Parvo "T"; it consisted of a model similar to the Parvo "L" with capacity for 1000 ft. magazines. This model had to be enclosed in a special blimp provided by the makers, owing to its noisy operation.

At the time that Debrie enlarged the magazine enclosure in order to take 1000 foot magazines, a sound padding cover was added. In 1941 a reflex viewing system was added and a high precision film drive movement was adopted, together with a special shutter and high quality internal optical system.

GENERAL DESCRIPTION. The several models of the Super Parvo consist of a soundproof camera body of box shape measuring 20 in. × 10 in. × 11 in. This body houses the film driving movements, the optical system, the film magazines, the motor, counters, etc. All these elements are assembled so as to form a single, vibration-free block, which is insulated by thick soundproof walls.

FILM DRIVE MOVEMENT. The film drive is effected by two sprockets, one at the top left corner and the other at the bottom right corner inside the camera front wall. Both are provided with pressure devices to ensure that the sprocket teeth penetrate the film perforations, and guide rollers. However the main element of the drive unit is the film track, i.e. the groove or channel formed by the aperture and pressure plates, at whose sides the shuttle claws and register pins successively penetrate the film perforations. Both claws and pins are of special alloy steel and work in synchronism with an intermittent pressure plate.

MOTORS. The motor is installed inside the central part of the camera. It is easily interchanged, is directly coupled to the camera and allows for forward and reverse drives. It is of the synchronous type for either 110 or 220 volts, but motors can be supplied for 24 volts to work from a battery source. A special speed reduction box allows for the use of two types of motor for working at different speeds.

CONTROLS. Most of the controls are located on the rear of the camera.

The focusing and framing tube allows for framing and focusing through the taking lens by means of a reflex system using mirror shutter blades. Inside the focusing tube there is a yellow filter which can be inserted at will to determine the contrast of the scene. A rubber eyecup protects the eye from external light and is mounted on an adjusting ring calibrated over a scale of ten diopters. Beneath and at both sides of the focusing tube there are built-in footage counters (normally expressed in metres) and a magnetic speed indicator. Both instruments have a zero setting knob at one side.

On top of the control panel there is a metal handgrip for carrying the camera. On the horizontal part of it is mounted an air-bubble level. Underneath the handgrip, to left and right of the camera, there are dials for focus control and for adjusting the lens diaphragm. The calibrations for focus control are marked on the dial itself, while diaphragm control is effected by exchanging plates with calibrations corresponding to the diaphragm of the lens being used.

The socket for connecting the power cable is at the lower right-hand side of the panel, together with a special on-and-off switch, which is also acted upon by the safety device. Beside the power socket and underneath the focusing tube, there is a handwheel which can be meshed onto the motor shaft when disconnected, so as to drive the camera manually while loading. The meshing of the motor shaft with the handwheel is effected by pressing the latter; a special lock ensures against accidental meshing.

On the sides of the camera are push buttons opening or closing the shutter aperture from 180° to zero, either automatically or manually. There is also an observation window for checking visually that the focusing scale, etc. is correct, also fitted are special locks for effective light sealing of all camera doors.

CAMERA FRONT. A sunshade and matte-box is installed at the front of the camera. The sunshade can be either an extendible bellows or rigid and the matte-box allows for inserting masks and filters. The whole assembly is swung to one side when the lens is changed. When the Super Parvo is to be used with anamorphic lenses, the manufacturer supplies a special adapter block with aperture dimensioned to 0·937 in. × 0·735 in. (23·8 × 18·67 mm).

Eclair Camé 300 Reflex camera

This camera was designed by the French engineers Coutant and Mathot and is manufactured by Eclair International Diffusion. It is a blimped, all metal, heavily built but compact camera. The body is of box shape and its front consists of a fixed plate provided with a specially treated glass through which light reaches the lens. Lenses with the special mount designed by the camera makers can be installed by means of this plate, and it furthermore affords easy access to the variable shutter control.

The intermittent drive consists of a two-claw shuttle with adjustable register pin; the adjustment for this is marked on a calibrated scale. It can operate in reverse, and under any working conditions the registration is highly accurate.

The new adjustable register pin system obtained an award from the Superior Technical Committee of the French film industry and many European operators have praised its advantage for multiple exposure takes, and for shooting in tropical regions where film frequently shrinks.

Fig. 6. Eclair Camé 300 Reflex mounted on a rolling pedestal manufactured by the same company.

VIEWING SYSTEMS. The Camé 300 Reflex camera is provided with three different viewing systems:

(i)   an integral, bright image, reflex viewfinder, with reflecting blade shutter placed at a 45° angle;
(ii) direct viewing through film;
(iii) side or monitor viewfinder with parallax correction.

Generally the reflex viewfinder is the one most in use, and its tube

71

swivels in order to facilitate viewing with the camera in awkward positions.

OTHER CHARACTERISTICS. The magazines are for 300 metres (1000 ft.) of film, and they are externally attached and are interchangeable (raw stock magazine and exposed film magazine). The magazines are provided with mechanical transmission for normal and reverse drive.

The variable opening of the shutter is calibrated from 180° to zero.

The camera is driven by an interchangeable electric motor, bayonet mounted at the rear, which can be either synchronous, 3-phase, for 220 v., 50/60 c/s, or variable speed from 22 to 26 f.p.s. at 24 v. DC.

The single lens mount is of the bayonet type. The minimum focal distance is 18 mm, but under certain conditions one can use 14 mm lenses. An extendible bellows sunshade and a matte-box are installed in front of the lens.

Other features of this camera are:

(i) exposed film-length counter in metres,
(ii) speed indicator,
(iii) automatic slating device,
(iv) threading safety switch,
(v) special warming system for working in extreme cold conditions,
(vi) synchronization socket for back projection.

Vinten Everest studio camera

This camera (now discontinued) was manufactured by the British firm W. Vinten Ltd. and its basic design was completed late in 1945. It was subsequently improved and thus obtained the official approval of the British Film Producers Association. It may still be found in use in some studios in the U.K., Italy, India, Scandinavia, etc. The main characteristics of the Vinten Everest Camera are its compactness, its professional design, its soundproof blimp and high quality finish.

The first Everest camera was the model I, which was an improved development of the Vinten "H". The Everest I was box shaped and included many improvements. The Everest II, described above, was of a sophisticated design including a new sunshade. It is worth pointing out that the Everest models included a concept introduced by the Russell camera: the aperture was placed near the rear of the camera, with the built-in magazines at both sides and in front of the unit. This brought about a critical limitation in the use of wide-angle lenses.

Fig. 7. Vinten Everest II camera which has reflex viewing and internally mounted film magazines.

The intermittent drive of the Vinten Everest consists of a two-claw shuttle and register pin ensuring very steady registration. The shutter is of the variable opening type, from a minimum 30° to a maximum 170°.

Lenses must be single mounted, and are of the bayonet type. They range from 28 to 100 mm focal length. The lens is protected by a special sunshade incorporating a matte-box.

Reflex viewing is effected by means of a shutter with shaft at 45° angle and mirrored blades; the image is viewed on a $2\frac{1}{2}$ × $1\frac{1}{4}$ in. screen with a special margin outside the frame to help the operator in preventing the appearance of unwanted subjects. A special device allows for inserting filters in the viewing system in order to work with different types of film.

The film is loaded in magazines which are internally installed side by side; they take 1000 feet of film. The camera is driven by a 220 v., 50 c/s 3-phase, permanently installed motor; for field work a converter is supplied for connecting to 24 v. batteries.

Among important features of the Vinten Everest camera are:

(i) special focusing control by means of a built-in telemeter (range finder);

(ii) synchronizing system for back projection shots;

(iii) self-lighted connection indicator and safety device.

Moskva KC 32 Soviet studio camera

This camera and the Rodina are part of the new cinema equipment manufactured in Soviet Russia. It has been designed to work in the studio, and is of box shape. It weighs approximately 132 lbs.

The intermittent movement comprises a two-claw shuttle similar to that of the Mitchell camera; there is one register pin at each side of the film. A special optical system affords direct viewing through the taking lens, but this is complemented by a side-placed monitor viewfinder, with device for parallax correction.

Film is supplied from and taken up by a double-compartment magazines which is attached to the camera top. However, each of the two magazine compartments can be withdrawn separately.

Both magazine compartments are mechanically driven by a special mechanism which also allows reverse drive. The camera is driven by a 220 v., 50 c/s motor, which can be interchanged with a 380 v. synchronous motor of 1440 r.p.m. (24 f.p.s.).

The variable opening of the shutter can be adjusted from a maximum 170° to zero. On the camera front plate, single mounted

Fig. 8. Russian Moskva Model KC 32 camera with direct viewing through the lens and a monitor viewfinder. The two film compartments can be detached separately.

74

Fig. 9. Russian Rodina field camera, a relatively small and easily transportable model with reflex viewfinding.

lenses are installed. These can be interchanged and the minimum focal length is 28 mm. The lens is protected by a rigid sunshade combined with extendible bellows, and the matte-box attached to it allows for the insertion of filters, etc.

Some of the other characteristics of the Moskva Studio camera are:

(i)   external focusing controls at both sides of the camera,
(ii) exposed film-length counter in metres,
(iii) correct threading safety device.

20th Century Fox camera

This camera was built by the Simplex Company under the instructions and requirements of 20th Century Film Corp. studios in 1939/1940. The studios wanted an instrument which should be noiseless, relatively light in weight, of high registration precision, and easy to operate. The camera was so successful that it was for many years standard equipment in the Fox studios.

The heart of the Fox camera is its specially designed intermittent mechanism whose absolutely noiseless running makes it possible to dispense with blimping, and which has the further advantage of high operating speed and light weight. It is based on the principle of a single-claw shuttle working in combination with an eccentric pin and cam, and two register pins.

75

Fig. 10. Side view of 20th Century Fox camera with lens turret and a rackover through-the-lens viewfinder.

Viewing is effected through the taking lens, or by using a monitor viewfinder. By moving a handle, the camera body is swivelled over an angle of 75° on the axis of the shaft of the shutter; this swivelling places the focusing tube directly behind the lens. The image seen through the monitor viewfinder is a reflected one, and parallax is corrected automatically.

The shutter opening is variable from a maximum opening of 200° to a minimum of 45°.

The magazines are attached externally, and are of the two-compartment type holding 1000 feet of film. The Fox camera is driven by a motor specially adapted to different types of supplies, which is attached to the rear of camera. This camera is provided with an automatic slating device, focusing control, synchronizing control for back projection, and other features.

Newall camera

The Newall camera was first built in England in 1946 by the Newall Engineering Co. at Peterborough, a firm which was later integrated into the Rank Organization through the Gaumont Kalee Co. and Rank Precision Industries Ltd. This instrument was manufactured until some years ago, to cover the needs of studios in the United Kingdom as well as for export to India, Australia, South Africa, Italy, etc. Its design is identical to the Mitchell NC camera, and this likeness is maintained throughout the instrument, and applies also to the high quality of the material and the excellent finish. As these two cameras are exactly alike, except for the British model's ingenious method of attaching magazine covers, the characteristics and features of the Newall can be found under the description of the Mitchell NC.

However, the manufacturer of the Newall supplied a soundproof blimp made of aluminium alloy, which provided focusing control, automatic parallax correction for the monitoring viewfinder, and great ease of operation.

Druzhba Soviet Studio camera

Among the recent Soviet made equipment, the most noteworthy are the Druzhba, for studio work, and the more simply designed Mir. These have been designed by engineers of various government divisions, such as the Cinematographic Equipment Construction Workshops, at Leningrad and Moscow (C.K.B. and M.K.B.K.), the Moskinap Unions and the Leningrad Optical Mechanical Organisation (L.O.O.M.P.). The Druzhba is being very intensively used in most Soviet Union studios, and is gradually displacing the older Moskva, not provided with reflex viewing. The Druzhba is very similar to the Mitchell BNCR, as is evident from its shape, almost identical intermittent drive, reflex viewing through the shutter, 1000 ft. sound-blimped magazine, focus control, lens hood with matte box, shutter opening, side viewfinder with automatic parallax correction, etc. As with all modern Soviet cameras, the Druzhba is painted in an attractive light grey.

Panavision camera

Panavision Inc. is a well known American firm which has developed up to date means for wide-screen filming, through its processes called Ultra-Panavision 70, Super Panavision 70, Panavision 70 and Panavision 35. For this last system it has created a modern studio camera with all refinements required by the latest techniques. These cameras are not for sale: they are rented together with the firm's services. Their most outstanding characteristics are: four-claw shuttle mechanism (two claws on each side of the film), double register pins, shutter with variable opening from 0 to 175°, reflex viewfinder built into the camera

77

access door, interchangeable motors, externally-placed blimped 1000 ft magazines, side viewfinder with automatic parallax correction, remote focus control, and special Panavision 35 mm lenses.

Field cameras

Mitchell Standard camera

The Mitchell Standard model is built with similar characteristics to the semi-noiseless NC model, but slight differences in the intermittent drive movement and in the controls must be pointed out individually.

INTERMITTENT MOVEMENT. Shuttle and register pin are operated by gears and eccentrics. Drive is effected by two claws on each side, and registration is obtained by two register pins, one on each side. The movement works equally well forwards and backwards.

OTHER CHARACTERISTICS. Shutter with variable opening from 170° to zero. Floating internal iris. Special disc with built-in filters.

Bell & Howell model 2709 camera

For the past forty years or so, the Bell & Howell Co. of Chicago have produced a first-rate camera with high precision register, offering excellent possibilities for process and high-speed filming. Production has now been discontinued but the camera is still often used in process work, as well as for animation and optical printing.

The intermittent movement of this camera is known as Unit I, and works with two register pins fixed at the side of the aperture which achieves a very high degree of registration steadiness. The Unit I intermittent movement can be exchanged for another one designed to operate at higher speeds up to 200 f.p.s.

Viewing is possible through the taking lens by displacing the camera body sideways while the lens turret remains in its rigid position. A parallax-corrected monitor viewfinder allows for framing and focusing while shooting.

In the older models of this camera, viewing was by rotating the lens turret till the taking lens was placed before the fixed position viewing tube at the camera side where the other controls are placed.

Fig. II. Bell & Howell Model 2709 seen from the side.

The shutter is of the variable opening type, ranging from 170° to zero.

Film is loaded by means of double compartment magazines attached to the camera top. The camera is driven by interchangeable motors of 115 v. AC or DC, or for 12 or 24 v. DC, for outdoor working.

Among other features of the model 2709 are:

(i)   the four-lens turret,
(ii) automatic dissolve,
(iii) shutter opening indicator,
(iv) capacity for adaptation to bipack systems,
(v)   slot for inserting masks and filters.

Vinten Windsor reflex

W. Vinten Ltd., the British camera makers who manufactured the Everest, produced another model at a later date. This instrument, the Windsor, was designed for shooting outdoors. It has an excellent, very steady and acceptably noiseless film-drive movement.

The viewing system of the Windsor is of the reflex type and

shows a bright and appreciably magnified image suitable for critical focusing. The image is reflected by the mirrored surfaces of a balanced, two blade shutter with an opening adjustable from 10° to 170°.

The two compartment magazine takes 1000 ft. film load and is attached to the camera top. The camera is driven by interchangeable synchronous and variable speed motors.

Rodina Model 3*KS Soviet Camera*

This is another Soviet camera very much used in field productions in that country. It is outstanding for its small bulk and compact shape. The intermittent drive works with shuttle claws on both sides of the film and a moving register pin on the emulsion side: the registration obtained is excellent. This camera can be reversed when necessary.

Framing and focusing is effected with a mirror single-blade reflex shutter and large viewing tube which protrudes behind the camera body. Normally this instrument is used with separate semi-internal, 400 ft. magazines, but 1000-ft. magazines can also be installed side-by-side. The shutter opening can be varied from 0 to 160°.

Its front carries an adjustable bellows sunshade with boom. The lens is single mounted and a filter insertion device is installed in front together with focus control. Lenses at 22 to 100 mm focal length can be used with this camera.

The motor is small and cylinder shaped and is installed on one side of the camera; it can be easily exchanged. This instrument can run at speeds from 8 to 48 f.p.s. and is provided with indicating speed counter. However, it can also work frame-by-frame with a special motor or with crankhandle drive. It is provided with an automatic device for dissolves. It weighs approximately 34 lb.

Lightweight cameras

Mitchell S35R (Mark II) reflex camera

One of the most recent newcomers in the motion picture market is the instrument designed and manufactured by the Mitchell Camera Corp. known as the Mark II. This was the result of fruitful research to fulfil the demand of the movie industry for a multi-purpose, noiseless, light camera, with a reflex viewfinder, which would be easily adaptable to studio work. To achieve this, the Mitchell company first designed and produced an experimental model, the R-35, and put it in the hands of camera operators, directors of photography and producers, so that they could try it out.

After a year's trials, during which the new features were tested out one by one, the Mark II was launched, taking into account the suggestions derived from the experimental runs. The result is a finely finished, easy-to-carry camera of modern design, capable of running at a wide range of speeds up to 128 f.p.s., just by changing motors, and which furthermore can easily be turned into a studio camera by merely attaching accessories.

The intermittent movement is similar to that of the Mitchell NC and BNC, and consists of a two-claw shuttle working with two register pins, one at each side of the film.

The intermittent unit is easily disassembled for quick interchange when required.

The Mark II incorporates reflex viewing for the first time in a Mitchell camera. The very bright image is reflected by polished stainless steel blades placed at a 45° angle to the film, these blades being rotated by the shutter shaft. The shutter is of the focal plane type, and its opening can be adjusted from 170° to zero, in

Fig. 12. The Mitchell R-35 reflex, a trial model which was tested by cameramen working in the film production industry.

segments of 5° each. The optical tube of the finder magnifies the image up to 10 times to afford critical focusing, and inside it there are filters which provide a very great help in studying lighting in the subject. The field of view is larger than covered by the lens, so that the operator can see unwanted subjects just outside the frame. The ground glass on which the image is projected can be easily interchanged to suit the aperture size being used.

The Mark II is loaded with film by means of an external 400 foot magazine, which is secured by an attachment plate onto the underside of the camera, at its rear, so that it rests on the operator's shoulder for hand-held shooting. The magazines take 100 ft. or 200 ft. daylight spools or cores for 400 ft. dark-room film loads. When a larger film-load is needed the typical 1000 ft. Mitchell magazine is installed on top of the camera or slant-back by means of adapter.

Interchangeable motors are supplied to drive the new Mitchell camera: 12 v. DC, 24 v. DC; 110 v. DC or AC (all for speeds ranging from 1 to 70 f.p.s.). Moreover there are synchronous motors of the following characteristics: single-phase 110 v., 60 c/s; 3-phase, 220 v., 50 c/s; 110 v. AC for animation filming; and 115 v. AC for high-speed shooting.

Fig. 13. Mitchell Mark II with 1000 ft. top mounted magazine, special sunshade and matte-box and viewfinder.

A sync-pulse built into the camera affords synchronization of camera operation with certain types of sound recorders working on this principle.

The lenses are specially made by the American firm of Bausch & Lomb and are installed by means of a special mounting (either single or on a lens turret, at choice) which can be combined with a manual focusing control.

Other characteristics of the Mitchell Mark II are:

(i) slot for inserting masks and filters,
(ii) mount for taking a special design of sunshade,
(iii) monitor viewfinder with automatic parallax correction,
(iv) hi-hat when the magazine is rear mounted,
(v) blimp of modern design,
(vi) closed circuit television system with built-in monitor tube and video-tape recorder (System 35),
(vii) water-tight cover for submarine shooting.

Debrie Parvo Model L and 58 cameras

Most of the studios in Europe, Asia and both American continents have one or more of the Parvo cameras manufactured by Etablissements André Debrie. Apart from their excellent quality, their reputation is based on having been standard equipment in the industry for over forty years. The most popular is the "L" model which still maintains the design characteristics that first made this camera famous.

Joseph Debrie founded his company in 1900 to specialize in making equipment for the newly born motion picture industry. They manufactured one of the most sought-after film punching instruments of the time. Their products were acquired by the best known manufacturers—Thomas A. Edison among them. In 1905 they produced the first professional printer, and in 1908, Joseph Debrie, together with his son André, designed the first Parvo camera.

The Parvo introduced the box-shaped concept in order to reduce bulk. It was readily accepted by cinematographers and through the years many models were turned out on the basis of the same solidly built bronze mechanism and specially treated wooden body (5-ply walnut). Years later the first all metal (aluminium) model appeared, and other improvements were gradually added, e.g. focusing device, automatic dissolve, etc. With the coming of sound films, many adaptations were made, leading to the model "L" which soon attained wide popularity.

Debrie-made instruments gave international renown to the French camera industry, and more than 8,000 units were sold in world markets. In America it competed with the then-reigning Bell & Howell and it was extensively used all over Europe in a large portion of films made in Britain, France, Spain and Italy. In the Soviet Union, Serge Eisenstein employed Parvos in many of his productions shot by Edouard Tissé. It was the typical instrument of the new-born cinema industries in Asia and South America, too. This popularity drove manufacturers in other European countries to copy the most important characteristics of the Parvo.

The all-metal body of the model L is of box shape, its dimensions being $27 \times 20 \times 13$ cms (approx. $10\frac{1}{2}$ in. $\times$ 8 in. $\times$ 5 in.), and its weight 22 lbs.

The intermittent movement consists of a special shuttle and register pin system, working beneath the aperture, their operation being complemented by a special pressure plate.

Viewing is effected by three means:

(i)   through the film and taking lens; whether the camera is stopped or running;
(ii) on a ground glass (both (i) and (ii) produce a magnified, upright image correct from left to right);
(iii) a side monitoring viewfinder to allow for quick framing.

Fig. 14. Debrie Parvo L camera, which provides three different methods of viewfinding.

The model 58 is further provided with a parallax corrected optical tube fixed on the right hand side of the camera. The shutter is of the variable opening type, adjustable over a scale calibrated from 1 to 7, corresponding to shutter openings ranging from 20° to 150°.

Lenses must be single mounted by means of a special mounting, with mechanical devices for external focus and diaphragm control, whose readings are shown on external interchangeable scales.

The film is carried in typical Debrie magazines, mounted side by side inside the camera body and with a capacity of 400 ft., emulsion wound outwards. The camera is driven by an easily mounted electric motor for 12 and 24 v. DC. A crank handle allows for hand operation of the camera at a speed of 8 frames per turn.

Other points to note are:

(i)   magnetic speed indicator,
(ii) crankhandle turn indicator,
(iii) capacity for adapting to anamorphic lenses,
(iv) automatic dissolve,
(v)   sunshade.

Eclair Cameflex M3 camera

One of the most outstanding innovations in the field of motion picture camera manufacture was the design of the Cameflex by the French engineers Coutant and Mathot for the Eclair International Diffusion. It was the result of several years research on the requirements of camera operators and on the combined possibilities of mechanics and optics. The originality of its conception lies in the attempt to achieve the ideal camera characteristics:

(i)   light weight,
(ii) high precision,
(iii) functional shape permitting easy handling,
(iv) extremely fast loading,
(v)   capacity for taking different drive motors,
(vi) wide range of applications.

With these aims in view, the Cameflex 35 was designed and built, and subsequently the Cameflex 16/35, the former having obtained an award from the Hollywood Motion Picture Academy.

The history of the Cameflex has a long tradition of ingenuity and perseverance behind it. The makers, Eclair of Paris, started work last century as a motion picture studio, and later as a laboratory.

In 1909 the company started producing cameras which were widely accepted in Europe and the USA. Among the many instruments they produced was the Cameraeclair, famous for its six lens turret, and the hand-held Camerette.

When sound films appeared, a new model was produced to record image and sound simultaneously on separate films. During the Nazi invasion of Paris in World War II, the Eclair Co. was immediately occupied and fruitless attempts were made to make the technicians of the company produce a camera for the German Film Service (UFA). Some time later, Eclair engineers started secretly to conceive an ideal instrument for all types of work, designed on the basis of totally different concepts from those applied at the time. These were kept secret and put into practice only after the war. The first units were manufactured in 1948 and obtained a prize at that year's Venice Biennale Festival. The "nouvelle vague" (new wave) surged in France through this instrument, which is also extensively used in Britain, in continental Europe (both East and West), the Soviet Union, India, and Latin America. In the USA it has a circle of addicts and it is known there as the Camerette, in honour of its old time ancestor.

Fig. 15. Eclair Cameflex CM3 with self-contained magazine.

DESCRIPTION. The outstanding feature of the Cameflex lies in the principle of the magazine camera system.

Certain mechanical devices are included in the magazine which permit the film to be threaded in the magazine itself, instead of through the camera. This principle had previously been applied to some 16 mm cameras, but was now improved so that even the continuous drive and the two loops are included within the magazine.

FILM DRIVE. The intermittent drive consists of a two-ratchet claw shuttle movement installed inside the camera body, and two pressure pads mounted in the magazine. Two spring-loaded guides acting on the loops in the magazine keep the film moving at a continuous and uniform rate. The patented registration principle of the Cameflex produces a remarkably steady image and allows for a wide range of temperature fluctuations with resulting film stretch or shrinkage.

The continuous drive which forms the loops consists of a single sprocket with several pressure rollers on top and beneath, making up an assembly installed in the magazine.

LENS TURRET. The lenses are bayonet-mounted on a spider turret, with diverging optical axes. The minimum focal length is 18 mm. The turret is rotated by hand, the taking lens being the one on the arm pointing down.

SHUTTER. The shutter is of the variable opening type, adjusting from a maximum opening of 200° to a minimum of 40°. It was designed so that the shutter blades stop the light rays very near the focal plane, which produces a very high degree of image definition.

VIEWING SYSTEM. The Cameflex reflex viewing system works with mirror surface shutter blades, a large magnification and eyepiece adjustment.

The viewing system can be pivoted horizontally, upwards and downwards, so as to allow for framing and focusing from any camera position. Moreover, viewing can be effected with either right or left eye by rotating the eyepiece. A special shutter shuts light out of the viewfinder when not in use, to avoid the possibility of light seeping through to the film.

MOTOR. The standard motor of the Cameflex is of small size

and is installed on the right hand-side of the camera. It also acts as a hand-grip. It is of the variable-speed type and works at 6/8 v., its rating being 55 watts. It is easily interchanged with other motors of similar dimensions, either for 24 v. DC or synchronous 110/220 v. For special processes an attachment is supplied for hand operating with a crank, affording speeds of either 1, 8, or 16 frames per turn.

APERTURE PLATE. The plate with standard sound aperture (868 in. × 631 in.) is of chrome plated steel. The Scope model of this camera is provided with a 0·937 in. × 0·735 in. aperture.

MAGAZINES. Three magazines sizes are supplied for the Cameflex: 100, 200 and 400 ft. respectively. The 100 ft. magazine, with 3⅝ in. spools can be loaded in daylight but the others must be loaded in a darkroom or changing bag. As explained above, the continuous drive movement is situated inside the magazine, which thus constitutes the second most important unit in the camera. The magazines are easily attached to and detached from the camera, thus allowing for changeover to different types of emulsion with negligible loss of film (about 2 in.), at the same time simplifying the record of exposed film, as each magazine is supplied with its own built-in footage counter.

SUNSHADE AND MATTE-BOX. The sunshade of the Cameflex is built throughout of light metal alloy, and is installed on two parallel rods which can be attached to the camera base; masks can be fixed on its front to reduce the field of view. The two-slot matte-box allows for the insertion of 3 in. × 3 in. filters and masks. Gelatin filters can also be inserted in a slot in front of the aperture.

CONTROLS. The controls are incorporated in various parts of the camera: the footage counter (in meters) is built into the magazine; the magnetic speed indicator is placed at one side, below the aperture; the shutter-opening adjusting knob is placed on one of the sides of the camera, and the switch is built into the motor.

BLIMP. The Cameblimp is a soundproof cover built of light metal alloy which permits the use of the Cameflex with 400 ft. magazines for direct sound recording. The Cameflex is installed on a sliding plate in the blimp, and the different functions are directly connected, either by rods or by flexible cables, to external

Fig. 16. Cameblimp. Visible are the controls for focusing and diaphragm, peepholes for observing footage indicator and tachometer, and the reflex finder.

controls on the outside of the blimp. The external controls provided are:

(i)   diaphragm control,
(ii) focusing control,
(iii) shutter control,
(iv) reflex viewing,
(v)   footage counter,
(vi) speed indicator window.

An extendible square-section bellows sunshade can be attached in front of the blimp. The Cameblimp including camera and 400 ft. magazine weighs approximately 110 lbs.

ANAMORPHIC LENS SCOPE MODEL. The manufacturers have released a model of the Cameflex called the Scope which allows for shooting with anamorphic lenses. It differs from the standard model in that:

(i)   the dimensions of the aperture are 0·937 × 0·735 inches (18·67 × 23·80 mm) (see p. 268) to suit Cinemascope or standard anamorphic ratios; the aperture dimensions can be modified by means of interchangeable plates;
(ii) a de-anamorphic viewer may be fitted to afford direct viewing through the anamorphic taking lens, but showing

89

an unsqueezed image. As in the standard model, this is a reflex viewfinder, but larger;

(iii) a special turret with one of its arms adapted to the anamorphic lens and corresponding aperture, while the other two arms are adapted to standard aperture.

The CM-3-T model of recent development allows the use of the Techniscope system by providing a quick change from four perforation pull-down to two perforation pull-down. Single perforation pull-down for 16 mm is also available in the 16/35 mm model.

Arriflex camera

In 1936 the German camera manufacturers Arnold & Richter A.G., introduced this excellently designed instrument, with its then revolutionary reflex viewing by means of a shutter placed at a 45° angle to the plane of the film. The first models were provided with 120° opening shutter, circular motion intermittent drive, and a rigid sunshade attached to a square shaft. Although its general design has been adhered to, improvements have been gradually

Fig. 17. Arriflex 35 Model IIC, with reflex viewing system and combined motor and handgrip and three-lens turret.

90

added, and today, the mechanical system generally is improved. The shutter opening has been increased to 180°, the intermittent movement has been changed for one giving high quality registration, a new optical system has been adapted for the viewfinder so that the resulting image is of greater brightness, and an extendible sunshade replaces the former rigid one. The most recent innovations are a variable opening shutter and the possibility in certain models of interchanging viewfinder masks and blimp for use with 400 and 1000 ft. (120 or 300 m) magazines.

Many important cameras were made in Germany over the years, but the most outstanding is, no doubt, the Arriflex, created by Arnold & Richter. Established in 1917 as laboratories and accessory makers, they brought out their first camera, the Kinarri, in 1925. Long research by the heads of the company, August Arnold, an engineer, Dr. Robert Richter and Erich Kaestner, led to their ingenious viewing system in 1931. After testing the principles on prototypes, they came out with the now famous Arriflex.

Designed mainly for news coverage, it had the sad task of recording the rise and fall of Hitler's regime: the Axis pacts, the invasion of France, the Russian disaster, Musolini's death, the Nuremberg trials. Many World War II documentaries include much German material shot with Arriflexes.

In spite of the war, many of its innovations leaked through to West Europe and America. From 1943, the almost identical American "Cineflex" (known as the PH-330), was made for the Armed Forces. The first Hollywood feature film employing the Arriflex, "Dark Passage" (1945), was directed by Delmer Daves, who had tried them out before, testing captured enemy material for the US Forces.

Arriflexes started crossing the Atlantic commercially in 1947, and Robert Flaherty was one of the first to adopt them for his "Louisiana Story" (1948). Some time later their makers could hardly cope with ever-increasing orders. It became standard equipment with the BBC, the Italian RAI, Polish Film News, and film units of the US Armed Forces. The Arriflex is used in many documentaries, commercials and "new wave" productions all over the world. Many critics mention this camera as the tool of new-generation film makers the world over. When the Government of The People's Republic of China decided to manufacture their own cameras, they set up a factory in Nanking to turn out an instrument identical to the Arriflex.

GENERAL DESCRIPTION. The shape of the Arriflex is asymmetrical and its compact body in the form of a right-angled triangle holds the film drive mechanism; the reflex viewfinder tube is mounted on the outside of the access door. The cylinder shaped motor is attached to the camera base and acts as a hand-grip. The three-lens turret can be rotated by means of three small wing grips (one for each lens), which also indicate the lens which is in the taking position. The taking lens is protected by either a rigid or an extendible-bellows sunshade with matte-box for holding three 3 in. × 3 in. (76 × 76 mm) filters. The compact film magazine is externally attached, and includes a built-in footage counter. Other controls, such as the on-and-off switch, speed indicator and variable shutter control, are placed at the side or the rear of the camera. The resulting instrument, a light-weight, medium-size camera, is perfectly suited to hand-held shooting, but at the same time is easily adapted to high quality studio work by adding the relevant accessories.

FILM DRIVE. Two sprockets built into the magazine effect the continuous drive of the Arriflex, both for film supply and take up. On attaching the magazine to the camera, a gear in the continuous drive movement meshes with the camera's main drive, thus providing mechanical power transmission from the latter.

The intermittent drive movement is a precision mechanism which produces images with a high degree of registration stability. It is based on the action of a "dwelling-time" shuttle which at the end of its downward stroke steadies the film for recording the image.

The aperture plate is combined with the pressure plate to form a hinged door which opens inwards and affords easy access for threading the film and cleaning.

VIEWING SYSTEM. As explained previously, the Arriflex was the first camera to incorporate a viewing system of the reflex type. When the shutter is in the closed position, its blades, set at an angle of 45° to the optical axis of the lens, reflect the image on its mirror glass outer surfaces onto a ground glass with vertical louvres to eliminate reflections falling on the film emulsion. An optical magnifying system (improved in the latest model II-C) shows this image exactly as it is recorded on the film when the shutter is in the open position. The ground glass is interchangeable and is marked to indicate the aperture it corresponds to. The viewing optical system is installed on the camera access door, and is furnished with an eyepiece having a rubber eyecup and adjusting ring for individual eyesight. In the latest model, the pressure of the eye on the eyecup opens an automatically closing shutter to protect the film from light coming in through the viewing system. When sighting the scene through the viewfinder before shooting, a small knob on the right-hand side of the camera is turned by hand to rotate the shutter and close it. The image shown through the reflex viewfinder is upright and correct from left to right, and is magnified $6\frac{1}{2}$ times.

MOTORS. The motor of the Arriflex is also the handgrip. It works at 16 v. in the latest models, and draws about 4 amps when working with a full film load. It is provided with a rheostat at the lower end for adjusting the operating speed, which is read on a built-in speed indicator, scaled from zero to 50 frames per second. The rheostat itself is calibrated from 1 to 9, a scale which furnishes a basis for operating-speed determination, given a constant voltage. Speeds greater than 32 f.p.s. can be attained by increasing the voltage of the supply source, or by exchanging the motor for another one specially designed for running at speeds up to 80 f.p.s.

Fig. 18. Arriflex converted for studio use by adding the Model 400 blimp with full external controls, and blimp basher attached.

Two switches are provided for starting and stopping the motor. One is of the push-button type, located near the motor socket, for short hand-held takes. The other is a toggle switch for long takes, or when operating on a tripod. The latest models are supplied with a switch for reverse drive, located near the power cable socket.

When the camera is operated in synchronism with a sound recorder, the variable speed motor must be changed for a synchronous one. A governor-controlled motor, or a transistor-controlled constant speed motor can also be used. The synchronous motor is a larger unit than the other ones, since it comprises a built-in footage counter, and a safety switch which is installed in the camera to switch off the power in the event of stoppage.

Fig. 19. Right-hand side view of Model 400 Arriflex blimp with matte box and sunshade.

ACCESSORIES. Of the accessories supplied by the manufacturers for this camera, the most important is probably the blimp. There are two models of blimp, for 400 ft. and 1000 ft. magazines. Both are built according to the most up-to-date sound-proofing techniques and are of streamlined functional shape. The 400 ft. model encloses the camera with synchronous motor and magazine for 200 ft. or 400 ft. colour film, or 500 ft. b & w. It is supplied with external controls for focusing, observation windows for lens markings, adjustable sunshade and matte-box. The 1000 ft. model converts this hand-held camera into equipment capable of turning

94

out studio work. One of its outstanding features is that it will take 1000 ft. rolls of film in Mitchell or Newall magazines; the magazine includes a special adapter with the continuous drive sprocket, guides etc. A small torque motor assures trouble-free take-up in the 1000 ft. magazine by means of reduction gears and a double friction belt. The controls furnished with the 1000 ft. blimp are the following:

(i)   three focus controls (located at both sides and behind the camera),
(ii) knob at front for diaphragm adjustment,
(iii) direct observation windows for lens marking,
(iv) pulsating pilot light,
(v)   sound signal when safety switch is operated,
(vi) dial for rotating shutter manually.

Among the many other accessories for this camera, the periscope attachment to the finder deserves special mention; its use is briefly described in Chapter 5.

Newman Sinclair Autokine cameras

The James A. Sinclair Co. Ltd, of London, of longstanding reputation in the photographic field, has for more than 60 years produced a series of excellent motion picture cameras for documentary, commercial and newsreel filming. Two of these models are still manufactured to special order.

Since Arthur Newman started producing them in the first decade of this century, Newman Sinclair cameras have had an excellent reputation in Britain, among scientific explorers and documentary film-makers. One of the first models was used by Herbert Ponting to shoot his Antarctic expedition. They were also taken on J. Noel's Mount Everest expedition, and their efficiency was also proved under different climates and difficult conditions by the Royal Geographical Society and the New York Zoological Society. A hand-held, spring-driven model known as the "Autokine" appeared in 1928 which also won great acceptance among cinematographers. Robert Flaherty shot his famous "Man of Aran" in 1933 in lonely Inishmore Island off the west Irish coast mostly with this camera. When Basil Wright travelled east and climbed the dangerous Sri Pada peak to shoot "Song of Ceylon"

95

in 1934–35 he also relied on this instrument to produce one of the classics of documentaries. This camera was almost the standard tool of a large portion of British documentaries produced at that time by the film units of the Empire Marketing Board and the GPO under the leadership of John Grierson.

The identifying characteristic of the Newman Sinclair camera is its box-shaped duralumin body ($9\frac{1}{2}$ in. × $4\frac{3}{4}$ in. × $9\frac{1}{2}$ in.). Four models were produced: the M, the E, the G and the N, as well as a high-speed model. The intermittent movement produces a very steady registration. It comprises a shuttle acting on a sector of the perforations, and a fixed pilot pin at the lower, right-hand corner of the aperture. In recent models viewing is effected through a bright-image reflex finder. In previous models a side-placed finder provided the viewing system which was parallax-corrected and had an interchangeable front lens. These old models also

Fig. 20. Newman Sinclair Model N, made in duralumin showing the lenses mounted on divergent axes.

incorporated direct viewing through the film by means of a special prism optical system.

The film is carried in internally-mounted, double-compartment 200 ft. magazines. Normally the shutter has a fixed opening of 160°, but the manufacturers can supply a shutter variable up to 170°.

96

Newman Sinclair cameras are driven by two springs which can be wound either at the beginning of the take or when the camera is running. The capacity of the springs ensures that 200 ft. of film is driven at constant speed with a single wind. For sound synchronization work, either a synchronous or variable speed motor can be used. Both types of motor include a speed indicator and sound sync-pulse, and are for 230 v. AC.

The lenses are mounted on a divergent-axis, three-lens turret (model N) or single mounted lens (models G and E), by means of a special sliding plate. Other characteristics are:

(i)   operating speed from 10 to 32 f.p.s.,
(ii) weight approx. 17 lbs.,
(iii) special sunshade with matte-box for 3 in. × 3 in. filters.

Newman Sinclair P/400 camera

The P/400 is the most recent in the range of hand-held cameras manufactured by the James A. Sinclair Company, and is totally different in shape and design from previous models. The intermittent movement is furnished with two register pins, and a special plate for normal drive and for reverse drive. Lenses are mounted

Fig. 21. Newman Sinclair Model P/400 with three-lens turret, reflex viewing and detachable magazine.

97

D

on a three-arm turret, rotated by a central control knob. The viewing system is of the reflex type.

Film is loaded by means of special magazines, in which the continuous drive mechanism is included. The magazines are easily and quickly attached to the rear of the camera. Some of the magazine models are adapted for reverse drive.

A special model with interchangeable film gates can be used for both 16 mm and 35 mm.

Drive for the P/400 is provided by a compact electric motor easily connected to the right-hand side of the camera. This motor runs with 12 v. DC and is rated at 0·9 amps. For studio work this is interchanged for a synchronous motor of 230 v. single phase AC.

For shooting with synchronous sound recording, the makers have designed a special blimp enclosing the complete camera.

Cameraflex

This American-built camera is of very similar characteristics to the Arriflex 35 mm camera, and was manufactured by the Cameraflex Corp. of New York. Its intermittent drive comprises a shuttle acted upon by an eccentric, and film registration is by means of side pressure elements which steady the film adequately during exposure.

Fig. 22. Cameraflex, first American camera produced with reflex viewfinder.

Standard lenses for this camera are f.2·3, in Goerz Apogar 35 mm, 50 mm, and 75 mm focal lengths. Reflex viewing is by a shutter placed at 45° to the optical axis, and the resultant image is magnified, upright and corrected left to right.

The continuous drive is built into the 200 or 400 ft. magazines, externally mounted and provided with a footage counter. The 200 ft. magazine is of the single compartment type, carrying the raw stock as well as the exposed film. The 400 ft. model is of the double compartment type: one chamber for raw stock and the other for exposed film take-up.

As in the Arriflex, the motor also acts as camera handgrip, and can be easily detached and re-attached at the side when the camera is mounted on a tripod. The standard motor is for 12 and 24 v. DC, but there is also a model for 115 v. AC with built-in signal generator.

Other features are:
(i) speed indicator calibrated from 8 to 56 f.p.s.,
(ii) shutter with fixed 135° opening,
(iii) adapter for spring motor,
(iv) adaptations to use the camera for scientific work,
(v) device to accept a crank-handle for driving the camera manually.

Sputnik Soviet camera

In 1962, the Soviet film equipment industry developed this new instrument, its design having been specially aimed at film reporting and newsreel shooting.

It is provided with a three-lens turret and a shutter installed at 45° to afford a reflex image, with variable opening from 160° to zero. The reflex viewing system is through an optical tube which can be adjusted to the position of the camera operator. It can take 200 or 400 ft. magazines of the automatic type. A 5-8 v. DC electric motor drives the film at speeds from 8 to 40 f.p.s.

Perhaps the most interesting novelty introduced by this camera is its ingenious controls system. All of them being installed in the camera handgrips, they enable the operator to change focus, rotate the lens turret and start the motor.

Kohbac Automat Model IKCP Soviet camera

This camera is also Russian-made and its design is similar to the structure and facilities of the Eclair Cameflex. It is used for

Fig. 23. Sputnik Soviet newsreel camera with reflex view-finder and handgrip controls.

newsreel and documentary films. It is furnished with a three-lens turret, and a shutter at 45° to afford reflex viewing through a non-swivelling optical tube.

Fig. 24. Kohbac Automat, a Russian camera extensively used in shorts and newsreel work. This 12 lb. camera was used during the flight of Vostok II by astronaut Titov for obtaining shots of the earth.

The model IKCP is driven either by an electric motor or by a spring-loaded motor installed at the side of the camera. The magazines are of the internally-threaded type holding 200 ft. of film. The outside is plated, and the camera gives the impression of sturdy construction and convenience for hand-held operation.

Bell & Howell Eyemo

The Bell & Howell Co. of Chicago has designed a series of cameras notable for sturdiness and portability, and intended for scientific, laboratory and field work, newsreel shooting and military use.

In the motion picture industry, the Bell & Howell Co. had become world famous for their Standard Camera which for the first time included in this type of instrument, an all metal body, an externally placed double chamber magazine, an excellent intermittent drive with register pins, and an all-ball-bearing mounted mechanism. For many years it was standard equipment with all Hollywood studios and the minion of many cinematographers. In 1923 this company decided to step into the 16 mm gauge market (which had been actively promoted by the Eastman Kodak Co.) for exacting amateurs, and launched their Filmo camera. This instrument won such widespread approval that the makers decided to apply the same design and characteristics to the professional 35 mm gauge. They called their new model the "Eyemo" and it was conceived for use by newsreel cameramen, scientific explorers and documentary producers. Its spring drive had so many advantages over the then reigning crankhandle, that it was universally adopted by documenary film-makers. During World War II it was one of the standard instruments used by the Allied Forces and is still a leading lightweight camera.

All cameras in the Eyemo series have the same essential characteristics and differ only in minor structural details (disc or spider turret, different operating speeds, drive motor, magazines, etc). For this reason, the details which follow apply to any of the seven cameras in the series.

Though the design of the Eyemo is compact, all but two of the models can be easily converted into studio equipment by adding a magazine and/or electric motor.

GENERAL DESCRIPTION. The dimensions of the main internal elements, the spring motor and the film spools, determine the shape of the camera. The spring motor, housed in the right-hand section of the camera body, consists of a powerful spring surrounding the driving shaft. One full wind will drive the film 50 ft. The winding is effected by means of a handle with safety catch connection to the driving shaft, so that when the latter turns on operating the camera, the handle remains motionless.

The film spools are housed in the camera body section opposite the driving mechanism. This section also affords access to the intermittent movement through an easily detachable cover. This part of the camera takes its shape from the circular shape of the spools and their positioning. The spools carry 110 ft. of film, of which 10 feet are lost when loading and unloading in daylight.

VIEWING AND FOCUSING TUBE. Present-day Eyemo models have a side-viewfinder built into the camera access door. This finder produces an upright image similar to that formed by the taking lens on the exposed film frame in the aperture. The tube is also furnished with a small three-lens turret, which is a miniature replica of the normal shooting turret.

Parallax errors when filming close-ups are corrected by a sideways displacement of the finder eyepiece.

Besides the side or monitor viewfinder, four Eyemo models incorporate a small focusing microscope for critical focusing through the taking lens, by rotating the lens to one side and displacing the camera by means of a rack-over device fixed on the tripod.

FILM DRIVE. The continuous drive for these cameras is provided by two sprockets, one above the other. The intermittent movement comprises a two-claw shuttle ensuring very accurate registration.

CONTROLS. Controls and dials are grouped on the right-hand side of the camera. The operating speed control scale is calibrated differently in the several models, from 8 to 48 f.p.s. These speeds are governor-controlled. On top of the speed control there is an exposed footage counter with a top scale-reading of 100 ft., the camera's maximum film loading without an external magazine.

LENS MOUNTS. The simplest lens mount is that of the K model, which takes only one lens in a single mounting. L and M Eyemo have a compact three-lens turret, but lenses must be carefully selected to ensure that they do not interfere with each other's field of view. Models N, O, P and Q eliminate the possibility of interference since they include a spider turret with its arms wide apart.

MOTORS. There are three motor-driven models for the Eyemo series: one works at 110 v. AC, another works at the same voltage but is synchronous and can be used only at 24 f.p.s. The third model is for 12 v. DC and works from a battery source. The electric motors are small in size, and can be easily mounted on one side of the camera.

Fig. 25. Bell & Howell Eyemo Model "Q" camera. Note the 3-lens spider turret.

MAGAZINES. When a film load longer than 100 feet is required, either 200 or 400 ft. magazines must be attached at the rear of the camera by means of a threaded bush. When external magazines are used, a speed indicator must be applied to the footage counter so as to complement the information given.

EYEMO REFLEX ATTACHMENT BY F. & B. CECO. A very useful improvement has lately been introduced for the Eyemo series cameras: a prism optical system, made by the American firm F. & B. Ceco, is inserted between the taking lens and the shutter, thus providing for continuous reflex viewing through the taking lens while shooting. The characteristics of this device are:

(i) lenses are single mounted,
(ii) modification of Eyemo models K, L, M, N and O to admit electric motors and magazines,

(iii) 10:1 magnification of the reflex image,

(iv) insignificant loss of light (less than $\frac{1}{4}$ stop) when working with colour film or with light below 125 ft. candles,

(v) silent film aperture with separate standard aperture mask,

(vi) TV size frame engraved on viewfinder ground glass,

(vii) image is completely free of flicker.

Sound-on-film cameras

From the birth of sound films to the surge of TV, a large number of cameras appeared which recorded sound directly on the film band itself or on a separate film. They were conceived to cover the new possibilities open to news filming, with the advantage of directly synchronizing sound and image to cover conferences, interviews, etc.

Many American and European manufacturers made models specifically designed for this purpose. We recall the Sound Cameraeclair with image and optical sound in separate bands; the famous cameras of the Movietone News, the Akeley Sound, widely used in America and which appeared for a long time in the head titles of the MGM newsreel; the Wall, described hereunder, the sound versions of the Mitchell and the Newall, the German Fernseh, and the Soviet Era 1.KOS., of more recent production.

The surge of TV with its daily crop of news, hastened the downfall of 35 mm newsreels and these cameras are no longer widely used. The two instruments described below deserve special attention because one is a classical model still in circulation, while the other is a new double system version applying the modern technique of recording sound on a separate perforated magnetic film.

Single system: Wall camera

This camera was manufactured by John M. Wall Inc. of New York, and was designed to cover the requirements of newsreel operators for simultaneous image and sound recording. It is of sturdy construction and the outstanding feature is its optical recording on the same film that carries the image.

Standard lenses for this camera are manufactured by Bausch & Lomb with focal lengths of 35, 50, 75 and 152 mm. The sound recording system is independent of the camera and is easily installed. The variable shutter opening is adjusted up to a maximum

104

of 170° (190° in some models) by a knob located on the right-hand side of the camera.

The high-precision intermittent movement was specially designed, and can be easily interchanged.

In its general principles the viewing system is similar to that of the Mitchell camera. The camera body is displaced sideways so that a special focusing and framing tube is placed behind the taking lens. When the camera is in the operating position, this tube acts as a side-mounted viewfinder; it is parallax-corrected at the eyepiece and is provided with different masks corresponding to the fields of the different apertures.

Fig. 26. Wall camera with built-in single-system sound recording.

The 400 ft. or 1000 ft. double chamber magazines are installed on top of the camera. Drive is supplied by a constant speed, 12 v. motor, with speed control at the back of the camera by a rheostat and tachometer.

Double system: Arricord camera

Arnold & Richter, makers of the Arriflex, produce this model to fill the need of newsreel camera operators for picture and sound recording on separate film and magnetic tape.

The Arricord comprises a special blimp housing an Arriflex 35 with 400 ft. magazine in one section, and a recorder using 17½ mm perforated magnetic tape in a separate section. Both elements are mechanically coupled to ensure perfect synchronization of picture and sound recording.

The camera section is furnished with external controls for focusing and iris diaphragm. Reflex viewing is retained by extending the finder tube through the rear of the blimp. Reading of the tachometer is through a window close to the finder eyepiece.

Constant speed drive at 24 f.p.s. is supplied by interchangeable motors for either 24, 110 or 220 v .An extendible bellows sunshade with matte-box protects the lenses against reflected light; it is adjustable for lenses of different focal length.

Fig. 27. Arricord double-system camera to record magnetic sound incorporating an Arriflex camera with 400 foot magazine.

The sound recording section houses a magnetic recorder carrying 500 ft. of perforated tape and works with a Klangfilm amplifier. Other features are:

(i) built-in illuminated indicators,
(ii) phone-type dial to operate shutter,
(iii) footage counter,
(iv) built-in ammeter,
(v) earphone plug for listening to recorded sound,
(vi) electronic slate.

106

Wide screen cameras

Technirama camera

The Technirama process was developed by the Technicolor Corporation and continues to be in active use. Its basic principle is the squeezing of a scene by an anamorphic prism block to print lengthwise on a 35 mm negative which travels horizontally. This system is similar to Vistavision, (see page 109), but has the added advantage that the picture can afterwards be reduced and turned 90° to convert it into a squeezed 35 mm film image, or it can be reprinted on 70 mm stock.

The use of a very high quality optical system, plus the advantage obtained by reduction, produces an image of high definition, free of graininess, and without distortion.

Technirama was based on the old "three-strip" Technicolor camera (see page 164).

The beam-splitter prism was replaced by a wide aspect ratio aperture for an 8-perforation frame, and the bipack system inter-mittent movement by a horizontal movement in which the film was moved forward 8 perforations at a time.

The optical system was designed by Professor Bouwers of the Onde Delft Company of Holland. It consists of a combination of

Fig. 28. Technirama camera using an anamorphic optical system and horizontal film travel for lengthways images on 35 mm film.

107

interchangeable primary lenses with a split rhombohedral prism with specially cut faces producing an anamorphic coefficient of 1·5 to 1 constant over the whole picture area and giving excellent definition.

The primary lenses were chosen from among different makes with the intention of obtaining a similar degree of definition, resolution and apochromatic quality. These comprise: 50 mm Leitz Summicron, 75 and 100 mm Cooke Taylor Hobson, and 135 mm Canon.

Primary lenses can be focused by the Selsyn motor remote control, as originally installed in the 3-strip cameras, or by individual control on the side of the camera.

Viewing is effected by a through-the-lens finder, and by an automatic parallax-corrected monitor viewfinder installed on the side of the camera.

Magazines are mounted side by side and have a capacity of 2000 ft. They are driven by a special torque motor with friction pulley transmission, thus eliminating film snatch when starting, and over-run when stopping.

The driving motor is installed at the rear, and can be inter-

Fig. 29. Another view of the Technirama camera. Observe the elaborate system for driving the magazines.

changed; the models supplied are of the synchronous type for AC or DC, three-phase, and for 220 or 96 v.

For filming with direct sound recording, a special large volume soundproof blimp is used, which is a modification of the 3-strip camera blimp, and is further provided with a special sunshade and other improvements.

More recently, a lightweight model of the Technirama camera has been introduced. It is of smaller volume, takes 1000 ft. magazines and allows the use of three primary lenses of 50, 75 and 100 mm focal length. For underwater shooting, the makers supply a watertight shell furnished with external controls, floats and stabilizers; this shell is built to withstand high water pressure and allows the camera to be very easily operated down to a depth of 230 ft.

Vistavision camera

The Vistavision system was developed by Paramount Studios of Hollywood, and makes use of an 8-perforation horizontal frame on 35 mm film. Vistavision is in many ways similar to the Technirama system just described. Most of the Vistavision cameras were produced by The Mitchell Camera Corp., and though the system is now obsolete, some of the cameras are still in use for matte shots and for producing transparencies for back projection.

Lenses are single mounted and their focal length varies from 21 mm to 152 mm. The shutter is of the variable opening type, with a maximum of 190°.

The film drive mechanism is a development of the Mitchell intermittent movement. The film travels horizontally from left to right exposing 1·485 in. × 0·991 in. frames which cover eight perforations and have an aspect ratio of 1·96 to 1.

Viewing is effected directly through the taking lens by mechanically displacing the camera body, complemented by a Mitchell monitor viewfinder on top of the camera provided with vertical parallax correction.

Magazines are equipped with their own drive motors and take a film load of 2000 ft.

The Vistavision camera is driven by a special synchronous motor installed with its shaft placed horizontally at the back of the camera. Its rating ranges from 96 to 220 v. and it is provided with reverse drive.

The most important accessories are:

(i) special design of blimp enclosing the complete instrument,
(ii) Selsyn motor remote focus control,
(iii) sunshade.

Vistavision field camera

The intermittent movement of this camera is similar to the Mitchell NC and BNC models. The shutter opening is fixed at 162°. Viewfinding is by means of a parallax-corrected finder equipped with a small turret holding several lenses installed on top of the camera.

The 400 ft. double-chamber magazines are mounted behind the camera. The instrument is driven by a lightweight variable-speed motor working at 28 v.; a built-in rheostat allows the camera to be operated at speeds from 12 to 24 f.p.s. For outdoor shooting, a DC supply can be fed from portable batteries. For special process work the motor can be interchanged for a 96 v. motor.

The Vistavision field camera weighs about 20 pounds, and therefore can be easily hand-held for locations where studio cameras cannot be employed.

Vintage cameras

With the progress of film technique, many excellent cameras have become obsolete. Examples of these, built in the period between 1920 and the coming of sound, are still doing stalwart work in scientific and technical institutes and laboratories in Europe and Latin America. Good specimens may still be found for sale or on exhibition in some camera stores and are fast becoming valuable collectors' items. In a short tabulation such as this, many less well-known makes and models must necessarily be omitted.

Akeley

Many critics consider that the twenties and the thirties were the golden age of motion pictures. Together with a large output of fiction films, many industrial and "travel" productions were made, and the major world events of the time were recorded. For the latter items, cinematographers had available a wide range of cameras made in the USA and in several countries in Europe. Britain was making Darling cameras, Williamsons, Newman Sinclairs, Cinchros and the Moy-Omnias used by Ernest Shackle-

110

ton in his Antarctic expedition. In France the Debrie Parvo and the Eclair were already reigning while in Germany they were making the Askania, the Bamberg, the Ernemann, the Zeitlinger, the Maurer & Waschke and the Ika Kinamo. We have already seen some of the instruments which acquired wide fame in America and still maintain their reputation; we shall see a few others yet, but at that time one of the most popular instruments was undoubtedly the camera designed by Karl E. Akeley, an outstanding American scientist, inventor, lecturer and sculptor.

Akeley was curator of the New York Natural History Museum, who sent him to Africa to study animal life in that continent and record on film. He took with him several camera models that were popular at the time. But he did not succeed in obtaining an effective filmed record of the expedition owing to the requirement for a camera that was immediately available in optimum operating condition and able to follow fast movement. On returning he tackled the design of an instrument capable of overcoming the difficulties he had suffered. He achieved an instrument which broke away from most of the established concepts at that time, and which included many improvements to follow rapid moving subjects.

The new Akely camera soon became a favourite with newsreel cameramen and documentary producers (Robert Flaherty took it to the Arctic in 1922 to shoot his first film "Nanook of the North"). It sold so well that for a long time its manufacturers could not cope with an increasing build up of orders. And when Hollywood returned to Africa with first-rate cinematographers like Fred Parrish and for spectacular feature films like "Trader Horn" (1932), the Akeley was in the front line, challenging the same difficulties that a few years ago had led to its creation. The camera's outstanding characteristics were: all metal, circular-shape body; focal plane shutter with 230° opening; intermittent movement with effective steadiness, the claw working on one side of the film only; framing and focusing system using a lens identical to the taking lens, with focus control and easily adjusted eyepiece; a 200 ft. magazine with built-in sprocket for installing inside the camera. It was crankhandle driven, but during World War II it was adapted to take electric drive.

Cameraéclair

This camera was manufactured by Eclair and became well known for the many facilities it afforded to the cinematographer

111

for special effects and process work. The lens turret mounted up to six lenses. Framing and focusing through the taking lens was effected by means of a mechanical device which placed a special viewfinder behind the aperture. Up to 400 ft. of film was loaded by means of magazines mounted inside the camera body. The camera was driven either by crankhandle or by constant speed electric motor, and counters were supplied for indicating exposed footage, exposed frames and crankhandle turns. The camera was equipped with sunshade and matte-box, built-in rangefinder, etc.

Newman Sinclair Standard

We have seen that Newman Sinclair cameras held a prominent position in British cinematography. The 400 ft. model was one of the first items this firm produced about 1910 and was widely used during World War I. It was also used on the trips made by the Duke of Windsor (then Prince of Wales) to Africa and South America, and by the well known explorer Major A. Radcliffe Dugmore, as well as by other cinematographers and explorers of that time, like Cherry Kearton, Harry Burton, Paul Rainey, and others. It went on a Mount Everest expedition with Capt. J. Noel and returned years later in Houston's flight. Throughout the years it maintained its reputation for its resistance to hard treatment and efficiency under all climates.

It was one of the first cameras to be adapted to take a small-size, battery-driven electric motor. Among its features the following are noteworthy:

(i)   automatic fade-in and fade-out,
(ii) three different systems for focusing,
(iii) bright finder for critical framing,
(iv) variable opening shutter,
(v)   intermittent drive with pilot pin registration.

It was driven by either crankhandle or electric motor and had a striking appearance since it was built of polished duralumin plates.

Askania Model Z

Over a period of many years, Askania Werke A.G. of Berlin manufactured a series of cameras for professional cinematography, of which the most outstanding was the Z model. The characteristics of this camera were very similar to the Debrie Parvo.

112

The demand for the Askania Z led to its mass-production for several years while it was the instrument preferred by many European operators and documentary film-makers. It was the camera most used by Hans Ertl to shoot notorious Nazi propaganda films like "Triumph of the Will" (1936), as well as "Olympiad" (1938), by Leni Riefenstahl. Many of these cameras covered the scenes of vast masses in these films. Leni Riefenstahl once employed up to 45 camera operators. At the same time, political films were being shot with Askania Z instruments in Italy, where the same system of simultaneously covering a scene with many cameras was applied. The Askania Z was well accepted in Italy, where it can still be found on animation benches and producing titles at some laboratories or documentary films for producers such as the well known Institute Luce.

The basic characteristics of this camera were very similar to the Debrie Parvo; its basic differences from the latter were the body finish, the lens hood and matte-box, the viewing system with double eyepiece, and critical framing effected only through the film.

Prevost

The motion picture industry became important in Italy during the silent era, and consequently many Italian manufacturers produced models of 35 mm cameras. Amongst them should be mentioned the Micro of the Societa Micromeccanica of Milan, the Standard camera produced by the Fotovita Company, also of Milan, and the Teck by the Serra Company of Turin.

But the Italian camera that was most widely accepted and sold in international markets was undoubtedly the Prevost made by the Attilio Prevost Company. This instrument was first produced in 1922 and was based, like many other designs on the principles of Joseph Debrie's Parvo L. However the Prevost boasted several improvements in form and mechanical design.

The lenses and lens mounts had been designed for quick change-over and furthermore allowed for shifting the lens along the optical axis. A diaphragm and iris system provided for special photographic effects. Fade-ins and fade-outs were produced by a variable shutter opening. Critical viewing was achieved through the taking lens with the loss of only one frame. The film-load was carried in separately mounted 400 ft. magazines. The other characteristics were similar to the Debrie Parvo L.

Institute Standard

Created in 1910, the New York Institute of Photography has acquired international reputation in teaching the arts of still photography and motion pictures. Distinguished professors and cinematographers like Herbert C. McKay, ARPS, Peter Milne, Carl Louis Gregory, FRPS and many others transmitted the most severe standards of cinematographic techniques to several generations, through this Institute and its associated Falk Publishing Co. Many of the cinematographers who have become active in the industry, whether commercial, documentary or newsreel were produced by the Institute's publications, corresponddence courses or practical lessons at its own premises.

To cover the requirements of specialized tuition and the demand of its pupils, and "shorts" producers, the Institute decided to undertake the production of a low-priced, lightweight, multipurpose camera. It was designed by the Institute's director, Carl Louis Gregory, together with Herbert C. McKay and William Nelson and it was manufactured at the Wilart Cinema Corporation's workshops, a firm which was already well known for the streamlined design of their cameras. The new instrument was called the Institute Standard and was widely used in the east coast of USA.

Its outstanding features were its four-lens turret, choice of fixed or variable opening shutter, high efficiency intermittent and continuous drive, critical viewfinding through film, 400 ft. double chamber magazine, etc. This camera introduced a concept now generally applied throughout the motion picture camera industry: that of a basic unit improved and complemented by accessories. The camera was sold with a single lens and small magazine, and could be gradually added to by means of a lens turret, large capacity magazines, rangefinder, etc.

DeVry

Over many years, the De Vry Co. won a reputation in the American market for its motion picture projectors, particularly the portable 35 mm model, which sold to many Armed Forces all over the world. Early in the twenties, hand-held, spring-driven, lightweight cameras were very scarce; the most popular was the B & H. Eyemo which had recently appeared and was selling very well. This persuaded the De Vry company to design a compact 35 mm gauge instrument, conceived for newsreel cameramen and exacting amateurs. It consisted of a leather-covered metal box of small dimensions weighing about nine pounds. Its main characteristics were:

(i)   single mounted interchangeable lens,
(ii) fixed opening (135°) shutter,
(iii) spring-driven motor,
(iv) daylight-loading 100 ft. spools of film.

The DeVry was much used by newsreel operators and the Allied Forces during World War II.

The company also built a camera for direct recording image and sound by the optical process, either on one or two strips. This camera obtained a very poor acceptance, but some of its concepts were later adopted by John M. Wall in his famous sound camera.

Universal and Box cameras

The Universal and Box cameras were very popular instruments for newsreel shooting, commercials and documentary films during the second half of the twenties. They were low-priced cameras of simple design built of seasoned wood as was usual at the time. The Universal carried a 200 ft. film load in square metal magazines, internally mounted. It was turned by a crankhandle. The Newton-type viewfinder was installed on top of the camera and was protected against reflections. The variable opening shutter could be adjusted from the back of the camera. The Universal was equipped with a 3-lens turret, and critical focusing was effected by a viewing system through the film.

The British-made Box camera was supplied in different models but its characteristics were very similar to those of the Universal.

Cunningham combat camera

Of all instruments of this type, the one which best deserves the name of combat camera is undoubtedly the Cunningham. It was designed with painstaking research by the U.S. Government, for use by film reporters covering the combat fronts in World War II. Its main features were:

(i)   magnesium alloy body with rifle-butt shoulder pad and pistol grip;
(ii) special turret with shockproof lens mountings;
(iii) intermittent movement consisting of a 2-claw shuttle and

115

register pin, which together with the continuous drive were included, in 200 ft. magazines;

(iv) viewfinder on top of the camera with frames for four different lenses;

(v) drive by electric motor for variable speeds from 16 to 32 f.p.s.

The camera could be operated in the taking position by grips and controls located within easy hand reach. Outstanding characteristics of the Cunningham were its sturdy construction and its anti-reflection treatment of all surfaces and components.

This instrument was manufactured by the American Camera Co., of Hollywood, and it is believed that Gregg Toland participated in its design on returning from shooting the well known "December 7th" war documentary. Military restrictions on this camera, known as the PH-530 PF, were withdrawn in 1954 and it then appeared for sale in the American market.

REFERENCES

[1] A.S.C. Cinematographic Annual, edited by Hall & Hall, Vol. I and II, Hollywood (1930).
[2] Cameron, J. R., *Sound Motion Picture Recording and Reproducing*, 8th edn., Cameron Publishing Company, Florida (1959).
[3] Mascelli, J., *American Cinematographer Manual*, 1st edn., A.S.C., Hollywood (1960).
[4] Rose, J. J., *American Cinematographer Hand-book and Reference Guide*, 8th edn., Hollywood (1953).
[5] Lutz, E. G., *The Motion Picture Cameraman*, Charles Scribner's Sons, New York (1927).
 Wyn, M., *Initiation aux Techniques du Cinema*, Eyrolles Ed., Paris (1956).

3

SURVEY OF 16 MM CAMERAS

Up to a few years ago, 35 mm film was the accepted standard gauge for professional film making, while 16 mm was used almost exclusively by advanced amateurs and a few professionals for scientific and other specialized work. The great upsurge of television with the consequent profusion of specially shot documentaries and news films, brought widespread popularity to 16 mm, adopted mainly because of its lower cost. Thus, though 35 mm is still standard for feature films and large-scale TV serials, the number of professional units working with 16 mm has now outrun the 35 mm units.

Technical developments over the past fifteen years have contributed to provide TV film units, and especially TV news cameramen, with a wide range of equipment to carry out their tasks rapidly and effectively. Manufacturers in the U.S.A. and Europe have taken great pains to design cameras with the characteristics required by TV coverage: light weight, high precision, sturdy construction and ease of operation.

Increasing demand in an ever extending market has forced manufacturers to improve their products constantly in order to incorporate the very latest developments as they appear from the research stage. Although in some cameras the original basic design has remained, new manufacturing processes open up infinite possibilities for the future.

TV requirements

From the long list of makes and models manufactured today, this survey covers only the instruments which TV crews and documentary film units use most frequently, to the extent that they have now become standard equipment.

TV coverage usually falls into one of three categories: on-the-spot coverage, the elaborated documentary and the interview, which implies simultaneous recording of sound and picture. Film production in each category makes different demands on the equipment, which must therefore be selected according to the type of work.

In the first category, the camera must be easy to operate and light enough for hand-held shooting, and consequently its film capacity should not be greater than 100 feet. It should allow for a quick and easy interchange of lenses, and the viewfinder must give a bright image covering the field of all these lenses.

When the camera is spring-driven, each winding should allow for at least eight takes of four seconds each. Finally, in cameras for on-the-spot coverage it is essential that both body and mechanism be of sturdy construction to withstand rough treatment without detriment to performance.

The filmed documentary calls for a number of further refinements in the camera. In the first place, it must be able to take 200 or 400 ft. magazines. A reflex viewfinder is also vital for this type of film, because of the rapid and exact framing and focusing it provides.

The variable opening shutter is also a useful feature for shooting fast-moving subjects and compensating for different film emulsion speeds.

A variable speed electric motor, a matte-box and a sunshade to allow shooting against the light, are other useful features.

Sound processes

Simultaneous recording of image and sound, required by interviews and similar films, can be done by one of two processes: optical or magnetic recording of sound on a track positioned next to the picture which is being recorded (single system), or recording on a separate tape or film (double system). The simplicity of single-system recording makes it the most effective medium when the material must be on the air very shortly after filming. This is the standard system for TV news programmes. It is when the material must be carefully edited that the double system shows its advantages.

Besides a focusing and framing viewfinder through the taking lens and a good drive mechanism, cameras for double-system sound recording must be able to run noiselessly and must be provided with effective sound synchronism. This can be achieved by interlock or synchronous motors, or by pulse or tone generators.

118

Silent 16 mm cameras

Bell & Howell Filmo

The Bell & Howell Co. designed this camera some 40 years ago, and to this day it keeps its original basic design principles, although some details have been modified. It has become standard equipment for many TV newsreel cameramen thanks to its sturdiness and ease of operation, and is still one of the most popular hand-held cameras.

The "70" series of this make comprises six different models: DA, DL, H, DR. SR and HR; the latest three of these include several refinements which considerably improve their ease of operation and general appearance.

Fig. I. Bell & Howell Filmo 70-DR news-reel camera with geared viewfinder turret and matched lenses.

The body is a single-piece aluminium alloy pressing, whose shape is determined by the main internal element, the drive mechanism and the film chamber. The sturdiness and rigidity of the body frame make possible a precision fitting of the different parts of the mechanism.

INTERMITTENT DRIVE. This mechanism comprises a cam operating a single claw shuttle, which penetrates into and withdraws from the film perforations at a right angle so as to avoid any up-and-down disturbance of the film. This produces a steady image without the use of a register pin.

119

SPRING DRIVE. Between 19 and 22 feet of film can be exposed with one winding of the spring, and a constant speed is ensured throughout the run by a high-speed governor. The intermittent shuttle is complemented by the two sprockets making up the continuous drive, which are gear-connected to the film take-up. The pressure rollers on the sprockets are interlocked so that on opening them up, the film gate is also opened. Thus a single operation makes the camera ready for threading.

SPEEDS. This camera can be operated at seven speeds: 8, 12, 16, 24, 32, 48 and 64 f.p.s., controlled by a dial on the side of the camera.

FILM STORAGE. Two classical type 100 to 120 ft. spools, one for supply and the other for take-up, are mounted on corresponding spindles inside the camera body.

LENS TURRET. Three lenses can be installed on the turret by means of C type thread mountings. When the turret has been turned, a safety device prevents the camera being started if a lens is not correctly in front of the aperture. In the DR, SR and HR models of this series, the taking lens turret is gear-connected to a turret on the viewfinder, so that the change of lens is synchronized with a change of viewfinder.

VIEWFINDER. Viewfinding and framing of the picture are done solely by a side viewfinder fixed on the camera access door and provided with a three-lens miniature turret corresponding to the three taking lenses. The finder's eyepiece is fitted with a control ring to adjust it to the operator's eyesight. The finder also allows for parallax correction down to 3 feet. The magnified image it provides is very bright and of the same proportions as that recorded on the film.

CRITICAL FOCUSER. When focus adjustment must be effected through the taking lens itself, its diaphragm must be opened fully and the turret rotated 180° to place it before a small critical focuser. The focus can then be checked by means of a small circle showing part of the image.

FOOTAGE COUNTER. Located on the side of the camera, near the speed control, the footage counter is a disc which can be set

120

directly by hand. It is scaled from zero to 100 feet and its calibrations allow for the length of leaders at the beginning and end of the spool.

CRANK HANDLE. The Filmo camera can be driven by means of a crank handle inserted into a hole provided for that purpose. This allows for continuous drive of the film, regardless of the 22 ft. maximum of the spring. Reverse drive can also be effected with the crank handle, but this winds the spring, which restricts the length of reversing. A frame counter indicates the number of frames exposed or reversed. The crank handle exposes 20 frames at every turn.

Paillard Bolex

This renowned Swiss-made camera is extensively used for news coverage in many European countries as well as by some TV stations in North and South America. It is precision built, with a fine quality of finish.

The body incorporates the drive spring and the film drive mechanism. As with other hand-held cameras, the film is loaded inside the body by means of two spools holding up to 100 ft. of film perforated on one or both edges.

Fig. 2. Bolex Paillard with fade device attached and showing lever-operated triple-lens turret.

121

INTERMITTENT DRIVE. This is a precision mechanism with a registration pin to ensure image steadiness. It is interlocked with the two continuous drive sprockets to form a combined automatic threading mechanism. This provides fast and foolproof threading, a great convenience to any TV cameraman working under pressure.

SPRING DRIVE. The spring is wound by means of a relatively long crank handle, and with each complete winding $16\frac{1}{2}$ feet of film can be exposed. A small battery-driven electric motor is provided, whose light weight makes it ideal when taking hand-held shots of long duration. An interlocking device disconnects the spring from the mechanism, so that the latter can be driven either by the electric motor or by the crank. The latter, provided with a constant speed governor, also makes possible reverse drive. A speed selector allows operation from 8 to 64 f.p.s.

LENS TURRET. The turret takes three lenses with C type mounting. It is rotated by a lever, and is provided with a device for holding it fast when heavy lenses are used.

FILTER SLOT. As with most professional cameras, the Bolex allows for the insertion of gelatin filters between the lens and the aperture, through a slot located at the side of the turret.

VIEWFINDER. In the latest models of the Bolex, the manufacturers have included a reflex viewing system by means of a beam-splitter prism inserted between the taking lens and the aperture. This gives an image identical to that recorded through the aperture, but magnified six times, and ensures accurate framing and focusing. There is adjustment for individual eyesight at the finder eyepiece, which can also be closed to avoid light seeping in.

Another side viewfinder, known as an "octameter" because it provides eight focal ranges, is installed on the camera access door. It shows a bright image and has a parallax correction device and a 10 mm supplementary lens. This finder is used when precision of framing is not essential, but image brightness is important.

COUNTERS. The camera is equipped with an elaborate system for indicating used footage and the number of exposed frames. The footage counter is placed on the right hand side of the camera and is interconnected with the camera door for automatic resetting to zero. The exposed frame counter is provided with two scales and a zero reset knob below.

VARIABLE-OPENING SHUTTER. The shutter is of the variable opening type, which is a help in exposure time control and when shooting fast-moving subjects. The opening can be adjusted by means of a sliding lever to give 1/65 second exposure at 24 f.p.s. when fully open, to 1/640 second when 3/4 closed. An accessory allows for automatic fade-ins and fade-outs over 28 or 40 frames.

OTHER ACCESSORIES. A wide range of accessories can be supplied by the makers, providing the camera operator with a large number of facilities. Among them are 400 ft. magazines (for H16 RX-5 model), a constant-speed electric motor Type MST, a lightweight rechargeable battery, a pistol grip with trigger starter, cable releases which are very handy when using a zoom lens, an underwater container and an adjustable sunshade and mattebox.

Bolex HRX-5

In response to the demand of TV producers for long takes with sync. sound, Paillard S.A. have produced a new Bolex model, the HRX-5, with accessories which include a 400 ft. magazine, a special motor and a portable battery. The camera itself is little changed from the standard Bolex model, but is built to take interchangeable magazines, though it will also accept 100 ft. spools.

THE 400 FT. MAGAZINE. This is a single chamber magazine for laboratory rolls or spools of up to 200 ft. It is attached on top of the camera, and its base is provided with a light-trap at the film slot, so that no light will seep in when the magazine is removed from the camera. The magazine is driven by its own drive motor, and is provided with a counter reading unexposed footage.

CONSTANT SPEED MOTOR. The new MST motor is the most important innovation of the HRX-5. It weighs only 2 lb. Its constant speed derives from an armature which rotates at a speed controlled electronically by a centrifugal governor. It is available in three models (24, 25 and 16⅔ f.p.s.) for commercial films or U.S. TV, for European TV, and special work respectively.

The 24 and 25 f.p.s. models are provided with a frequency generator to facilitate sound synchronization by means of a pulsed signal.

Fig. 3. Bolex H-16 Model
RX-5 with 400 ft. magazine
and external motor.

Consequently, when ordering, the buyer must specify the type of magnetic synchronizing head used: Pilotton, Neopilotton, Perfectone or Rangertone.

The MST motor runs at 11 to 15 v. DC, and is provided with connections for the magazine motor and for the special starting switch (other than the one built into the motor) which can be operated from the hand-grip- or by remote control.

BOLEX BATTERY. This is a 10-cell, nickel cadmium battery (Saft-Voltablock), weighing $3\frac{1}{2}$ lbs, and rated at 12 v. The unit also comprises a charger for connecting to AC at 100 to 250 v. and 50/60 c/s with voltmeter, and which also acts as "buffer" and thus allows the camera motor to be connected while the battery is being recharged. The capacity of the battery is enough to shoot twenty-five 100 ft. spools or five 400 ft. magazines.

Bolex 16 Pro

This most recent Bolex camera is totally unlike its predecessors in conception and appearance, and incorporates the most up-to-date ideas in automation, view finding, and hand holding.

GENERAL CHARACTERISTICS. This camera has been conceived fundamentally for hand-held shooting, although provision has

124

also been made for tripod mounting. The 400 ft. coaxial magazine has been designed to provide adequate support on the shoulder. At both sides of the camera body there are hand-grips with switches for starting the motor and controlling the various devices.

The reflex viewing system using a revolving mirror shutter is so arranged that the image is always visible, even when the camera is stopped.

There is a × 20 magnifier for ease of critical focusing, and the swivelling periscope eyepiece. The diaphragm setting can be read through the finder.

MOTORS. The camera is driven by a 12 v. Synchro-Vario type motor installed inside the camera body. It provides both forward and reverse drive, as well as single-frame and its speed range is from 12 to 50 f.p.s.

The motor speed is regulated by means of transistorized governors. The double function claw intermittent movement gives a very steady image.

Three servo motors may be operated without moving the hands from the grips. Two of these focus and zoom the lens within a wide range of speeds.

The third motor is designed to automatically set the diaphragm in accordance with the prevailing light conditions. This motor is controlled by light through the lens (the TTL method) deflected from the viewfinder. This device allows for a film speed range of 12 to 1600 ASA, and a running speed of 12 to 50 f.p.s. as well as single-frame exposure.

Fig. 4. Bolex 16 Pro camera designed for hand and shoulder support, with reflex viewing and through-the-lens exposure control.

The lightweight, easily inserted magazines take either rolls or daylight-loading spools. When the film run is nearing its end, the operator is warned by a red lamp.

The camera is usually equipped with an Angenieux f. 2·2 12-120 mm zoom lens, or a Schneider-Variogon f.2 16–80 mm zoom lens.

Other lenses can also be used, and the mounting is of the bayonet type and of rugged design. The lenses are provided with special rubber sunshades.

Other features are connections for sync-pulse recording, magnetic recording head, adaptations for special accessories, electric start mark on film, etc.

ACCESSORIES. The most important accessories provided are: battery with control unit and charger, amplifier for magnetic recording on the film itself, radio microphone and receiver, "monopod" for hand-held shooting, ×15 magnifying eyepiece, electronic viewfinder, tachometer.

Arriflex ST camera

Arnold & Richter, German camera makers since 1917, have for many years had a reputation for well designed instruments to cover the requirements of scientific and documentary film units and newsreel cameramen.

The first 16 mm camera made by this firm was the ST model. The shape of its body is compact and designed for hand holding. It houses the intermittent drive mechanism, the reflex view-

Fig. 5. Arriflex 16 ST. can be converted for recording single-system magnetic sound with Gaumont Kalee recording equipment.

finder, and space for the film, while the lens turret is mounted on the front. The body is a single-piece, light alloy casting, weighing no more than 6½ lbs.

INTERMITTENT DRIVE. This mechanism comprises a single-claw shuttle pulling down on one side of the film, and a register pin to steady the film during exposure. All parts are made of high quality steel and are precision balanced and finished to ensure image steadiness.

FILM GATE. The pressure plate is spring loaded to ensure freedom from weaving and breathing. All surfaces in contact with the film are of alloy stainless steel with hard chromium plating. The pressure plate is hinged to allow access directly to the aperture and to the film guides.

REFLEX VIEWFINDER. This type of viewfinder with all its advantages of rapid focusing and accurate framing was first introduced on the Arriflex in 1936 and has been adapted to the 16 mm cameras. It produces a very bright image, even when the diaphragm is stopped down for shooting. The optical tube gives a 10 × magnification. The eyepiece is adjustable, and is closed automatically when not in use, to prevent fogging.

LENS TURRET. The turret takes three lenses with mountings of special design (identical to those for the Arriflex 35). Minimum lens focal length is 5·7 mm. The turret is compactly designed with divergent lens axes so that their fields will not interfere. To change lenses, the turret is rotated by pressing on wing grips jutting out of the turret edge, with inscriptions on their rear faces to indicate which lens is in the taking position.

CONTROLS. Located at the back of the camera: tachometer calibrated from 0 to 50 f.p.s.; footage counter and frame counter, both with zero reset knob.

MOTORS. The Arriflex ST is driven by an electric motor of small size which can be easily installed and interchanged to suit the operator's need. The standard motor is rated at 8 v. DC, and is provided with a rheostat for adjusting the camera speed from 4 to 48 f.p.s. It can also reverse at any speed. The following motors can also be supplied: synchronous motor for 110 or 220 v., 50 or 60 c/s driving the camera at 24 or 25 f.p.s.; governor-controlled motor for 8 v., also running at 24 or 25 f.p.s., and stop-frame equipment for animation.

ACCESSORIES. The makers produce many accessories for these cameras which turn it into a complete studio instrument. Among the most important are the following:

(i) the 400 ft. magazines which can be mounted in a slot on top of the camera, and can take 200 ft. or 400 ft. spools. An easily-detachable separate motor drives the take-up spool and is connected automatically to the camera power supply when the magazine is attached to the camera; these magazines are fitted with their own footage counters;

(ii) the blimp for this camera is very complete: it is equipped with a device for focus control and an extension for the reflex viewfinder tube and is designed to allow for the attachment of external magazines (as above), and for interchangeable motors;

(iii) periscope viewfinder attachment which swivels in any direction and allows the operator to view through the finder tube when standing in almost any position in relation to camera and subject.

Arriflex Model M

The wide popularity attained by the Arriflex 16 ST led to the introduction of two new 16 mm models, the M and the BL.

The M model is designed on the basis of the "magazine-camera" principle introduced on the Arriflex 35 in 1936. The motor is mounted on the camera body which houses the intermittent drive mechanism. The interchangeable magazine unit carries the continuous drive sprockets. After threading in the magazine the loop is inserted into the camera when attaching the magazine.

The other characteristics of the camera, such as the bright image reflex viewfinder, tachometer, frame and footage counters, lens turret with divergent axes, register pin, intermittent movement, etc., remain the same as for the ST model previously described.

However, in order to meet the needs of modern sound synchronization systems, together with certain specialized requirements, the makers have added several new facilities.

BUILT-IN TONE GENERATOR AND SLATING MECHANISM. This device allows for sound filming by synchronizing the camera to the sound recorder through the tone generator. A frame or its edge is exposed as reference between the sound track and the film at the start. To employ the pilot-tone generator built into the camera body, one of the special 24 or 25 f.p.s. motors must be used.

128

Fig. 6. Arriflex 16-M, with 200 and 400 ft. magazines. It has a built-in pilot-tone generator for synchronizing sound.

THREE CONNECTOR SOCKETS. These are located at the rear of the camera and are:

(i)   socket for the 5-pin plug of the pilot generator;
(ii)   socket for the 3-pin plug for parallel connection to the camera feed circuit (for special purpose work);
(iii) empty space for installing 2- to 12-prong connections for scientific work.

THE 1200 FT. COAXIAL MAGAZINE. This magazine is of ingenious design, with the two film spools mounted on the same axis, so that a large film capacity is enclosed in a comparatively small space. At sound filming speed 1200 ft. of film gives 30 minutes of continuous shooting, often a necessity when covering conventions and conferences, and in certain types of scientific work in which frequent reloading must be avoided.

MOTOR TRIP SWITCH. An item usually found only in more elaborate cameras, this acts as a safety switch which stops the motor in the event of film jamming inside the camera.

129

E

Fig. 7. Arriflex 16-M with 1200 ft. co-axial, double compartment magazine.

Arriflex model BL

The is the second and latest addition to the Arriflex 16 mm line. It combines the characteristics and advantages of the M and ST, as described above but has the added advantage of noiseless running mechanism and a zoom lens of special characteristics.

A new drive mechanism has been devised which runs much more silently than the standard one and the camera body is built with very effective noise deadening material, so that as much as possible of the little noise made by the mechanism will be absorbed.

The great improvement in the image quality of zoom lenses has brought them into almost universal use. So the Arriflex has been provided with a single mounting designed to take a special Arri zoom lens.

These modifications have resulted in alterations in other characteristics, such as changes in the reflex viewing system, addition of a built-in light meter, and a variable shutter device which can be adjusted even when the camera is running.

In short, the Model BL is a versatile, relatively light and virtually noiseless camera, well suited for TV news cameramen, documentaries and all types of shooting calling for direct sound recording.

130

Fig. 8. Arriflex 16 mm BL model with battery in separate case and shoulder strap.

Amongst the many accessories for this instrument are a DC motor with constant-speed governor, a magnetic sound head, and sunshade and matte-box

Eclair NPR (*Noiseless Portable Reflex*)

When Eclair of Paris conceived their new design of 16 mm camera, they broke away from long established concepts in camera making. In the first place, they abandoned the classical system of installing the film magazine on top of the camera, and instead attached it at the rear so that it rests on the operator's shoulder. This coaxial magazine (i.e. with both film spools on the same shaft) houses the camera's continuous drive mechanism; thus threading takes place in the magazine instead of in the camera body.

As in the firm's Cameflex 35, (see p. 85) the magazine is very quickly attached to the body, even while the instrument is running, which is important when switching to different types of emulsion, and when there is a need to save seconds at critical moments.

Framing and focusing are by a reflex viewfinder taking its image from a variable shutter made of Lucite, with brightly plated outer surfaces. As the image field on the ground glass is 20% greater than that of the aperture (whose field size is marked by a rect-angle with the TV safe area engraved on it) the operator can check the subjects that will come into the frame or are just out of it. The image on the finder is very bright and is twelve times magnified. The finder allows for sighting with either right or left eye, and as it can be swivelled 360° it is very useful for "candid camera" shots, where the operator has his back to the subject.

Eclair make a special point of the careful research behind the design of each part of the camera. This can be appreciated in the position of the shutter shaft below the aperture, so that the shutter blades close the aperture in a horizontal direction, i.e. from one

Fig. 9. Eclair 16 NPR camera, a self-blimped instrument basically designed for hand held operation.

side to the other, thus working like the focal plane shutter in many still cameras. This layout permits faster panning free of stroboscopic effects.

Various types of motor are available for driving this camera. The standard one is a transistor model for 12 v. DC with constant speed regulation, and it comprises a pulse generator for synchronizing the camera with Perfectone or Nagra type recorders. Other available motors include a variable speed type, an AC synchronous motor, and one with a crystal speed control.

The outstanding characteristic of this camera is its careful engineering, which provides in effect, noiseless running without sacrificing portability by the use of blimps. This has been achieved by simplifying to the utmost the noise producing components in the mechanism. These mechanical modifications have created the

132

camera's particular shape, which contributes to its convenience for hand-held shooting.

The supply and take-up compartments of the separate magazines are placed side by side. The raw stock can be supplied in 100 or 200 ft. spools, or in 400 ft. darkroom loads. Footage counters (either in feet or metres) are built into the magazines.

Many accessories are provided for this camera to meet various requirements. Among them are: sunshade and matte-box, hi-hat, magnetic sound recording system built in a special case, 1200 ft. magazines, and a case for carrying camera assembled ready for immediate use.

Beaulieu RC–16

This French camera, though of recent design, has already won wide acceptance in Europe and America. It is a compact instrument, intended for all-purpose shooting. The smart body is a one-piece casting in a very light but highly resistant alloy. The various controls are easy to identify and most of them are situated on the two sides of the camera.

Fig. 10. The Beaulieu camera, ideal for hand-held shooting

The reflex viewing system gives a very bright image even at small diaphragm settings, owing to a new type of ground glass

133

developed by Eastman Kodak and to a special design of mirror shutter working on the guillotine principle. The image on the viewfinder is $10 \times$ magnified and the eyepiece can be adjusted to the operator's individual eyesight.

The mechanism is driven by a small speed-regulated 6-v. motor with a range of 2–64 f.p.s., which can also be reversed to provide special effects. A built-in tachometer facilitates the adjustment of the working speed.

The rotating lens turret takes three lenses mounted so that they will not interfere with each other's fields of view. An attachment allows for mounting long focus lenses without need for special supports.

The Beaulieu takes 100 ft. daylight-loading spools, but also has provision for the attachment of 200 ft. external magazines. A small window near the camera controls indicates exposed footage in feet and metres. A frame counter, which also reverses up to 100 frames, is useful for trick work.

A particular advantage of the Beaulieu for newsreel work is the light meter built into the optical system, so that readings are made through the taking lens, thus compensating for transmission of light through various lenses. This meter is power operated by small dry-cell batteries with enough capacity to last a year. A special device checks instantly whether the meter is operating correctly.

Finally, the speed rating of the film used is related to the taking speed by means of a special selector.

Additional features are: built-in mechanical sync pulse connection, noiseless running, device for controlling input voltage, ease of hand-held shooting due to light weight and pistol grip. Among available accessories are a device for making frame-by-frame takes, an intervalometer, for precisely timed stop-frame exposures, batteries, and remote control.

Doiflex

The Japanese camera industry, already famous for its still photo and 8 mm motion picture cameras, has recently entered the international market with a new 16 mm camera designed to cater for the requirements of TV newsmen as well as documentary and industrial film-makers. It is the first Japanese attempt in the field of professional motion picture cameras.

Of compact design, sturdy construction and excellent finish, the Doiflex incorporates typical modern professional character-

Fig. 11. Doiflex camera with a reflex viewing system and three-lens turret, shown here with a zoom lens attached.

istics: very bright reflex viewing by means of a special device synchronized with the focal plane shutter, shuttle and claw pull-down mechanism and register pin, three-lens turret with "C" mount lenses, lightweight cast aluminium body, built-in tacho-meter and footage counter, 8 v. interchangeable motor for speeds from 2 to 48 f.p.s., fixed shutter with 1/57 second exposure at 24 f.p.s., capacity for 100 ft. film spools.

Various accessories are supplied by the makers, amongst them 400 ft. magazines, rewinding device for producing double ex-posures, adjustable sunshade and filter holder, pistol grip with built-in switch portable 8 v. battery and charger, synchronous motor, governor controlled motor, barney and a bracket for the zoom lens.

Pathé Model PR16-AT/BLT

The Pathé company of France has been world-renowned since 1896 for their film studios, their newsreels, laboratories, their film production and distribution and for the many items of equipment they manufacture both for amateur and professional cinematography, thus covering all fields of the industry. Their latest contribution to the 16 mm field is an all purpose instru-ment, known as the PR16-AT/BLT, which shows a wide range of improvements over their previous model, the well known

135

Pathé Webo. The many refinements and accessories make this instrument one of the most complete cameras of its type.

The mechanism is of simple design and produces very good image steadiness. It comprises a device for automatic film threading which forms the loops by itself. When switching to externally placed preloaded magazines, or when the camera must be cleaned or overhauled, this device can be easily removed.

Fig. 12. Pathé PR16-AT/BLT camera with 400 ft. magazines, electric motor and special matte box and sunshade.

The camera's spring motor drives up to approximately 23 ft. of film. An ingenious device is provided to avoid accidents while winding the spring: a warning bell tinkles about three complete turns of the handle before the spring is completely wound; the bell also tinkles about three feet before the completion of the spring's drive.

An adapting device allows for the use of variable speed electric motors, either 6–8 v, DC or 110–250 v AC. These motors are easily attached at the side and they allow for reversing and for speed regulation by means of a built-in rheostat. The speed counter is calibrated from 8 to 80 f.p.s. For work requiring direct sound recording, the motor can be adapted to the Piloton system by

136

exchanging the speed tachometer for one scaled from 8 to 64 f.p.s. and containing a signal generator.

The camera body is designed to house the typical 100 ft. spools, but as professional film-making now demands a larger film capacity, the design also allows for adapting an ingenious two-chamber magazine, installed on top of the camera, after removing a special cover plate. The two chambers are separate parts and can be withdrawn from the unit independently of each other; each chamber is provided with its own footage counter and independent drive connections. Mechanical drive is effected by means of a flexible shaft connected to the motor, and if the connection is inverted the camera runs in reverse.

The shutter has a maximum opening of 180°. A lever placed in front allows for controlling the opening angle in four positions: fully open, 3/4 open (135°), 1/2 open (90°) and 1/4 open (45°).

Pathé's well known reflex viewing system, working with a semi-reflecting, mirrored crystal placed between the lens and the film is also used in this model, but it has been considerably improved in order to obtain a much brighter image and larger magnification. Moreover, the optical system includes a photo-resistor to measure the light reaching the film. With film speed, filming speed and shutter opening preset, an external finger control is used to adjust the lens diaphragm until an indicating needle seen in the finder is placed in the correct position.

OTHER CHARACTERISTICS: Three-lens turret rotating in both directions and with a special catch for using zoom lenses; a device for checking state of batteries; housing for spare dry cells for exposure control system; crankhandle for hand drive and reversing; counter showing footage, frames and available raw stock, and speed selector scaled at 8, 16, 24, 32, 64 and 80 f.p.s. Many accessories are provided for the Pathé PR16-AT/BLT, among which are the special lens hood and matte box, compact 60 ft. magazines, a periscopic viewing tube which can swivel 360°; adapting device for miscroscopic takes, cable for remote control, extension tubes for big close-ups and handgrip.

Canon Model Scoopic 16

This is another Japanese camera for the professional or advanced amateur. The manufacturers have introduced all possible advantages of automation within an attractive, functionally

137

shaped body conceived for hand-held shooting, which makes it ideal for news coverage.

The body holds 100 ft. spools, which are automatically loaded. The operator need only cut the spool's trailing end, and introduce it into a slot of the mechanism, which automatically forms the loops. This is a great advantage to the newsreel reporter.

Fig. 13. Canon Scoopic, 16 mm news camera with 6:1 ratio zoom lens, automatic threading, reflex viewing and fully automatic electric eye.

Very bright image, reflex viewing is effected by means of a prism built into the instrument's optical unit. This is a Canon zoom (varifocal) lens with focal lengths ranging from a wide-angle, 13 mm to 76 mm telephoto (zoom range of 5.85:1) with f1.6 diaphragm opening. A large portion of this lens is built into the camera body so that only a short length juts out, which allows for reducing bulk and improving the instrument's balance.

The optical system incorporates a photoresistor which measures light going through the lens and allows for film speeds ranging from 10 to 320 ASA. The photoresistor is fed from the power source driving the motor and can be adjusted from the camera's outside. Diaphragm regulation can be either automatic or by hand.

Among the other facilities offered by this camera are: socket for connecting sound synchronization systems, device for checking

138

state of batteries, set of filters and close-up lenses, special grip for hand-held shooting, lens hood, and a light-tight, aluminium case. The latest accessory provided by Canon for this camera is an acrylic water-tight, small size shell, for underwater takes.

Sound-on-film cameras

During the past few years, the simultaneous recording of picture and sound on a single film has become an urgent requirement in covering news events. Long before the advent of TV, several camera manufacturers in America and Europe met this need with satisfactory 35 mm models. But these were heavy and took a long time to get ready, which made them unsuitable for rapid recording.

When 16 mm film began to replace 35 mm the size of equipment was immediately reduced, and an opportunity arose for creating more functional designs. The first attempts to produce simultaneous image and sound recording equipment for 16 mm film are already more than 35 years old. But it was TV which encouraged the development of 16 mm as most suited to many kinds of film reporting.

Optical recording in sound systems of this type was very popular up to a few years ago, and great improvements were made in the design of galvanometers, or modulators, which are their most critical components. Siemens-Klangfilm, Zeiss-Ikon's Ikophon, Mouillard et Deshayes' MD16, Meopta Somet, and Sonoretta in Europe; RCA, Maurer and Berndt-Auricon in the USA, were pioneers in this field.

But today, optical recording is obsolescent, having been largely replaced by magnetic. Portability is constantly being improved by using light alloys for camera and recorder bodies, by incorporating solid-state amplifiers, and by applying improved drive mechanisms and viewing systems.

Auricon Cine-Voice

The American firm of Berndt-Bach has been a pioneer in this field for many years, producing for TV news reporters a series of cameras capable of efficiently covering any type of filmed journalism with minimum effort. Their present range comprises four models progressing from the small Cine-Voice to the Super Auricon 1200. The Cine-Voice is designed for short duration reporting where ease of transport and rapid installation have precedence over all other factors.

The Auricon Cine-Voice was adapted by many companies to work with a large film capacity. For this purpose, a 400 ft magazine has been added, as well as special devices for supporting the instrument on the shoulder, grip with trigger-switch, 12 v AC motor and others. Some such adaptations leave the camera body intact, but others include a new special body to facilitate hand-held shooting. Among American firms who are specialists in these adaptations are F. & B. Ceco, General Camera Corp, S.O.S. Cine Optics Inc.

Fig. 14. Auricon Cine-Voice sound-on-film camera with side viewfinder and 100 ft spool chamber.

DRIVE MECHANISM. The intermittent drive is of the sinusoidal type, which is of very simple design and provides excellent picture steadiness. There is a patented pressure system with steel balls round the aperture edges and a removable pressure plate ensures the smooth passage of the film. The continous drive is by a single sprocket with suitably positioned guide rollers and a pressure roller opposite the sound recording head. The whole mechanism is mounted on Neoprene bearings in a compact light-alloy body with lined internal walls to silence noise. Two 100 ft. spools of film are accommodated in the camera body.

MOTOR. This camera can be supplied with either a constant

140

speed or a synchronous motor. Both are of the noiseless running type, 115 v. AC, either 50 or 60 c/s as required.

SHUTTER. This is of the fixed opening type at 173°. A special model for recording TV images can be installed on request.

LENS TURRET. This camera can be supplied either with a three-lens C type, or single mounting for zoom lenses.

VIEWFINDER. Viewing is through a side viewfinder, with parallax correction device, which gives a bright image covering the field of a 13 mm lens. Amber colour plastic masks can be inserted at the front to frame fields corresponding to various lenses: 17 mm, 1 in., 2 ins. and 3 ins.

SOUND RECORDING SYSTEM. The makers supply this equipment with galvanometers for either variable-area or variable-density optical sound recording. A Filmagnetic magnetic recording head can also be easily installed for use on raw stock with pre-striped magnetic track. The amplifier system is fairly compact and works from a battery source. The model for magnetic recording is fully transistorized and is very easy to carry. The cable connection system between camera and amplifier is foolproof, and

Fig. 15. A typical transistorized amplifier for magnetic sound-on-film cameras.

in the latest models the connectors are of the Canon type to avoid faulty contacts. A wide range of accessories considerably extends the range of this instrument.

Several American accessory manufacturers for cinematography have built transistorized amplifiers for use with optical sound recording on Auricon cameras. They are all small-size units for installing between the camera and the tripod head, thus dispensing with the bulky amplifiers supplied with the camera.

Auricon Pro 600 and Pro 600 Special

The Pro 600 is based on the Cine-Voice, but the design is more sophisticated to facilitate shooting of professional standard. The film drive mechanism is identical to that of the Cine Voice, together with the aperture plate and most of the threading system. But there are important changes and additions in the camera body and the film loading and viewing systems.

CAMERA BODY. In its general lines the body is similar to that of the Cine Voice, but larger in size.

The connections for the amplifier and the motor are placed on

Fig. 16. Auricon Pro 600 with separate 600 ft magazine, three-lens turret and three systems for viewing.

142

one of its sides. The other side carries the camera access door, which opens sideways on special hinges allowing a quick and easy interchange of door and viewfinder.

The lens turret takes three lenses with C type mounting, as well as the corresponding three small lenses for the viewfinder. The turret is 4 in. in diameter and the lenses are mounted wide apart so that their respective fields will not interfere. The film is not carried in the body, as on the smaller model, but in a 600 ft. magazine on top allowing 16 minutes continuous shooting.

However, in the Pro 600 Special the film capacity is reduced to 400 ft., and the lens turret has been replaced by a single mounting to allow for the installation of zoom lenses. Both features contribute to reduce the weight of the instrument.

VIEWING SYSTEM. These cameras are provided with three systems for checking focus and framing. A bright image viewfinder can be looked through with both eyes; it allows for parallax correction, and masks are inserted to delimit the fields corresponding to different lenses. Another viewfinder uses small auxiliary lenses on the turret equivalent to those for taking; it gives a ten times magnified image which is helpful when using telephoto lenses. The third is a side-placed viewfinder for critical focusing; it is brought into use by rotating the turret until the taking lens is placed before it.

MAGAZINE DRIVE. These cameras are provided with independent magazine drive (called Electromatic) which starts operating at 1/3 power rating when the camera is connected to the power source, even when the camera motor switch is in the off position. This provides a constant tension on the film and prevents it slacking off when the camera is not running.

OTHER CHARACTERISTICS. The Auricon Pro 600 Special has been conceived as light equipment for newsreel work and is 30% lighter in weight than the standard model; its magazine is smaller and can take daylight loading spools. As both the standard and the Special models run so noiselessly, they are provided with a safety device to stop the camera should anything go wrong with the threading.

Auricon Super 1200

This model of the Auricon sound camera series is a heavy piece of equipment with all the refinements of a studio camera. Its basic characteristics are those of the preceding models, but it has several important additional features.

LARGE CAPACITY MAGAZINES. Magazines of 1200 ft. capacity provide 33 minutes of continuous shooting. This is a great help in covering conferences, shows, long interviews, etc.

FILM GATE. To prevent emulsion build-up on the film gate, polished sapphire inlays are used and they also minimize wear. The removable pressure plate system is the same as in the other models.

Fig. 17. Auricon Super 1200 camera designed for studio use, with large capacity magazines and through the lens viewing.

CONTINUOUS DRIVE. The extra large magazines call for a somewhat larger diameter sprocket to drive the film effectively. The smaller sprocket located beside the sound recording head has undergone no change.

DIRECT VIEWING THROUGH TAKING LENS. Accurate framing and critical focusing through the taking lens is effected in this camera by means of a device which, before shooting, inserts a mirror at 45° between the lens and the aperture. The viewfinder optical tube magnifies the image ten times. Before the camera is

144

started, the mirror must be withdrawn from the viewing position, after which the optical tube acts as a side viewfinder working through small auxiliary lenses installed on the turret, and equivalent to those used for taking.

VARIABLE OPENING SHUTTER. The control is mounted on the right-hand side of the camera and allows for in and out fades, or for shutter speed variations from 1/50 to 1/200 sec. The higher shutter speeds are extremely useful when shooting with highly sensitive emulsions.

THREADING FAILURE INDICATION. As the Super 1200 runs so silently, failures in the threading or take-up systems are indicated by sound and lamp alarms.

OTHER CHARACTERISTICS. Two red lights go on when the camera is operating. Footage and frame counters are self-lighted. Another light indicates when the camera is connected to the power source and the take-up motor is running at one third power rating.

There are also connections for plugging in earphones, a device for automatic shutter opening when focusing, and withdrawing shuttle automatically when threading.

Other features are push-button starter, framing position safety device, special design sunshade, electric heater with light indicator.

Mitchell SSR

This camera is the result of a research project started by the Columbia Broadcasting System to produce a new type of camera intended for all kinds of work with 16 mm gauge film. The goal they set themselves was to achieve a versatile instrument which would also record on a magnetic track with highest fidelity to the original sound.

For this purpose they joined forces with the Mitchell Camera Corp., who designed the mechanical parts of the camera, while the sound system was handled by CBS and RCA. The result was the New Mitchell SSR-16 (Single Sound Reflex 16 mm).

The camera's main body is a magnesium alloy casting, housing the film drive and the reflex viewfinder, on which a divergent-axis three-lens turret, as well as the main controls, are installed. The magazine is attached to the top of the camera body, and the interchangeable motor is mounted on the right hand side.

The silent running intermittent mechanism is based on the famous Mitchell shuttle and register pin movement. The reflex viewfinder makes use of a highly polished stainless steel shutter, which is separate from the focal-plane type shutter used to close the aperture. The shutter opening is fixed at 170° and produces a shutter speed of 1/51 sec. at 24 f.p.s.

The finder's optical tube produces a very bright, ten times magnified image whose field is larger than that taken through the aperture, and shows objects just outside the frame.

At the back of the camera are the tachometer, footage and frame counters, starting switch, and connections to the power source and the amplifier for the built-in magnetic sound recorder. The easily

Fig. 18. Mitchell 16 mm SSR model. (Single System Reflex) with magnetic sound unit and lenses mounted on divergent axis turret.

interchangeable motors supplied for this camera are: 12 v., DC, standard model with transistorized constant speed control; and a three-phase, synchronous model for 110 v. AC.

The sound unit consists of an RCA portable transistorized amplifier with interchangeable heads built into the camera.

Many accessories are offered by the makers, including magazines of up to 1200 feet, built-in pulse generator, monitor viewfinder, and special battery power source.

146

Other 16 mm cameras

The cameras just described are those in most general use at present, especially in the field of television. But many older models are still in use, while some newer ones are today emerging from the experimental stage, and a number of these deserve some mention. (See also Table of 16 mm Camera Characteristics on p. 306).

For several years the Mitchell Company has been producing the well known Mitchell 16 with characteristics identical to those of the 35 mm Mitchell Standard, and one of the first cameras to provide the narrow-gauge professional with an instrument of standard gauge quality and efficiency. The 16 mm camera includes all the refinements that went with the Mitchell Standard, ranging from an identical intermittent drive to the same full range of accessories.

Fig. 19. Mitchell 16 mm field camera with full standard gauge camera facilities.

Another U.S.A. manufacturer of great reputation in the field of 16 mm optical sound recording, J. A. Maurer, Inc., produced an excellent instrument based on similar principles.

The Eastman Kodak Co., of Rochester, having introduced professional concepts into the field of light portable instruments

147

with its Cine Kodak Special, developed in 1962, the Kodak Reflex Special, which incorporates modern improvements such as reflex-shutter viewing, interchangeable motors, automatic turret, external magazines of up to 1200 ft. capacity, and magnetic sound attachment.

At the request of the American Broadcasting Company, Beckman & Whitley, an American firm who specialize in high speed cameras, has recently built a remarkably noiseless standard speed instrument, with radically different concepts embodied in the film drive and the arrangements for hand-held shooting.

Fig. 20. Beckman & Whitley 16 mm single-system sound camera in operation.

Sound is recorded magnetically on the film. This camera has been exhaustively tested by operators working for the ABC but has only very recently appeared on the American market.

Many 16 mm cameras have been produced in France. The Etablissements André Debrie first created the Sinmor, for combined picture and magnetic sound recording, and later the CS16 which is a similar model showing a great improvement in some features, and more recently a still further developed model with the same basic features.

Tolana, another French company, has for a number of years been producing two instruments which have been much used by Radio Télévision Française: the Sincroflex and the Sonoflex.

Fig. 21. Debrie CS-16 single-system sound camera with reflex viewing and zoom lens attached.

Fig. 22. Debrie CX-16, a recent introduction. Note the three-lens divergent turret and on-the-shoulder magazine.

Magnetic recording of sound in these cameras is effected alongside the image. Many technical refinements can be added to these instruments to convert them into studio equipment.

149

Several cameras for 16 mm gauge film are also manufactured in the Soviet Union. Among many models one should note an instrument very similar to the 35 mm Sputnik, with controls in the handgrips as well as the 16ST and the 16SS, the last-mentioned of a bulky design, including reflex viewing, synchronous motor and external focus controls on both sides of the camera.

Among the very latest 16 mm models, the most outstanding is one manufactured in Japan by the Seiki Company. It was specially designed for professional use, and includes large capacity magazines, intermittent drive with register pins, reflex viewing, semi-self-blimp, manual dissolve shutter, miniature shutter indicator, single system magnetic recording in detachable unit, etc.

Finally, mention must be made of the Orafon camera which has for some years been manufactured in Bergamo, Italy. This instrument records sound and picture, the former on an optical track. Its compactness renders it very practical for conferences, interviews and similar coverage.

REFERENCES

[1] Still, R., Fletcher, J., *Television Newsfilm Standards Manual*, Time/Life Broadcast, New York (1964).
Fletcher, J., *J'ai tourné dix mille metres en 16 mm en 1960—Vers Une Releance du 16 mm*, Le Technicien du Film. No. 69 p. 8 (1961).
[2] Ham, D., The Arriflex 16, *U.S. Camera Magazine*, p. 92 (March 1954).
Forbes, J., Single System sound for the Arriflex 16, *American Cinematographer Magazine*, p. 491 (August 1958).
[3] Henry, J., The new Arriflex 16 M, *American Cinematographer Magazine*, p. 28, (January 1964).
[4] Bronson, G., *The candid photography of "The Fabian Story"*, *American Cinematographer Magazine*, p. 582 (October 1964).
[5] Connaissance des cameras 16 mm, *Le Technicien du Film*, No. 72 p. 9 (May-June 1961).
[6] Mitchell New SSR16, *American Cinematographer Magazine*, p. 218 (Apr. 1964).

4

SPECIALIZED CAMERAS

THE development of cinematography towards techniques such as matting, animation, scientific work, etc., gave rise to the need for cameras of specialized design. The basic mechanical principles of these instruments are the same as those of standard cameras, but they differ in certain important characteristics, and thus require separate discussion.

Low- and high-speed cameras

Low-speed cameras

At one end of the speed scale is the "time-lapse" process, and the adaptations of it used in animation. All these processes employ standard equipment, and none requires structural changes in the camera itself but only in the drive motor.

TIME LAPSE CAMERAS. The time lapse system is based on the automatic printing of a few frames at preset intervals (minutes, hours, days). When projecting the film at normal speed (24 or 16 f.p.s.), the time elapsed appears to be more or less contracted according to the frequency of the takes. This process is a great, help in all sorts of scientific research, medicine, biology, astronomy industry, etc.

Time-lapse cameras can be either spring or electric-motor driven. Those with spring drive require a special trigger device to operate the camera automatically, frame by frame. The system works under the action of a solenoid switch on an armature which stops the camera's mechanism. Each time the solenoid receives electric power, the armature is withdrawn from its position and the mechanism is thus free for a fraction of time enough to expose one or more frames. A spring drives the armature back to stopping position as soon as the solenoid ceases its action. This is the principle used on many 16 mm cameras like the Cine Kodak Special, the

151

Bolex Paillard, the Pathé and others. But the problem with spring driven cameras is that the spring requires periodic windings without the slightest framing modification. Therefore such instruments must be firmly seated on a rigid base.

Electric motor driven cameras work with a special time-lapse (or animation) motor designed to rotate only once each time it receives an electrical pulse. Thus the camera is operated frame by frame by adequately coupling the motor shaft with the camera's main shaft.

There are also other frame-by-frame devices using a "Bodine" type synchronous motor connected to a gearbox and working on the Geneva Movement principle.

INTERVALOMETER. Whether the camera is spring-driven or electric the fundamental item is the electrical pulse which shoots off the camera or acts on the electric motor. The instrument producing pulses at pre-set intervals is known as an intervalometer.

Fig. I. Time-lapse device made by John H. Waddell Inc., suitable for programming a camera to operate according to specific requirements.

There are many types of intervalometer. Some operate by clockwork, others act under synchronous motors, and some models work by the action of electronic circuits based on the properties of certain gas discharge valves or on the accumulation of electric power in condensers. Whichever the process, the intervalometers must be capable of:

(i)   supplying electric pulses at intervals ranging from one second to several hours, to act on solenoids to trigger off the camera;

152

(ii) operating the animation motor, at intervals from one second to 25 minutes, for frame-by-frame takes;

(iii) regulating the exposure time of a take frome one to ten seconds;

(iv) acting synchronously on special shutters in co-ordination with the camera;

(v) starting off a system for lighting up the scene to be shot, so that it goes on a few seconds before exposure and goes off immediately after;

(vi) indicating the number of exposures actually effected.

Among a wide range of intervalometers made for various purposes we should point out the one made by Arriflex for their 16 and 35 mm cameras; the Roger, used extensively for time-lapse, animation and slide film; the multi-purpose Seco; those manufactured by the Eastman Kodak Co. for their Cine Kodak Special or Kodak Reflex Special; and the motor intervalometers made by the Industrial Timer Company, of the USA.

DESIGN CHARACTERISTICS. Although most cameras may be adapted to time-lapse work, there are some points to bear in mind. Reflex viewing is a great help, as it allows for easy checks on the exact framing and on sharp focusing. But the shape of some reflex shutter blades may allow light to leak in during long periods between each exposure. In such cases a separate shutter unit is placed in front of the lens and is synchronized with the camera's reflex shutter. This allows for long exposure takes by the double-pulse process: a pulse opens both the camera and the secondary shutters, and after exposure another pulse recloses both shutters.

Time-lapse work often requires exposure adjustments for each frame. Cameras with variable opening shutter allow for exact exposure time control disregarding whether it works at a wide range of speeds or not.

ANIMATION CAMERAS. Except for the mechanism and the motor drive, cameras for animation are of a very similar design to standard cameras. Their mechanism design must include:

(i) fixed pilot pin intermittent mechanism;

(ii) interchangeable mechanism for 16 mm and for 35 mm gauges;

(iii) automatic safety switch in case of threading failures;

(iv) direct through-taking-lens viewing system (either reflex

153

prism or sideways rack-over), with device for projecting the frame onto the animation bench;

(v) automatic fade-in and fade-out device;
(vi) exposed frame counter, whether forward or reverse motion;
(vii) magazine with individual mechanical drive to each chamber to keep constant tension and allow for effective take-up running forward or reversing.

The drive motors must have the following characteristics:

(i) they must be interchangeable;
(ii) selector switches for forward and reverse motion;
(iii) operating speeds of 1, 2, 3, 4 or more f.p.s.;
(iv) remote control starting switch;
(v) capacity for continuous operation (for titles or for winding film).
(vi) exposure time selector device from $\frac{1}{4}$ sec. to 4 seconds);
(vii) selector switch for working at speeds from 1 to 3 r.p.s. (for shooting in black and white or colour film with tripack system),

Among the best known animation cameras are the American made Richardson-Bowlds R-500, the Acme Animation, and the Oxberry, working both with 16 and 35 mm film, the German 35 mm "Trick-Kameras" by Askania and Crass, the French instrument designed by Armand Roux of the SAMOPRA, and in Japan two instruments of more recent design—one for 35 mm by Seiki, and one for 16 mm by Doi Works Co. Besides these instruments specifically conceived for animation benches, many American studios use the Bell & Howell 2709 for this purpose, while in Europe and Latin America the Debrie Parvo L and the Askania Z are used.

Intermediate-speed cameras

Intermediate-speed cameras are those relying exclusively on a conventional intermittent drive system to attain speeds above the standard 24 f.p.s.

Most of the commonly used cameras can reach maximum operating speeds around the 80 f.p.s. mark. To work at higher speeds, specially devised intermittent mechanisms must be used, but mechanical limitations, together with the breakage resistance qualities of film base, set a maximum of approximately 300 f.p.s. for 35 mm and 400 f.p.s. for 16 mm.

154

Fig. 2. S.D.S. 16 mm 6050 camera. A typical instrument for aerospace or missile test photography. Used on drone aircraft during test firing to photograph the missile for trajectory determination, miss-distance and relative velocity to drone.

Fig. 3. 35 mm Cameraflex Radar Boresight camera. Used to photograph targets being tracked by radar. The Mirrotel lens is rigidly mounted and the whole unit is aligned with the radar antenna.

155

Generally, the operating characteristics of intermediate-speed cameras are quite similar to standard ones; their difference lies mainly in the extra strength of the mechanical parts, and in the elimination of refinements unnecessary for scientific applications.

Among the film formats on intermediate-speed cameras are the following:

(i)   16 mm full frame (perforations on both edges)
(ii)   35 mm half frame
(iii)   35 mm full frame
(iv)   35 mm frame with margin for recording additional data
(v)   35 mm double-height frame
(vi)   70 mm half frame
(vii) 70 mm 4/10 frame
(viii) 70 mm full frame.

The shape of intermediate-speed cameras is often the result of adapting them to specific requirements, such as installation in reduced space, or subjection to extreme vibrations or pressures. Moreover some models must undergo very high or very low temperatures and rapid accelerations or decelerations without detri-

Fig. 4. Debrie Cine-Theodolite camera, with built-in theodolite for missile study. The film travels horizontally and the image is recorded on a 24 × 36 mm frame.

Fig. 5. Eclair Camematic GV 35 mm camera. A recording camera for speeds from 24 to 120 f.p.s.

ment to their performance. It is often essential that these instruments allow for the simultaneous recording of additional data such as time and speed, temperatures, distances, and other information necessary for analysing the recorded images.

Fig. 6. Debrie GV High Speed camera designed for industrial and scientific work.

157

Fig. 7. Newman Sinclair 35 mm high-speed camera (120 f.p.s.).

Further details of cameras of this type will be found at the end of this book.

High-speed cameras

This term is applied to cameras in which film is exposed at speeds higher than those attainable by intermittent drive systems. They have an application in countless scientific studies where the subject matter moves far too rapidly for direct human observation. Among these are: ballistics (missiles and satellites), aerodynamics (flight testing and rocket tracking), atomic fission and thermonuclear energy, electrodynamics, hydrodynamics, biology, medicine, instrumentation, and even sports analysis and similar subjects.

High-speed cameras may be classified thus according to their mechanism:

    (i)   rotating prisms,
    (ii) rotating lenses or mirrors,
    (iii) cameras synchronized with intermittent light flashes,
    (iv) extreme high-speed cameras.

ROTATING PRISM SYSTEM. The working principle of rotating prism cameras is a prism synchronized mechanically to the continuous film drive, so that its speed of rotation coincides with the displacement speed of the film.

Behind the lens is placed the rotating prism which refracts the image to "follow" the continuous displacement of each frame as it is exposed.

This method of alternation of exposure and blanking off is effected by the different positions of the prism. The characteristics of this type of camera are determined by the size of the frame, the number of faces on the prism, and the refractive index of the glass.

Some manufacturers have added a supplementary shutter to the system just described; this is a rotating disc placed betwen the prism and the film. This gives a very steady image of better quality at all speeds. As the aperture of the rotating disc can be regulated, there is effective control of the exposure time on the film.

Speeds of up to ten thousand frames per second can be attained with rotating prism cameras, and as the mechanical system employed is relatively simple, the camera can be of small

Fig. 8. Debrie Speedex high-speed camera for industrial applications.

159

size and light weight. These two factors are naturally of very great importance when cameras must be installed on missiles or in crowded aircraft cockpits.

It is worth noting at this point that a camera has been recently designed and built for TV interview coverage, based on the principle of the rotating prism which provides not only the advantages listed above, but also that of running noiselessly.

CAMERAS WITH ROTATING LENSES OR MIRRORS. Rotation of a ring made up of lenses or mirrors is another means of achieving high speeds in recording images on film, and enables speeds of up to forty thousand frames per second to be reached with 16 and 35 mm film.

The German Pentazet 35 is typical. It makes use of a rotating ring of mirrors, which are interchangeable and can be varied in number from a minimum of 30 to a maximum of 120.

The subject is filmed through the lens and the image cast on a prism which, in its turn, deflects it onto the mirror ring. The film is displaced continuously behind a frame placed at the rotating axis of the ring, where the mirrors produce an upright image correct from left to right.

CAMERAS SYNCHRONIZED WITH LIGHT FLASHES. The application of the stroboscopic principle to motion pictures has extended the possibilities of high-speed cameras. Intermittent flashes of light at pre-established intervals record an image on a film which is moving continuously. The gaps between each flash correspond to the period the shutter is closed. With such cameras as Dr. Ing. Frank Frungel's Stroboskin, up to 300,000 flashes per second can be electronically produced, each having a duration of 1/1,000,000 sec.

Recent stroboscopic cameras incorporate a rotating prism to give appreciably better image quality.

EXTREME HIGH-SPEED CAMERAS. The highest speeds are attained by very elaborate instruments whose distinguishing characteristic is that the film remains stationary while the image is recorded on sensitive surfaces of 4 × 5 in. or larger. The operating principles vary considerably, but in most cases a mirror scanning system is used, applied in different forms and sometimes combined with a number of lenses (up to 94 in one French camera). The rotating elements are frequently driven by turbines running in helium gas.

The speeds reached with specialized equipment of this kind

160

range from one to forty million frames per second. These instruments are as a rule very heavy, extremely expensive and are not built on a commercial basis.

Often their technical characteristics are well kept secrets.

An analysis of the images obtained is effected by transferring them to a conventional motion picture film by means of a special printing process in which each image is repeated several times before passing on to the next one.

Multiple Film Cameras

Bipack system

The bipack filming process derives from some of the multiple image experiments carried out in the early days of colour cinematography. Its operating principle is simple, and consists of the simultaneous passage through the aperture of two films in close contact. These two films must be threaded with their emulsion sides inwards and touching, so that focus is the same on both. Hence, light entering through the lens must also pass through one film base.

Bipack films were employed in early colour processes to obtain a chromatic selection of the scene being taken. This was achieved by placing one film with orthochromatic emulsion face to face with another coated with panchromatic emulsion. The first film was tinted to act as a selecting filter so that a different region of the spectrum was recorded on each emulsion. Nowadays, the standardization of colour monopack films has made the bipack system obsolete, and it is now used only for process matting and similar special techniques. The technical requirements of bipack filming necessitate that the camera be adapted to the simultaneous travel of two films, have good registration steadiness, and take double magazines.

Suitable cameras are: the Acme Process, the Askania Color, the Bell & Howell 2709, the Mitchell NC, the Newall, the Oxberry, the Debrie Super Parvo, and others.

The adaptation of some instruments requires only minor adjustments (e.g.: the Super Parvo, whose normal 1000 ft magazines must be changed for special ones with double capacity chambers but of smaller capacity), while the B & H 2709, the Mitchell and the Newall must undergo major modifications. By way of example we detail hereunder the adaptations that must be effected on Mitchells and Newalls.

161

F

CONTINUOUS DRIVE. The sprocket component called the "stripper" must be replaced by a device known as a "cutaway".

APERTURE. It is of vital importance that the pressure plate should work efficiently when two films travel in the film gate. Apart from the constant and even pressure needed for film steadiness, the pressure must be sufficient to eliminate any air bubbles formed between the two films. For Mitchell and Newall cameras, it is advisible to replace the standard pressure plate with two guide rollers with a 4-roller plate similar to that patented by Cinecolor Corporation.

LENS MOUNTS. As the two films travel through the aperture with their respective emulsion sides in contact. With both film bases outwards, the frontmost film base displaces the image plane backwards a distance equal to the thickness of the base. The lens must therefore be mounted 0·0045 in. behind its normal position. Lenses with S.L mountings need not have their position altered.

VIEWFINDER. As a result of the backward displacement of the image plane, the viewfinder ground glass of the Mitchell camera must also be displaced backwards by 0·0045 in.

MAGAZINES. The typical magazines for these cameras must be exchanged for a special four-chamber model. The Mitchell Corp. and the Rank Precision Industries (who sold the Newall) provide such "double" magazines, placing two chambers on top of the others, which are easily installed.

Tripack system

Like bipack, the origins of the tripack system go back to the early days of colour cinematography. Apart from the difficulties of film drive and registration steadiness, this system presents the additional problem of how to obtain three identical and equally sharp images. If the three films face the same way and are superimposed in the same aperture, the focal plane will coincide with the emulsion of only one of them, and the other two will record images slightly out of focus. If two of the films are placed with the emulsion face-to-face (as in the bipack system), the third film is inevitably out of focus. If more than one aperture was to be used, there would be parallax errors. These problems were solved with the invention of the beam-splitting prism.

The beam-splitter principle, as originally used in Technicolor,

Dufaychrome, and other cameras, works in the following way. Three images are obtained through two apertures by the use of a special optical system. It will be seen that the printing of three images through two apertures implies the use of the bipack system in one of them. The apertures are placed at right-angles to each other, and so of course are the corresponding drive mechanisms.

The beam-splitter optical system consists of a glass cube made up by two cemented half-cubes whose diagonally joined faces are treated with gold so as to form a semireflecting mirror at 45°. The optical system is assembled in a metal casting installed in the space between the lens and the angle made by the two aperture plates. The prism must be precision centered behind the lens and at the angle of the two apertures, so that the image reflected by the mirror to the bipack aperture at 90° is identical to the one formed on the aperture placed on the axis of the lens.

The insertion of a glass cube behind the taking lens means a considerable increase in the minimum space between the plane of the film and the rear elements of the lens. Lenses for this camera with short focal lengths of 25 and 35 mm had to be designed specially to have the characteristics of an inverted telephoto lens, i.e., that their real focal length was greater that their effective focal length.

Fig. 9. Diagram showing the basic principle of the Technicolor beam-splitter system.

Another point to take into account in tripack cameras is the drive mechanism. The use of a bipack system and a separate single pack film necessitated two shuttle and register pin movements, synchronized in their motions, at 90° to each other. Since the requirements of colour register demanded maximum steadiness, the register pins had to be either of the full fitting or of the fixed type, while the apertures needed constant pressure plates, one of which had to be of special bipack type.

THE THREE-STRIP TECHNICOLOR CAMERA. Tripack Technicolor cameras were first used in 1932, and some years later, after a thorough programme of testing, they were produced at a cost of $25,000 each. They were very sturdily built with a high degree of precision. The body was box shaped, and the mechanical and optical systems were based on the principles described in the preceding paragraphs. Several innovations were included to ensure maximum film steadiness and to establish a more perfect contact of the film in the bipack aperture.

The lenses were made by Taylor & Hobson of Leicester, England, and were carefully corrected for colour and calibrated photometrically according to an arithmetic scale; the lenses supplied were of 25, 35, 40, 50, 70, 100 and 140 mm focal length. Viewing was possible either by a direct finder or by a special monitor

Fig. 10. Three-strip Technicolor camera (now obsolete) many of which were later adapted to the Technirama system.

finder, affording parallax-corrected viewing with both eyes. Film had to be threaded through both sections of the camera, one section with monopack and the other with bipack film. The compact magazines were arranged to hold the three films side by side; take-up was by belt.

The camera was driven by a motor mounted at the back; the motor was of the interchangeable type and eight separate models were supplied for different speeds and voltages, as well as for reverse drive.

As the Technicolor camera was too noisy for direct sound recording, it had to be blimped, and since the blimp was very large, special blimp mounts were needed. The camera was provided with a sunshade and matte-box, and could be furnished with remote focusing control operated by Selsyn motors, special lens mounts for aerial filming, watertight shell for submarine takes, etc.

The Technicolor tripack cameras were made in a wide range of models (C, D, E, F and G) to cover all the requirements of three-strip colour cinematography. They have, of course, been out of use now for many years. Some were later adapted to the Technirama system.

DUFAYCHROME TRIPACK CAMERA. The now abandoned Dufaychrome process was created by Jack Coote a British expert in colour techniques, and operated by Dufay Chromex Ltd. some years ago; it made use of a special tripack camera, designed by the creator together with Gilbert Murray, which was very similar to the Technicolor tripack, but with the following differences:

(i)   the beam-splitter was removable,
(ii)   film storage was in two independent magazines, one for normal monopack film and the other for bipack film,
(iii) direct viewing through mirror at 45° and Mitchell-type monitor viewfinder with automatic parallax correction,
(iv)   remote control of focusing by means of Magslip motors.

Dufaychrome cameras have been used by some laboratories and studios for special effects or process filming, especially for the type known as the "travelling matte".

Special effects cameras

Effects or process filming demands the use of instruments properly adapted to the many special requirements of these techniques. The camera is mounted on a stand in front of what is in effect a projector, and the two together carry out work very similar to that of a film printer.

No fundamental modifications to the camera mechanisms are

Fig. 11. Acme process camera. *Above:* side view showing the shutter control knob, viewing device and drive motor at right. *Below:* showing threading of film (drive motor removed).

necessary, but they must meet very high precision requirements and incorporate various special features.

Intermittent movement

In these cameras, the intermittent drive mechanism must achieve the highest possible degree of registration steadiness. This

166

is vital for special optical effects, where the image is continuously modified as a result of combining takes with masks and multiple exposures. The shuttle claws are therefore made to act on both sides of the film in synchronization with register pins, which can be either moving or fixed to the gate.

Two of the best known special effects cameras, the Oxberry and the Acme, have individual register pin systems working on similar principles.

The Oxberry makes use of fixed register pins similar to those devised for Bell & Howell 2709 cameras. Two pins are provided: one with a cross-section exactly the same size as the film perforations while the other fits the vertical dimension of the perforation but allows a clearance in the horizontal dimension to allow for film shrinkage or expansion. Both pins together adjust the exact positioning of the frame, vertically and horizontally.

The two-pin registration method of the Acme camera is similar: one pin fits the perforation exactly while the other fits vertically but leaves a clearance horizontally. These pins are made to

Fig. 12. Oxberry process camera mounted on an optical printer. Note the bipack magazine and the numerous controls.

167

penetrate the perforations in synchronization with the intermittent vertical drive of the shuttle and with the spring action of the pressure plate, so as to avoid damaging the film perforations. The pressure plate design permits the use of bipack film.

Viewing system

The Acme camera is provided with reflex viewing through a mirror set at an angle of 45° which operates as in the cameras previously described. Through a right-angled optical tube, the finder produces a sharp upright image, correct from left to right and twice magnified. Subsequent improvements include the provision of two pins on the finder window in order to fit a previously processed film frame in exact registration, for use as a reference when inserting mattes and masks. It is now possible to dismount the optical tube from the viewfinder window, and install in in its place a housing with a light source so as to project a film which is to be used as a matte through the taking lens. This also allows for painting-on a mask in exact registration.

In the special effects model of the Oxberry camera, viewing is effected by the reflex method, and in the animation model, by the sideways rackover displacement method.

Shutter

The variable shutter is an essential accessory in special effects cameras. It can be either manual or automatic, but must have a wide range of openings. The Oxberry camera is equipped with a 170° shutter whose control allows for selection of the number of frames in a fade from 8 to 120. The Acme camera shutter has the same opening angle and is adjusted by two controls allowing for automatic fades over film lengths of 1, 2, 3, 4 and 8 feet.

Magazines

Special effects cameras take 400 and 1000 ft. magazines, which admit couplings for working with the bipack system. They are driven by two sets of gears for forward and reverse drive, and for different speeds at a constant tension.

Motors

The motor is an important element in special effects cameras, and its constant speed regulation must be extremely accurate. It must be capable of working at minimum speeds of one frame per second, as well as at very high speeds in order to produce a

168

slow-motion effect, and furthermore must be capable of reversing. As it is normally difficult to obtain such a wide range in a single motor, motors are generally furnished in interchangeable units.

Other features

Other notable features on special effects cameras are:

(i)   disc for inserting filters between lens and aperture. Different types of filters are supplied for colour shooting, and by means of a lever the disc can be synchronized with the shutter rotation, so as to facilitate the recording of three frames exposed in succession;

(ii) because of their special design, effects cameras do not permit the use of wide angle lenses. The minimum focal length adaptable to the Acme camera is 62 mm while the Oxberry admits lenses of 47 mm focal length, when using 35 mm film. When the camera is installed on a special effects stand or animation table, focusing is controlled either by hand or automatically;

(iii) interchangeable movements which allow the same camera to be used with either 35 mm or 16 mm film (this feature only in Oxberry cameras).

(iv) footage counter, exposed frames counter, and totalizing counter, with discounting effect for reverse drive.

Other special cameras

The above cameras are used exclusively in the laboratory. But process filming often requires the use of adequate equipment in the studio itself. Thus cameras were designed with the characteristics necessary for special effects as well as those demanded by direct shooting. The special effect most commonly used is the travelling matte, i.e. the addition of a background to separate scenes with actors, by combining filmed shots in a complex laboratory process. This requires the "two-strip" system, effected with a camera incorporating a beam-splitter prism and two apertures at right-angles to each other to take the scene on two negatives simultaneously.

In Hollywood, this process is effected with the old Technicolor Tripack camera, while in Europe they use the British JARO made by the Rank group, the French Camé Twin, and a few cameras built in Spain some years ago by the Aragonés brothers for their Cinefotocolor system. An idea of the possibilities of these

169

instruments may be gained from the characteristics of the Camé Twin, designed by the French engineers Coutant and Mathot:

(i)   the image is recorded on two films through two apertures placed at right-angles to each other, by means of a fixed beam-splitter prism; the film gates are provided with a slot for filters and intermittent action pressure plates;

(ii)   two-claw intermittent movement and fixed register pin;

(iii)   two viewing systems, one direct through film with magnified image for critical focusing and framing, and a side monitor viewfinder with automatic parallax correction;

(iv)   double magazines for 1000 ft film in each compartment or receptacle;

(v)   externally controlled variable shutter;

(vi)   lenses for various focal lengths from a minimum 35 mm;

(vii)   special synchronous motor;

(viii) correct threading safety device;

(ix)   soundproof blimp.

Cineradiology cameras

Cineradiology is the cinematographic recording of images produced by X-rays on a phosphorescent screen. It allows for a careful analysis of the moving subject, either by projection, or by frame-by-frame study.

For some years now, manufacturers have been able to adapt their cameras to X-ray equipment, thanks to the development of image intensifiers. Some firms, Arnold & Richter for example, adapted their instruments to suit Philips equipment with 15, 21 and 27 cm diameter image intensifiers.

For this work the Arriflex 35 is fitted with a 22 × 18·67 mm aperture, and it works with small, 200 ft magazines; it can be reversed and generally used with medium focal length lenses. The 16 mm Arriflexes have similar characteristics including reverse motion, a periscope designed specifically for this work, and 35 to 75 mm focal length lenses, according to the diameter of the image intensifier they must be aligned with.

One of the most serious problems of cineradiography is the poor quality of the images on the intensifier, due to their limited capacity for reproducing all the details on its phosphorescent screen, with the required definition and symmetry. It is therefore necessary that the cinematographic reproduction of such images should not have appreciable losses which could impair a subsequent correct analysis. With this end in view a special 35 mm gauge camera was built in Australia some time ago by the National Heart Foundation, making full use of possibilities afforded by this gauge. As this instrument comprises several concepts which may guide those interested in the subject, we detail hereunder its main innovations:

(i) square frame covering the height of six perforations, allowing for full coverage of all of the circular surface of the image intensifier at the appropriate magnification;

(ii) 180° angle shutter opening synchronized with pulses emitted by the X-ray equipment;

(iii) specially designed drive mechanism, with double claw shuttle and register pins;

(iv) magazine with easily-removable, independent chambers, and a maximum 400 ft load;

(v) working speed up to a maximum of 100 f.p.s. for studies with slow motion projection;

(vi) variable speed motor, separated from the camera but connected to its mechanism by means of a flexible shaft;

(vii) speed and exposed-frame counters.

The NHF camera is part of a group of instruments for improving the recording and reproduction of images in the field of cineradiology as well as for electrocardiograms and phonocardiograms. Negatives can be viewed either frame-by-frame or in specially devised viewing apparatus. The processed film can also be projected for large audiences if it is reduced to 16 mm, which requires a special reduction optical printer.

Several cameras were designed specially for recording X-ray images. The most complete of such instruments is the British made Acmade. It prints images from a Marconi intensifier on to 16 mm film. The unit was designed to operate with a fast pulldown and is installed on top of the X-ray equipment itself, with large film-load capacity chambers.

Kinescope cameras

Nowadays it is frequent practice to shoot scenes directly from a television kinescope tube for a wide field of applications. It allows for recording permanently all sorts of transmissions, both in black and white or in colour, and whether they are sent out from a station or in closed circuit. It affords reference records of all sorts of transmitted events, as well as of educational, industrial and commercial applications of TV. Moreover it allows for retransmitting the same program through one or several stations.

Electrical current is supplied in either of two frequencies: 50 or 60 Hz (hertz, or cycles per second), depending on the electrical standards adopted by each country. The established frequency determines the characteristics of TV transmission stations and of closed circuit systems. This imposes design characteristics on motion picture cameras for taking images from a kinescope tube (generally known in Britain as telerecording).

The image on a TV screen is produced by phosphorescence when its surface is scanned by an electronic beam. The beam sweeps the screen from left to right and from top to bottom forming a certain number of lines. The combination of these lines and the resulting contrasts produce the image. The screen is scanned twice during each TV picture. Of the total number of lines, half are used in one *field* and half in another *field*. Thus a complete TV picture is composed of two fields. Both scans of the beam are interconnected so that the even number lines are used on one field while the odd number lines are used on the other field. The combination is made during the lapse of each cycle and each time a scan is completed the screen is blacked-out so that it should not show the beam going up to start the next scan.

The number of cycles per second (frequency) determines the fraction of time in which the complete image is formed. One half of this value is the time taken by the beam to scan two fields. For example, if AC is supplied at 50 Hz each complete image is formed in 1/25 sec. and only one field in 1/50 sec.

When printing kinescope images with a motion picture camera, its sound film standard speed (24 f.p.s.) must be adapted to the above values. In the case of 50 Hz, since each complete image formed by two half-fields is obtained in 1/25 sec. it suffices to increase camera speed to 25 f.p.s. to make each film camera frame coincide with a complete TV image. However, where 60 Hz is used the problem is not so easily solved. In this case the image is produced in 1/30 sec. Consequently during one second, 30 TV images are shown while the camera is printing 24 frames, thus one out of every five TV images is "palmed off". This may form a bar across the frame (known as a "splice") produced by printing the top part of one frame and the bottom part of another.

There are several means to reconcile these two sets of values. For one method the camera is fitted with a shutter with 144° opening which at 24 f.p.s. renders an exposure time of 1/60 sec. Thus only one half field is taken, eliminating the problem of the "splice". But this solution renders images of poor definition in the vertical section, since only one half of the lines of a complete scan are taken.

Another solution is to increase the vertical shuttle travel on the intermittent mechanism, so as to make the most of the short shuttering time and lose no more than one half field. This solution can be achieved either with an electronic or mechanical shutter. The electronic shutter blanks out the image on the kinescope after each complete scan and it can be synchronized with any camera speed by means of pulses coming from the receiver. The mechanical shutter must provide an exposure time of 1/30 sec to expose the complete image, and blank out the aperture in 1/120 sec so that the shuttle can pull down the exposed frame in that extremely short fraction of time. For such timing, shutters must have an opening of 288° and a closing (blacking out) sector of 72°. In some cameras these shutters are driven by a separate

Fig. 13. Debrie Kinescope recording camera. Designed for recording images from a kinescope picture tube onto 16 mm film.

synchronous motor working independently of the camera's intermittent drive mechanism.

Various models of cameras for shooting from kinescopes are made according to the above requirements. In America the best known makes are: Acme, Auricon, GPL (General Precision Laboratories), Harvey, Milliken, Mitchell and RCA, all for 60 Hz frequency and 24 f.p.s. camera speed. In Europe where the frequency is generally 50 Hz, several special cameras have been built for this work, among which one should note the British-made Moy (four models) and the Marconi, and the Eclair Cameflex Television and the Debrie Kinescope, both made in France; all European models run at 25 f.p.s.

In the instruments like the RP-15 made by Ernest Moy in the U.K., the intermittent movement is designed so that the vertical action of the shuttle is effected in 0·0014 sec. The complex mechanism of the Marconi camera designed by Arthur Kingston achieves a time of 0·0013 sec. These values were attained in order to adjust the 25 f.p.s. camera speed to British TV standards, using 50 Hz, 405 lines.

Of all special features of these instruments, the following are noteworthy:

(i)   large load capacity to cover long duration programs;
(ii) high precision intermittent mechanism with maximum reduction of vertical unsteadiness, typical shortcoming of this cinematographic medium;
(iii) synchronous motor drive;
(iv) special system to facilitate fast phase adjustment;
(v)   critical framing and focusing devices.

Underwater cameras

The growing interest in submarine films over the last few years has induced manufacturers to produce instruments to meet the exacting requirements of underwater shooting. As far back as 1954, several Hollywood studios had to tackle the construction of special shells to hold cameras for shooting "Twenty Thousand Leagues Under the Sea", "The Big Rainbow" and "Jupiter Darling". Intensive research aud practical trials produced underwater camera covers for R.K.O., Metro Goldwyn Mayer and Walt Disney Studios, but they demanded an effort and investment which only the larger studios could afford.

At the special request of the U.S. Navy, Birns & Sawyer, one of the American companies specializing in studio equipment, built an underwater cover for Arriflex cameras. This was a big step forward, because it allowed for the use of an already widely accepted hand-held camera, easily operated in this type of work. This cover (or shell) was soon put on the market as an accessory for Arriflexes. Since then many accessory makers have produced different watertight shell models in aluminium, glass fibre, and other materials, both for light and medium weight cameras. The best known are probably those by Milliken, Gordon Enterprises and Jon Hall.

Fig. 14. Eclair Aquaflex underwater camera with stabilizing fins and special handgrips for underwater control.

In Europe and especially in France, there was a widespread development of underwater documentaries and scientific films, among which the work of Commander Jacques-Yves Cousteau was outstanding, specially in his film "Le Monde du Silence" (The Silent World). This expert's name had already been associated with a camera, the Cousteau-Girardot, made by the Compagnie de Travaux Mecaniques which won deserved renown.

The Cousteau-Girardot underwater camera is distributed in USA by Gordon Enterprises and uses a modified LeBlay camera in its interior. Commander Cousteau's initiation in motion

175

pictures was a documentary "Par Dix-huit métres du Fond"
in 1943.

For his film "Le Monde du Silence" Louis Malle, the well
known director, was retained as cinematographic consultant, and
he used another well known camera of this type—the Aquaflex,
made by the Eclair Co. of Paris. It obtained wider recognition and
was included in the company's normal production range in order
to fulfil orders from the navies of several countries. This instrument is of ingenious design and has become the favourite camera
of many underwater specialists. It thus deserves a fuller description:

   (i) egg-shaped metal shell, measuring $27\frac{1}{2}$ in. overall length, by
      $13\frac{1}{2}$ in. maximum diameter;

  (ii) all controls located on outside of shell to allow for any type
      of underwater operation;

 (iii) houses a Cameflex with special long-shaped magazine (see
      Figure 14), 6–8 volt motor, and adapted reflex viewfinder
      tube;

The various controls provided for shooting operations are:

   (i) motor switch,

  (ii) shooting speed control,

 (iii) distance setting control,

176

(iv) diaphragm setting,
(v) indicator of focal length of lens being used;

other controls included are:

(i)   tachometer,
(ii) footage counter (in metres),
(iii) built-in photoelectric cell,
(iv) gauge for checking pressure inside shell;

buoyancy control system comprising:

(i)   compressed air bottle,
(ii) de-compressive valve,
(iii) air distributor;

other characteristics of the camera are:

(i)   facility for framing and focusing through special reflex viewfinder which can be observed through diver's mask,
(ii) stabilization fins,
(iii) special grips for handling the camera,
(iv) pressure-resisting, specially treated optical front glass,

Total weight, 86 lbs.

The 65/70 mm wide screen systems

The 70 mm gauge has earned a very wide and complete acceptance from both technical and commercial points of view. Multimillion dollar productions especially, both in Europe and the U.S.A., have appeared to an increasing extent in the 70 mm format, which may now become the standard for very large screen presentation.

But when 70 mm is referred to in feature films, it is to be noted that this is a gauge exclusively for projection in theatres; 65 mm negative is nearly always used in the camera. An exception is Super Technirama 70, filmed on 35 mm film (see Table). Thus when the copy is printed onto 70 mm film, space is gained for the sound track.

Another exception is provided by the Russian motion picture industry, which makes use of 70 mm film both for shooting and projection. Several cameras have been built in the U.S.S.R. for this gauge, of which the foremost is the heavily built but noiseless Rossiya studio model.

The 70 mm positive copy is contact-printed from the 65 mm negative, since the dimensions of and distances betweeen the perforations are identical on both films, the difference lying in the width of the edge beyond the perforation on both sides.

In the history of motion pictures there are a few early attempts to use 65 mm film, with the well known Magnafilm system tried out in 1929 by Paramount (then known as Paramount Famous Lasky Corporation). At that time Paramount commissioned a 65 mm camera from the French firm of André Debrie. Debrie first designed and built a 65 mm printer, and then after over-coming many difficulties, developed a very compact camera which was first put to work on October 23, 1930. This instrument had been conceived with the latest design developments in mind, such as double chamber magazine attached to the back of the camera (and thus different from this firm's classical model), special shutter with 230° opening and a projected image viewfinder.

Fig. 16. Mitchell 65FC camera. Note similarity to 35 NC model.

About the same time, Mr. Fear of the Fearless Camera Company in the U.S.A. developed a 65 mm camera with a top-mounted magazine, a noiseless film-drive system of original design, and other refinements. This instrument was intended for series pro-duction at the rate of one per week, and provided the then new and outstanding characteristic of having interchangeable parts so as to work also with standard 35 mm film.

178

This was the first era of popularity of the "wide film," in which the contending gauges of 65 mm and 70 mm (the latter in Fox Grandeur) vied for public preference. The Mitchell Camera Corp. had built an instrument for 70 mm which was very similar in its characteristics to its later and now well-known Standard model.

But the fantastic success of sound films, the development of fine-grain emulsions which improved the quality of large screen projection, as well as the effects on the motion picture industry of the world economic crisis in the late twenties and early thirties, led to the abandonment of wide-gauge film.

Twenty-five years later, spurred by the competition of TV, the 65 mm gauge re-appeared. One of its most enthusiastic early promoters in this second period was Michael Todd, the American

Fig. 17. Mitchell 65-BFC camera.

producer, who patented the Todd-AO system in 1954. At present, 65 mm negative film is standard for large-screen systems such as Panavision 70, Ultra-Panavision, MGM Camera 65, Cinerama and Dimension 150. The 65 mm cameras most widely used are made by two American manufacturers, the Mitchell Camera Corp. and Panavision Inc.

The Mitchell Company has long-standing experience with wide film, dating back to the times of Fox Grandeur. Besides scientific and industrial instruments, they manufacture several cameras for 65 mm gauge: the 65-BFC, an adaptation of their popular 35 mm BNC, and a lighter model, the 65 FC, also similar to the 35 mm NC. Both instruments have been tried out in several Hollywood and European feature films.

Todd-AO AP-65 camera

Todd-Ao Co., producers and distributors of technical media for making 65 mm gauge films, commissioned the Mitchell Camera Corp. to design and manufacture a camera which should be light and adequate for hand-held shooting. The result was the new AP-65, of streamlined appearance, which incorporates many recent developments in the field.

The intermittent mechanism of this camera works on four perforations; its adjustable type register pins can be withdrawn to facilitate threading through the film gate. Its shutter has a fixed, 175° opening. The single-unit 250 ft film-load magazines are

Fig. 18. The new Mitchell-made, Todd-AO system, AP-65 camera.

easily coupled mechanically to the camera. Reflex viewing is effected by means of a bright-image beam splitter prism covering a larger field of view than the aperture; the viewing system affords facilities for focusing and inserting filters for studying illumination.

The AP-65 can run at 12, 18, 20, 22, 24, 28 and 32 f.p.s. and it is driven by a built-in, 28 v. motor with electronic, constant-speed governor. The motor can be interchanged for others such as: synchronous model (110 or 220 v. AC), multi-duty motor (96 v. DC) a variable speed one (110 v. AC) and a motor for animation (110 v. AC).

Other features of the AP-65 are: exposed film counter behind the camera; available raw-stock indicator placed on the magazine; slot in front of film gate for inserting gelatin filters; built-in heater; sockets for remote control connections; signal generator for sound synchronizing; special design lens hood; grip with starting switch and automatic zoom; total weight of the instrument including film-load 16 lb. Among the many accessories designed for the AP-65 are: watertight shell for underwater takes, 1000 ft magazine, monitor viewfinder allowing adjustments of focus and field of view; belt supported battery with special charger; focus control device; and several lenses including a zoom.

German 70 M.C.S. camera

Other 65 mm cameras have been built in the German Federal Republic. Their designer was Jan Jacobsen, who conceived two models: a lightweight one for hand-held shooting, and a more elaborate model. The latter item was proved in many European productions. It has a very compact body on top of which 500 or 1000 ft two-chamber magazines are seated slant-back.

Viewing is effected by the reflex method and the tube is attached to the camera body access door, in a fashion similar to the Arriflex. The simplified design movements include a high efficiency intermittent mechanism. The camera can run at speeds from one to 40 f.p.s., and is driven by interchangeable motors: either variable speed (16 v. DC), synchronous or high speed. Lenses for this camera are supplied in nine different focal lengths and are single mounted. The long-bellows lens hood allows for the insertion of filters.

Panavision cameras

Panavision Inc., well-known as specialists in anamorphic lenses, have developed their own 65 mm cameras for Panavision 70 and Ultra-Panavision. This company was already well advanced when it reached an agreement with Metro-Goldwyn Mayer to join forces in the development of a high quality image recording

TECHNIRAMA PROCESS

Camera with anamorphic prism 1.5/1 Sq. ratio

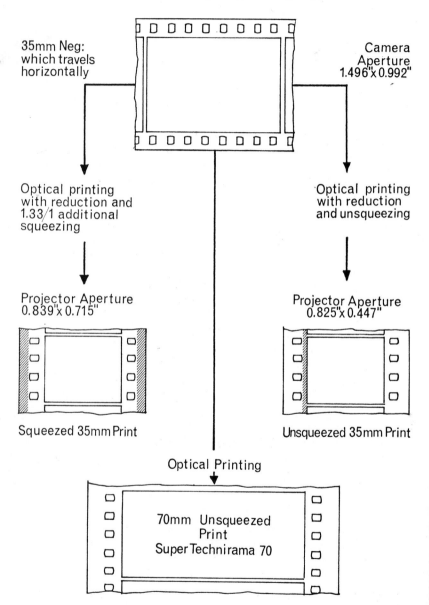

35mm Neg: which travels horizontally

Camera Aperture 1.496"x 0.992"

Optical printing with reduction and 1.33/1 additional squeezing

Optical printing with reduction and unsqueezing

Projector Aperture 0.839"x 0.715"

Projector Aperture 0.825"x 0.447"

Squeezed 35mm Print

Unsqueezed 35mm Print

Optical Printing

70mm Unsqueezed Print Super Technirama 70

PANAVISION AND MGM CAMERA 65

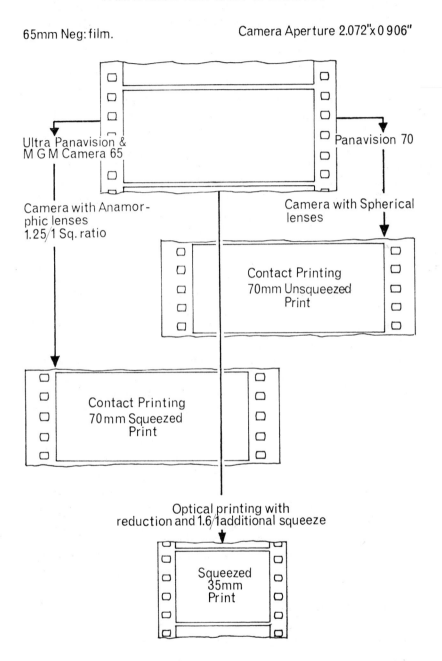

65mm Neg: film.

Camera Aperture 2.072"x 0 906"

Ultra Panavision &
M G M Camera 65

Panavision 70

Camera with Anamor-
phic lenses
1.25/1 Sq. ratio

Camera with Spherical
lenses

Contact Printing
70mm Unsqueezed
Print

Contact Printing
70mm Squeezed
Print

Optical printing with
reduction and 1.6/1 additional squeeze

Squeezed
35mm
Print

process for spectacular productions. During these investigations, new lenses were developed for the 65 mm negative, which achieved appreciable improvements in image quality and in freedom from distortion. The new system was called MGM Camera 65 and was first used in the production of the film "Ben Hur". The first instruments for this system were built by other makers to specifications by Panavision. Subsequently the design was totally revised and the cameras built at Panavision's own plant.

The 65 mm cameras built by Panavision are hired to producers for shooting with their Panavision 70 and Super-Panavision processes. Panavision 70 is for shooting directly on 65 mm film with spherical lenses, while Super-Panavision is the application of anamorphic lenses to 65 mm film while shooting. Both systems use the same types of camera, which this company supplies in two models: the heavily-built, noiseless-running studio model, and the lighter, hand-held, multi-purpose model.

Studio model

This has a noiseless intermittent drive designed by the makers, with dual registration pins, a shutter with variable opening ranging from 50 to 215°, critical focusing by means of a rack-over system with built-in contrast filters and variable magnification, top-mounted, 1000 ft., double chamber magazine. Motors are various 110 v. and 220 v. models, either synchronous or variable speed from 8 to 24 f.p.s. There is a parallax-corrected side viewfinder and an adjustable sunshade with matte-box. The anamorphic or spherical lens is single mounted by a bayonet system.

Portable model

This model is very useful for complementary takes and has recently been re-designed. The 500 ft. magazine is mounted at the rear at an angle of 45°. Other features are intermittent mechanism which produces rock-steady images, mirror type reflex viewfinder, wide assortment of interchangeable motors and a focus control device which corrects parallax of auxiliary viewfinder. The camera is supported on the operator's shoulder for hand-held shooting and can also be mounted inside an underwater shell.

Soviet 70 mm cameras

In 1959 the Soviet motion picture industry adopted 70 mm negative film for shooting their wide screen productions. Several

184

cameras were immediately manufactured for this gauge, among which the best known are the 70 SK and the Rossiya, both for studio work, and the KSRSH hand-held model, of very functional design. For special effects they have also built the high-speed 70 KSK camera, which can run up to 90 f.p.s. and the 70 KCK model for travelling mattes by the infra-red process. All these instruments are very well built and include several accessories to increase their scope.

The latest development for this gauge in the Soviet Union is the Varioscope system, making use of a larger than standard image (48·5 × 46 mm), to which masking can be applied subsequently according to frame requirements. Several of the above mentioned cameras have been adapted to this new process, and a few experimental models have also been built.

The 8 mm format

Over the last few years important progress has been made in the evolution of better quality 8 mm gauge filming, long popular with amateurs. The Eastman Kodak Co. pioneered a means of gaining more area for recording the image by fundamentally modifying the perforation dimensions. The old 0·172 × 1·29 in. frame thus became 0·211 × 1·58 in.

This system, called Super 8, has opened a vast field for the utilization of 8 mm film for certain types of sales promotion, industrial control, and even TV news.

Super 8 is today universally accepted, and many makers besides Kodak are manufacturing cameras for this gauge, incorporating the latest developments in mechanics, optics and automation, and thus meeting the need for easy-to-operate equipment. Such cameras are still destined for amateur use, but they are provided with some of the latest refinements, enabling them to rival and sometimes surpass professional equipment. Among these are:

   (i)   miniature electric motors driven by dry-cell batteries,
   (ii) zoom lenses of wide aperture with automatic operation,
   (iii) automatic diaphragm control,
   (iv) variable shutter opening,
   (v) reflex viewfinder,
   (vi) small size and light weight.

Since the market for 8 mm is already very large and is constantly

Fig. 19. Bolex Macrozoom Super 8 mm camera. Typical of the new generation of 8 mm instruments, this camera incorporates a revolutionary zoom lens capable of filming distances ranging from 1 inch to infinity.

growing, the effect of competition will undoubtedly be to widen the professional scope of Super 8, and compel manufacturers to bring their 16 mm cameras into line with these latest 8 mm advances.

REFERENCES

[1] High Speed Photography, S.M.P.T.E., New York (1949).
[2] Garrec, J., Connaissance des Caméras Ultra-Rapides, *Le Technicien du Film*, Nos. 64, 65, 66, 67, 68, 69, 75 (1960–1961).
[3] Garrec, J., Eclairage en Cinematographie Ultra-Rapide, *Le Technicien du Film*, No. 70–71 (March-May 1961).
[4] Cornwell-Clyne, A., *Colour Cinematography*, 3rd ed., Chapman & Hall, London (1951).
[5] Ball, J. A., The Technicolor Process of Three-Color Cinematography, *Journal of The Society of Motion Picture and Television Engineers*, Vol. XXV, No. 2, pp. 127–138 (1935).
[6] Hoch, W., Technicolor Cinematography, *Journal of The Society of Motion Picture and Television Engineers*, pp. 96–108 (August 1942).
[7] Kiel, J. P. A 35 mm Process Camera, *Journal of The Society of Motion Picture and Television Engineers*, pp. 551–558 (May 1951).
[8] Palen, V. W., The New Oxberry Combination 35/16 mm Process Camera, *American Cinematographer* (May 1956).
[9] Coutant, A., La Camera de Prise de Vues Double-bande, *Bulletin de L'Association Francaise des Ingenieurs et Techniciens du Cinema*, No. 17 (1958).
[10] Delaye, J., La Camera Sous-marine Aquaflex, *Cine-Sciences Photographie*, No. 31 (1956).
[11] Moon, A., Everest, F. A., Time-Lapse Cinematography, *Journal of the Society of Motion Picture and Television Engineers*, pp. 81–87 (February 1967).
[12] Hood, J. H., Jones, P. R. W., Cinematographic Instrumentation in Cine radiology, *Journal of the Society of Motion Picture and Television Engineers*, pp. 1090–1094 (November 1967).

5

HOW TO OPERATE THE CAMERA

The purpose of this chapter is to provide detailed information on how to operate a number of actual camera models. Obviously not all cameras can be so described. The present selection includes some of the cameras most widely used in America and Europe, with emphasis on lightweight models popular with newsreel cameramen, documentary film crews, and low-budget production units. Moreover, these are the cameras with which newly initiated professionals usually start their careers, and the information presented here may help to give them a more comprehensive knowledge of their equipment.

Operation of 35 mm cameras

Operation of the Mitchell NC & BNC, and Newall

MOUNTING THE CAMERA. Place the camera body on the tripod head so that the latter's retaining screw penetrates the threaded bush in the camera base. Never hold the instrument by the lens or focusing tube, as the precision mounting of these delicate parts will be damaged by the weight of the whole instrument bearing down on them. The camera should be supported by grasping the hand-grips supplied at the front and rear.

Holding the camera in correct position on the tripod head, turn the head retaining screw clockwise until it is firmly secured.

MOUNTING THE MOTOR. These cameras are driven by various interchangeable motors: synchronous, interlock and variable speed. However, the motors must be those specially made for the specific camera model, since a motor for the NC cannot be installed on the BNC, and vice versa. The motor is fitted into the recess at the right-hand side of the camera; it is first tilted so that the lower flange on the motor fits into the slot of the camera's retaining latch, then it is firmly set in position and secured by screwing in the two top corners and sliding the latch home. After installing the motor, it is advisable to try turning the flywheel by hand, to test that meshing is functioning correctly.

VIEWFINDER.
(i) Side Viewfinder in NC Model or Newall.

To attach the viewfinder, slide the dovetail male support into the female dovetail slide built onto the side of the vertical section of the camera base.

(ii) Viewfinder and Parallax Corrector on BNC Model.

In general, the same procedure as for the NC model should be followed, but with allowance for differences in mounting the automatic parallax correction device. The BNC viewfinder is provided with additional plates attached to a frame beneath the finder. These plates are marked with the focal lengths of the lenses to be used; there are plates for 25, 30, 35, 50, 75 and 100 mm lenses. Another individual characteristic of the BNC viewfinder is an automatic focusing control connected to the automatic parallax corrector.

When installing this viewfinder, first of all attach the plate corresponding to the lens being used; then turn the focusing and parallax control ring (working in combination with the plates) to the end of its run. Next, connect the sliding roller to the corresponding plate. Mount the lens securely in position and bring the infinity marking in line with the zero marking. Bring the white line on the pinion into line with the lens gear system, by which the latter will be set at infinity. Lift the focusing support forward so that the lens gears will mesh with those of the transmission pinion.

LOADING THE MAGAZINE. Magazines must be loaded in a dark room or changing bag. In order to become familiar with the different operations, it is advisable to rehearse them previously in daylight with a roll of exposed film.

Before loading it is advisable to clean out the magazine chamber thoroughly, taking special care with the light-trap rollers. Every so often these must be checked by placing them before a light, and adjusted if they allow the passage of light which may fog the film.

188

Fig. 1. Front view of Mitchell BNC showing (1) lens focusing mechanism release, (2) lens gear connection, (3) focusing dial and vernier adjustment knob.

The following sequence must be adhered to when loading the magazine:

(i) remove both lids and place the magazine with its base towards you;

(ii) insert the roll of film in the left-hand side magazine chamber, with the film unrolling clockwise;

(iii) thread the end of the film through the opening in that chamber, so that it will go round the first guide roller and run through the two plush rollers (see Fig. 2);

(iv) leave a free length of film of about 20 in.;

(v) close the lid of the film supply chamber and complete the operation in daylight;

(vi) reverse the process described under (iii) when threading the film into the take-up chamber, taking care that the film is threaded round the upper roller;

(vii) insert the contracting spool on the shaft of the right-hand side chamber. Insert the end of the film in the slot on the spool hub, and to obtain a more effective grip of the film end, fold it once or twice so that it fits the slot tightly.

Finally, rotate the spool anticlockwise a few turns so that it starts winding the film;

(viii) rotate the pulley behind the magazine, by hand, a few turns, to check that film is properly adjusted and wound;

(ix) close the lid on the film take-up chamber.

MOUNTING THE MAGAZINE ON THE CAMERA. Open the camera door thus gaining access to the camera drive mechanism. To avoid accidental tripping, disconnect the buckle trip by swivelling the trip plate to the side. Place the front end of the magazine base on the front end of the magazine attachment recess plate, on top of the camera. Tilt the magazine until the small film loop can be slid through the slot which leads to the interior of the mechanism. Lower the magazine, taking care that the edges of its base and the camera top plate do not pinch the film. Secure the magazine firmly by turning the screw at the rear of the recess plate.

THREADING THE CAMERA. Before threading the film through the camera, run the latter for a few minutes to warm up the mecha-

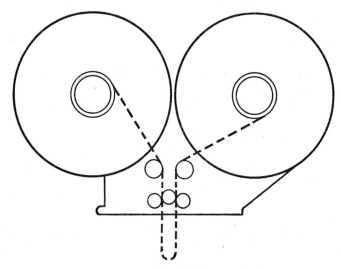

Fig. 2. Correct threading path for Mitchell magazines.

nism and to ensure a constant speed when taking the first shots. Before starting, check that the buckle trip is in the correct position and that the magazine transmission belt is connected.

After warming up the mechanism, proceed in the following sequence (see Fig. 3):

(i) disconnect the buckle trip:

(ii) clean the aperture and pressure plate carefully

(iii) rotate the upper and lower sprocket guides half-a-turn clockwise;

(iv) take the loop coming out of the magazine and draw it up to the camera door latch when in open position; this will draw out the approximate length for threading;

(v) rotate the motor flywheel until the shuttle claws are away from the aperture plate;

(vi) insert the film between the sprocket and the upper pressure roller, taking care that the sprocket teeth penetrate the film perforations correctly;

(vii) withdraw the register pin shifting it towards the rear and towards the right, so that the film can be threaded between the aperture and pressure plates (film gate);

(viii) after threading the film under roller (7), thread it over roller (6) and under roller (2); allow for a loop comprising twenty-four visible perforations from roller (2) up to the aperture plate inlet; passing the film under roller (1).

(ix) insert the film between the aperture and pressure plates, and make the shuttle claws penetrate the perforations; then shift the register pin towards the left and press it home;

(x) form a loop of about twelve perforations up to roller (4), and thread the film over (4) and under roller (5) and mesh the sprocket teeth into the film perforations; next, thread the film over the sprocket guide and roller (8) then return the sprocket guide to its working position by pressing it home;

(xi) the operation is completed by threading the film between rollers (9) and (3) and under the roller guide.

The excess film in the loop is taken up by rotating the take-up spool anticlockwise by means of the corresponding pulley. The take-up belt should be immediately placed in position to prevent it being forgotten later on.

ADJUSTING THE SHUTTER OPENING. The shutter opening is adjusted by means of the lever and knob at the back of the camera. The knob is pulled out slightly and is slid over the scale to the required calibration, and then pressed back into the corresponding

191

Fig. 3. Threading chart for Mitchell cameras. Figures indicate the series of film roller guides which the film is passed around.

hole in the scale. The shutter can be adjusted from minimum to maximum openings or vice versa while the camera is operating. The BNC Model is provided with two push-buttons for automatic dissolves: the in button is for fade-ins and by pressing the out button fade-outs are effected; these automatic dissolves are spread over a film length of some five feet. (see Fig. 4).

STARTING SWITCH. In Mitchell NC and BNC, and Newall cameras, the starting switch is mounted on the power cable feeding the motor. Before starting the camera make sure that the camera body is in the correct shooting position and *not* in the focusing position. Make sure also that threading has been done correctly, and check that the magazine belt is in position.

ADJUSTING THE MONITOR VIEWFINDER. Set the mattes so that they correspond to the taking lens being used by means of two knobs placed on top and at the side of the finder. Markings on the edge of these knobs indicate their position in order to determine the field of view corresponding to different lenses. Should there be red markings, an adapter must be fitted to the viewfinder to work with the 25 mm or with the 152 mm lens.

In the monitor finder for the NC model, a knob at the front end

192

1 —————— 5
2 —————— 6
3
4 —————— 7
—————— 8
—————— 9

Fig. 4. Rear view of Mitchell BNC. (1) Focusing eyepiece, (2) telescope magnification lever, (3) footage counter, (4) frame counter, (5) automatic dissolve controls, (6) hand dissolve lever, (7) miniature shutter (8) shift-handle, (9) spirit level.

adjusts the focus of the image projected on the ground glass. In the BNC the focus control is automatic. In the NC and Newall, parallax correction is effected by making the graticule lines in the direct focusing tube coincide with those in the monitor viewfinder.

Operation of the Debrie Super Parvo reflex models

PRELIMINARY PROCEDURES. Before transporting the camera, the motor must be detached, since its weight may bear excessively on the mechanism and harm it. Attaching or removing the motor is not difficult, but the proper sequence of operation must be followed. To install the motor:

(i)   remove the handwheel and cover plate, then take the motor and position it behind the camera, making sure that the oil holes are uppermost;

(ii) mesh the motor into the coupling which connects with the gearbox shaft, and fix it by means of its two locks;

(iii) if the motor does not go right in, the coupling has not meshed correctly; release the locks and rotate the motor shaft until it is properly positioned;

(iv) insert the plug in the socket at the side of the support; check that the power supply is connected correctly by

observing the direction of rotation of the motor shaft (if it turns clockwise, contacts (1) and (3) must be reversed);
(v) replace the handwheel.

LENS MOUNTING. Open the camera door by means of the lock on the right-hand side. Disconnect the focusing knob by turning it beyond the infinity mark until it disengages. Loosen the lens retaining ring and withdraw the lens from its seat. Return the focusing control device to its working position, and close the door.

Fig. 5. Top view of Super Parvo camera. (1) Take-up magazine, (2) film supply magazine, (3) motor, (4) mechanical unit.

THREADING. Open the three camera doors and proceed as follows (see Figs. 5 and 6):
(i)   take off the film supply magazine and load it in a darkroom or changing bag, making sure that the loose end comes out of the appropriate film slot; replace the magazine;
(ii) open the shutter assembly door and then the film gate by releasing the pressure plate lock;
(iii) draw about three feet of film from the magazine;
(iv) thread the film over the first pressure roller, under the sprocket, and over the second pressure roller;
(v)   check that the film gate is thoroughly clean and insert the film, forming a loop as it enters the gate;

Fig. 6. Front view of Super Parvo camera showing film threading path.

Fig. 7. Controls of Super Parvo Color camera. (1) Focusing knob, (2) diaphragm knob, (3) reflex viewing eyepiece, (4) footage and frame counters, (5) handwheel, (6) special on-off switch, (7) film punch, (8) lock, (9) footage mirror.

195

(vi) form another loop as the film leaves the gate, and thread it over the first roller, under the second roller, over the sprocket, and under the pressure roller;

(vii) thread the film through the slot in the take-up magazine and fit the end into the magazine shaft, then close the take-up magazine and insert it into the camera;

(viii) close the film gate and secure the lock on the left-hand side, then turn the handwheel to verify that threading is correct;

(ix) close the shutter assembly door and the remaining camera doors.

STARTING. The Debrie Super Parvo camera is started by pressing its switch lever right down and keeping it there for about three seconds.

REFLEX VIEWFINDER. The eyepiece for the reflex focusing view-finder is placed at the back of the camera and can be adjusted to suit the operator's individual eyesight. Normally, when the camera stops, the shutter closes the aperture and consequently reflects the image; but should this not occur and should nothing be seen through the finder when the camera is stopped, rotate the motor handwheel in the direction of the arrow to bring the shutter to the closed position, whereupon it will reflect the image to be focused and framed. (see Fig. 7).

Operation of Mitchell S35R (Mark II) camera

LOADING THE MAGAZINE. This is identical to the previous Mitchell models.

MOUNTING THE MAGAZINE ON THE CAMERA. This can be effected by one of three methods:

(i) on top of the camera;

(ii) on a side, slant back on the camera, by means of a special adapter;

(iii) under the camera, for hand-held shooting, for which only the special, 400 ft capacity magazine can be used.

THREADING THE CAMERA. Whichever the position of the magazine, the threading of the camera is the same. The Mark II is threaded in a very similar method to the other Mitchells. The main difference is that the sprocket is placed somewhat further below and somewhat nearer the intermittent mechanism.

196

Fig. 8. Rear view of Mitchell S35-R with base-plate attachment and large matte box and sunshade

SETTING UP THE UNIT. The Mark II can be used in five different set-ups:

(i) as a hand-held, lightweight camera, in which case the magazine is mounted on the instrument's underside. The monitor viewfinder and special sunshade cannot be attached;

(ii) as a semi-portable camera, mounting the magazine on top and permitting the installation of the monitor viewfinder;

(iii) for more exacting requirements, use is made of a base plate attachment to take the lens hood; the camera is mounted thereon and is secured with two screws and the monitor viewfinder is then attached; this method affords a variation; the magazine can be installed slant-back by means of a special adapter;

(iv) as a noiseless instrument for studio work, for which the magazine is installed on top (but without the lens hood base plate) and over this the blimp, after which the monitor viewfinder can be installed;

(v) "System 35"; this is a special device added after installing the blimp which turns this camera into a complex instrument with remote control of the image by means of a closed TV circuit connected to the reflex viewfinder.

197

SHUTTER OPENING CONTROL. The shutter can be opened from 0 to 170° in both directions (increasing or decreasing the angle), and with the camera either stopped or running, just by turning a knob placed on top of the camera.

LENS MOUNT. Either a single mounting or a three lens turret can be used. Removal of the turret unit is effected by releasing locks placed at each end of the assembly. When changing the single mounting for the turret or vice versa, the viewing system's ground glass can also be exchanged.

Fig. 9. Threading path of Mitchell S35-R with 400 ft rear magazine.

MOUNTING LENSES. Super Baltar lenses are used. To install, place focus indicating arrow in 6 o'clock position and fit lens to orifice, rotating clockwise until the bayonet seats home. To remove lens, press on the lever placed on the turret, above the lens and rotate it in the opposite direction (anticlockwise).

CONTROLS. The built-in tachometer, and footage and frame counters are placed side by side on the top rear of the camera.

MOTORS. These are installed on the camera's right hand side, by means of four screws. The variable speed motor, with rheostat for speed regulation, is the model most used for general purposes. Its body includes sockets for power supply and remote control.

MONITOR VIEWFINDER. Is installed the same as for the model described above. It makes use of a special finder clamp and harness for coupling to the automatic focus and parallax control.

198

SPECIAL LENS HOOD. This unit is supported on twin booms for extension and retraction. Its left-hand side has a hinged sector for permitting the use of the monitor viewfinder. The lens hood is supplied with a special based support for seating on the tripod platform, and on which the camera and the focus control system is installed.

OTHER OPERATIONS. The insertion of gelatin filters in front of the film gate and the operation of contrast filters for lighting study built into the viewing system, are very much the same as for the other Mitchells. The magnification control of the viewing system is placed between the two knobs operating the contrast filters.

Operation of Eclair Cameflex CM3 and Scope model

MOUNTING THE CAMERA. To mount the camera on an Eclair tripod, mate the end of the flat dovetail base of the camera to the appropriate end of the slide on the tripod, then push the camera onto the slide, making sure that the dovetail is inserted correctly.

SHUTTER ADJUSTMENT. The following sequence must be followed to alter the shutter opening:

(i) rotate the lens-turret so as to place it in an intermediate position;

Fig. 10. Aperture plate of Cameflex showing: (1) reflex shutter regulator, (2) shutter knob.

(ii) slightly loosen the screw which secures the adjustment of the shutter blades; this screw can be seen and reached through the opening for mounting the taking lens;

(iii) press the knob marked "reflex" and turn it until the shutter shows through the lens orifice;

(iv) press the knob marked "obturateur" and turn it to obtain the desired shutter opening value marked at the edge of the reflex mirror.

Care must be taken that neither the "reflex" nor the "obturateur" knobs are touched while operating the camera.

Fig. 11. Method of forming internal magazine film loops and flattening film against magazine plate.

MAGAZINE THREADING. Loading and threading the film into the magazine is the most important operation in the handling of Cameflex cameras. As this loading and threading requires some practice, it is advisable to rehearse the procedure several times in daylight with blank film before carrying out the operation itself in the darkroom or changing bag:

(i) take off the lid of the magazine and keep it within easy reach;

(ii) release the pressure rollers above and below the sprocket by lifting the clips;

(iii) insert the film (wound emulsion out) on the top shaft, so that it will unwind anticlockwise (see Fig. 12);

200

Fig. 12. Film path in Eclair Cameflex CM3 and Scope magazine showing formed loops, ready for attachment to camera.

(iv) insert the end of the film through the upper slot and draw out some 32 inches;

(v) insert this end through the lower external slot of the magazine;

(vi) thread the film above the sprocket so that it goes under roller (A) and under the pressure rollers, then meshes with the sprocket teeth; next take it over the upper roller and close the pressure rollers;

(vii) adjust the external film loop by inserting a finger into it (Fig. 11), and pressing down the film until it touches the magazine attachment knob;

(viii) hold the film inserted through the lower magazine slot by pressing it with a finger, so that the length of the loop is not changed accidentally;

(ix) thread the film over the remaining two pressure rollers, and mesh it to the lower side of the sprockets, checking that the sprocket teeth penetrate the film perforations fully;

(x) close the lower pressure rollers;

(xi) insert the film in the core so that it winds anticlockwise;

(xii) replace the magazine lid;

201

(xiii) in daylight, look at the footage counter reading and verify that it corresponds to the length of the unexposed roll of film;

Fig. 13. Attaching Cameflex magazine to camera. Once in position it is automatically secured by a catch.

(xiv) the extended loop must now be pushed into the camera; this is done by pressing the rear of the loop with the finger, and flattening first one end and then the other with the other hand; when doing this, push the film through the light-trap slots so as to form two internal magazine loops (see Fig. 11); when the film is flat against the magazine base plate, the magazine is ready to attach to the camera.

MAGAZINE MOUNTING. This is a very simple operation. Take the camera body in one hand, place the magazine on its slot and push it home with a jerk. To position the magazine correctly it is advisable to present it to the slot using the edges of the tachometer and speed indicator as guides. Once the magazine is pushed home,

Fig. 14. Method of inserting aperture plate when using 16 mm film in Cameflex 16/35.

it is automatically secured by means of the catch placed on the upper right-hand side.

CAMEFLEX 16/35. In the Cameflex 16/35 mm model, when changing from 35 mm to 16 mm film, set the 16 mm aperture plate in the film gate and fix it by means of a retaining plate inserted through the filter slot.

Use 16 mm film magazines. Lenses need not be changed.

HAND DRIVE. The Cameflex can be crankhandle driven by means of a unit comprising an externally controlled gearbox which allows for regulation at three speeds: 1, 8 or 16 frames per turn. The crankhandle drive unit is installed in the same position for coupling the electric motor and is secured by the same means.

INSTALLING THE CAMEBLIMP. The specially designed blimp for the Cameflex can be installed either with 200 or 400 ft magazines, though the latter are normally used. Access is afforded by a single door on the blimp's right hand side; its lock is on the curved top sector. The camera is placed on a plate sliding along rubber guides which is pulled out of the blimp; this not only facilitates installing but also gives the operator access to all parts of the

203

instrument. When the camera is pushed home, it will be automatically in line with, and connected to, the inside portions of the blimp's external controls, such as viewfinder, diaphragm control, main drive shaft control, focus control, etc. A device for installing glass filters or 3 × 3 inch masks is provided on the sliding plate, in front of the camera.

The blimped Cameflex is generally used with synchronous motors, either 220 v. 3-phase, AC or 110 v. 60 Hz AC. All internal circuits are 6-wire throughout in order to take any type of electrical current.

The Cameblimp can be illuminated inside by means of special lamps for observing the camera's operation, installation, etc. from the outside. The external controls on the Cameblimp are:

(i)   reflex viewfinder eyepiece;
(ii)   starting switch;
(iii) shutter opening control;
(iv)   knob for operating shutter by hand;
(v)   internal light switch;
(vi)   focus control;
(vii) diaphragm control with two retaining catches and three observation windows, respectively for:
(viii) lens setting,
(ix)   speed counter and
(x)   exposed footage counter.

Operation of Arriflex Models IIC and IICV

THREADING THE MAGAZINE. Arriflex magazines require careful threading. Before loading, check that the roll of raw stock does not exceed the stated magazine capacity (a longer length of film may rub against the magazine walls, or cause the footage counter to stick, or the camera to run irregularly). Make sure that the film has been wound emulsion side in, and that the roll is tight and its surfaces perfectly flat.

To remove the magazine from the camera body, loosen the catch by turning it clockwise and pulling it out; the magazine can then be withdrawn.

To open the magazine, set the latch to position "A" and then remove the lid. Next, take the footage-counter roller seated on the left-hand core, and shift to the right as indicated by the arrow. Subsequent operations must be carried out in a darkroom or changing bag. As with the Cameflex, it is advisable to practice loading with blank or exposed film before attempting the following operations with raw stock:

(i)   take the end of the roll and cut the perforations by means of the special template provided by the manufacturer;

Fig. 15. Proper threading of Arriflex magazine. Arrow shows how footage counter arm must be seated on film roll.

should this template not be available, cut the end of the film straight between two perforations;

(ii) push the prepared end of the film through the slot on the left-hand side of the magazine, taking care that the film is kept parallel to the magazine walls, so that the sprocket teeth mesh correctly with the perforations;

(iii) mount the film on the left side of the magazine, making sure that the core seats firmly on the spindle;

(iv) check that the roll of film rotates freely on its spindle, then draw the free end out of the magazine base and wrap it round the magazine until the end reaches the engraved marking (this ensures the right length of loop);

(v)   holding the film roll steady, insert the end of the film through the slot on the right-hand side of the magazine, taking care that the sprocket teeth mesh correctly with the film perforations;

(vi) secure the end of the film to the take-up core with one turn, so that it will not slip;

(vii) return the arm of the footage counter to its working position (otherwise the magazine cannot be closed), and fasten the magazine lid by turning its catch; make sure that the lid edges are properly seated to avoid fogging.

THREADING THE CAMERA. To avoid the risk of accidental starting, disconnect the camera from its power source. Next, open the camera access door by turning the lock to position "A". Remove the door and put it in a safe place to avoid damage to the optical system built into it. Then,

(i) rotate the inching knob until the claw is moved completely away from the aperture plate to the top of its cycle; open the film gate and check that the aperture and pressure plates are thoroughly clean;

(ii) place the magazine on the camera, taking care that the loop

Fig. 16. Threading diagram of Arriflex 35 camera.

passes completely through the slot on the camera top. The best way to position the magazine is to tilt it first and place it on the rear end of the magazine housing slot, and then seat it completely until the lock snaps back into position; finally turn the lock;

(iii) insert the film into the film gate; with a finger, carry the film over the aperture plate until the loop thus formed reaches the indicating mark on the camera wall; this upper loop must comprise 15 perforations from the top position of the claw to the magazine slot;

(iv) turn the inching knob by hand and check that the claw engages the film perforations;

(v) close the film gate, turn the inching knob and so make sure that the film is moving freely; connect the camera to its power supply and with the switch run a few feet of film;

(vi) replace the camera access door and secure it by turning the lock to position "Z".

INTERCHANGING LENSES. The turret has three lens positions and the taking lens is the one just beneath the plane of the magazine base. To rotate the turret, press on one of three grips which are placed halfway between the lenses.

To remove a lens, press simultaneously on two locking grips placed at each side of the lens mount, and at the same time withdraw the lens very carefully from the turret. When installing a lens on the turret, check that the slot on the lens mounting is in line with the protruding pin which will be inserted into it.

Fig. 17. Front view of Arriflex camera showing locking grips for changing lenses and external grips for rotating turret.

The standard lenses on the Arriflex are 30, 50 and 75 mm. These are the markings jutting out of the turret edge to inform the operator which lens is in the taking position. If other lenses are used, be careful they do not interfere with each other's fields of view. The 25 mm wide-angle lens must be used without the rigid sunshade and without the 85 mm lens.

VARYING SHUTTER OPENINGS IN MODELS IIBV AND IICV. In models IIBV and IICV the shutter opening can be changed by a knob placed at the side. To alter the shutter opening, stop the camera and for safety's sake disconnect the power source. Next withdraw the taking lens from its mounting. Then press the shutter knob and turn it until the desired aperture angle appears in the lens mounting orifice. Finally replace the lens. The camera is again ready for shooting, but the makers recommend that the shutter knob *should not be pressed* while the camera is running, since this may damage the mechanism. To avoid accidents due to the shutter knob action, the knob is provided with a spring to return it to position after it has been pressed; however, it is advisable to check the positioning of this knob before restarting.

USE OF ANAMORPHIC LENSES. To use the camera with anamorphic lenses, the standard size aperture must be changed for one of the required dimensions: 18·67 × 22 mm (0·735 in. × 0·937 in.).

The aperture plate must first be replaced by one specially supplied for use with this lens. Since the photographed image will be squeezed by the anamorphic lens it is advisable to replace the normal viewfinder tube, which is integral with the camera access door, by another designed to unsqueeze the image. Model IIC is equipped with a door already prepared to accommodate this device, which takes the form of a prism. The unsqueezing viewfinder gives an upright image correct from left to right with an aspect ratio of 2·66 to 1. Anamorphic viewing can be changed back to normal by pressing a lever.

CHANGING VIEWFINDER FRAMING. The framing graticule is on a ground glass placed at right-angles to the lens mount orifice. In the IIC cameras the ground glass can be easily changed to adapt the viewfinder to Cinemascope, widescreen or television frames. The ground glass is removed by hooking a piece of wire or paper clip in a perforation and drawing it out.

VARIABLE SPEED MOTOR. This motor works at 12–16 v. and is

provided with a lever at the power socket to change from forward to reverse drive. It must be used in combination with the appropriate 400 ft. magazines, designed to work with reverse drive.

PERISCOPE ATTACHMENT FOR VIEWFINDER. This accessory can only be used with the latest IIC model Arriflex. It is installed on the standard eyepiece of the viewfinder and can be swivelled in any direction, to allow the camera operator to view from any angle, in relation to the camera and the subject. The periscope attachment gives a circular field of view, of approximately 22 mm diameter. This attachment is installed at the rear of the finder eyepiece system by means of a retaining ring.

Operation of Bell & Howell Eyemo cameras

To load the camera, remove the door by simultaneously turning the locks placed above and below the viewfinder. This will afford access to the interior of the camera and its various components. Next, open the film gate by pressing the arm on the pressure plate fully away from the aperture plate. Pull out about one foot of film from the spool of raw stock, and place the spool on the upper spindle. Then proceed as follows:

(i) insert the film under the upper sprocket, taking care that its teeth penetrate the film perforations;
(ii) form a loop and place the film in the gate between the aperture and pressure plates;
(iii) form another loop at the gate outlet and put the film over the lower sprocket, verifying again that the sprocket teeth penetrate the perforations;
(iv) wind the end of the film clockwise onto an empty reel and fit the latter onto the lower spindle in the camera;
(v) check that the upper loop comprises nine visible perforations and the lower loop eleven, then close the film gate; also check that on closing the film gate, the pressure plate has been seated correctly, otherwise the camera door will not shut tightly;
(vi) wind the spring motor fully and press the operating button (placed underneath and at the rear of camera) to check that the camera is working properly;
(vii) replace the access door and secure it by returning the catches to their original position;

(viii) set the footage counter at 95 ft. and run the camera till zero is reached (the 5 ft. that have been allowed to run correspond to the film leader);

(ix) set the lens as required and then adjust the viewfinder parallax corrector (on the latest models) to the correct

Fig. 18. Threading path in Eyemo cameras when using daylight-loading spools.

Fig. 19. Bell & Howell Eyemo with 400 ft. magazine. (1) Footage counter, (2) critical focusing eyepiece, (3) electric motor, (4) coupling.

camera-subject distance (do not forget that the viewfinder lens must correspond to the taking lens);

(x)   in the models with a three-arm spider turret, the lens is changed by loosening the spider shaft, then disengaging the lens from the camera lens orifice and rotating the spider in order to place another lens in the taking position;

(xi)   on Eyemo models that will accept 200 or 400 ft. magazines, the magazines are installed at the back of the camera by loosening the screw which secures the magazine slot protecting plate, and screwing the magazine screw into a threaded bush;

(xii)   the magazine supply chamber must be threaded in a darkroom or changing bag. After placing the roll of film in the upper chamber and withdrawing the leader, the end of this is inserted in the take-up chamber core, and after rotating it a few times, the lid is replaced and sealed; a loop of about eight inches is drawn out and used to thread the camera as already described.

Eyemo models L, M, N, O, P and Q can be operated by a

Fig. 20. Bell & Howell Eyemo. (I) Turret lock, (2) magazine bushing, (3) coupling, (4) rack-over device.

crank-handle supplied on request. This is inserted in a hole provided at the right-hand side of the camera. Eight frames are exposed at every turn of the crank-handle. Therefore, sound filming speed is attained by turning the crank-handle three times every second. A counter has been incorporated in this crank-handle to indicate the number of frames exposed.

The crank-handle can also be used to reverse the camera for making superimpositions. When reversing with the crank-handle, the operator must bear several points in mind:

(i) the reverse drive action winds the motor spring, so be sure that the motor is well run down before starting to reverse;

(ii) the lens must be closed with a lens cap during the reverse crank-handle operation;

(iii) during the reverse drive action, the footage counter keeps on adding instead of subtracting, so the length of run-back must be carefully calculated.

When external magazines are used the camera must be driven by an electric motor, which will drive not only the camera but the magazine take-up as well. The motor is attached to the camera behind the curved part of the body by inserting the motor shaft into the same coupling that takes the crank-handle.

Operation of 16 mm cameras

Operation of the Arriflex 16 M camera

The 16 M Arriflex is designed to provide very rapid adjustment and operation. The magazines are of the type in which most of the threading is internal, so that they can be mounted on the camera with only a few moments' loss of shooting time.

THREADING THE MAGAZINE. The magazines supplied for the 16 M are for 200 or 400 ft. darkroom-loading rolls, or for 100 or 200 ft. daylight loading spools. Film is wound emulsion inwards.

The film spindles in the magazine incorporate a device which accepts either the square hole in a spool or the round hole in a normal core.

The following are the operations required to load and thread a magazine. Unless daylight loading spools are used, they must be carried out in a darkroom or changing bag.

(i) Open the magazine and lay the lid aside keeping it handy;

212

place the open magazine before you, with its base nearest to you;

(ii) lift the arm of the footage counter;

(iii) place the film roll or spool on the left-hand spindle in such a way that it will unroll clockwise (film perforated on one side only has its perforations next to the magazine wall);

(iv) insert the end of the film through the left-hand slot in the magazine base; rotate the sprocket making sure the teeth penetrate the perforations, until the end of the film comes out of the magazine base;

(v) pull out a length of film long enough when curved round the magazine to just reach the engraved mark; then insert the end into the magazine through the right-hand slot, rotate the sprocket, making sure the teeth penetrate the perforations, until the film goes in, thus ensuring that a 39-frame loop has been formed;

(vi) insert the end of the film into a core or spool and place it on the take-up spindle; rotate the sprocket a few turns to check that threading has been done correctly;

(vii) replace the lid, making sure that it is seated properly so as to avoid fogging.

Mounting the magazine on the camera takes only a few seconds. First turn the magazine lock to the left, so as to detach the plate protecting the magazine housing. Release the catch beneath the viewfinder on the access door by pressing it to the left, then open the camera access door. After pushing the loop through the slot into the camera body, mount the magazine by tilting it slightly, so that the rear end rests first, and then press it home. Turn the magazine catch to the right to secure it firmly.

Next, open the film gate. Rotate the motor shaft until shuttle and register pin are away from the film gate. Insert the loop in the film track so that the lower loop edges round the curved inside wall of the camera body. Close the film gate.

Rotate the motor shaft to check that threading has been carried out correctly, that the shuttle claws penetrate the perforations, and that the loop keeps its shape and position. Replace the camera access door and lock it.

CHANGING LENSES. The turret with its divergent axes takes three lenses which do not obscure one another's fields. The turret can be rotated by pressing on one side of the wing clips jutting out from the edge.

213

To mount a lens in an empty socket, press together the two clips on the lens, and when inserting it make sure that the slot on the mounting is uppermost.

MOTOR. Dismounting and interchanging the motor is a simple operation. Turn the side lever to the left. Withdraw the motor carefully. If another motor is to be installed, check that the pin at its side coincides with the hole at the side of the motor housing. A ring at the back of the motor can be turned to reverse its rotation, and thus, the direction of film travel in the camera. The motor speed can be altered over a range of 5–50 f.p.s. by turning the black striped band on the top.

STARTING THE CAMERA. In order to start the camera proceed as follows:

(i)   connect feed cable end with Canon connector to lower, three-pin male contact, and the other end to 8 v. battery terminals;

(ii) adjust motor speed by turning the rheostat until the chosen speed is shown on the tachometer;

Fig. 21. Arriflex model M showing threading path. (1) Reflex eyepiece, (2) matte-box boom, (3) start switch, (4) magazine release lever, (5) optical system, (6) film loop, (7) switch connection, (8) variable speed motor, (9, 10, 11) external electric connections, (12) motor hand-knob.

(iii) press down lever switch placed above reflex viewfinder; this locks automatically, so that, to stop the camera, the retaining clip must be released.

REFLEX VIEWFINDER. If, before starting the camera, no image appears in the viewfinder, rotate the motor shaft until the image appears. There is an adjuster ring on the viewfinder eyepiece to correct for the operator's eyesight. To avoid fogging the film by light seeping in through the viewfinder tube, the eye should be placed closely against the eyepiece when shooting with strong backlight. When the viewfinder is not in use, the eyepiece should be closed. The latest models are equipped with an automatic device which opens up when the eye is pressed against the eyepiece, and closes again when pressure is withdrawn.

INSTALLATION OF SUNSHADE AND MATTE-BOX. These are mounted on a boom which is inserted in a slot located above the turret close to the magazine lock. The boom is secured by turning the fixing thumbscrew at its forward end. The bellows are then adjusted to suit the field of view of the lens in use.

Operation of the Eclair NPR

As already explained, the Eclair NPR (Noiseless Portable Reflex) makes use of a coaxial magazine, which houses the continuous drive mechanism and the footage and frame counters. The magazine consists of two side-by-side chambers (instead of the usual fore-and-aft arrangement, and the supply and take-up rolls are mounted on the same spindle which is supported by the internal wall separating the two magazine chambers. The magazine takes 100 or 200 ft. daylight loading spools, or rolls of film up to 400 ft. loaded in the darkroom. These are wound emulsion in.

LOADING.
(i)   Place the magazine flat on a table with the base to the right, and the lock of the top lid nearest to you;
(ii) press the safety lock (1) and push-button (2) simultaneously and remove the magazine lid to give access to the supply chamber;
(iii) raise the arm of the footage counter, until it locks in the "up" position;
(iv) if daylight loading spools are to be used, the plate (3) must

215

Fig. 22. Eclair 16 NPR self blimped camera. (1) Safety lock, (2) button catch, (13) finder retaining ring, (14) friction adjuster for finder, (15) finder position lock, (16) eyepiece magnification adjuster, (17) Motor Switch.

be removed; if the film is perforated on one side only, the perforations must be nearest the magazine lid.

(v) open the pressure roller (4) by pushing its retaining catch and feed the film onto the sprocket, checking that the teeth penetrate the perforations on the first inch of film.

(vi) close lid on upper side of magazine, but do not lock it and push safety catch back; the footage counter arm will then jump into position automatically;

(vii) turn the magazine upside down and remove what is now the top lid, and rotate take-up shaft (5) anticlockwise to make about 4 in. of film pass from the supply chamber to the take-up chamber;

(viii) edge the film end along the loop-marking engraved on the magazine wall;

(ix) open guide roller and insert film onto sprocket and then close pressure roller;

(x) keep rotating shaft (5) until film comes out of base-plate (6) and pressing it against the base-plate to facilitate the next steps;

(xi) insert film end in through lower slot; open lower pressure roller; and insert film onto sprocket again, leaving a loop comprising about twelve perforations (approximately enough to allow the insertion of two fingers); this loop should protrude from the magazine base-plate;

(xii) clip the lower pressure roller back into position and keep

216

rotating the shaft until there is enough film inside the take-up chamber to insert the end into the slot in the spool core; check that the film goes over the guide roller;

(xiii) after completing threading on the take-up side, check it by rotating drive shaft (7) [never use take-up shaft (5) for this purpose after the film end has been secured to it];

(xiv) close lid on magazine, engaging the left-hand side first,

Fig. 23. Eclair 16 NPR Magazine supply chamber and film path. (3) Film spooling plate, (4) pressure roller, (7) Film drive shaft, (9) magazine release.

Fig. 24. Magazine take-up chamber of Eclair NPR camera showing film path. (5) Take-up shaft, (6) Base plate, (8) Operating pin.

217

thus pushing in pin (8); adjust lid firmly and push back safety lock (1);

(xv) using your fingers (see Fig. 11), divide film loop into two halves, and push one into the upper and one into the lower slot in the magazine base (this is important and must not be neglected).

ATTACHING MAGAZINE TO CAMERA. Place magazine baseplate against camera's magazine-plate. Tilt magazine slightly and seat lower end of baseplate first, and then swing it forward until the upper catch clicks into position. To detach magazine from camera, press button (9).

ADJUSTING THE SHUTTER. Shutter opening can be adjusted from 5° to 180°. Proceed as follows:

(i) rotate turret until it is in horizontal position;

(ii) turn lever (10) up to "Reflex" position;

(iii) turn knob (11) until shutter edge shows through lens opening;

(iv) turn lever (10) to "Shutter Adjustment" position (R.O.) and push in;

(v) rotate shutter control (12) until the desired shutter opening setting can be read on shutter edge through lens opening;

(vi) release lever (10) on which its spring will return it to its neutral "Motor" position, thus unlocking the pull-down mechanism.

Fig. 25. Shutter control panel in Eclair NPR camera. (10) Shutter adjustment lever, (11) Shutter inching knob.

Fig. 26. Eclair NPR 16 mm camera mounted on a tripod adaptor. (2) Button release for magazine lid, (12) Shutter control, (14) Friction adjuster.

MOUNTING LENSES. The Eclair NPR takes lenses with three types of mounting: bayonet mounting, C type mounting, and Cameflex and Arriflex mountings.

(i) insert the bayonet mounting so that the narrow flange is nearest the turret shaft, and then turn clockwise;

(ii) screw C type mounting lens into central orifice of turret mount;

(iii) lenses with Cameflex or Arriflex mountings must be fitted with an adapter which is then screwed in like a C type mounting.

The turret is rotated by pressing on the central shaft in the direction of arrow "D", and then pulling out and rotating the turret clockwise. After fitting the desired lens return the turret to its shooting position by rotating the central shaft in the direction of arrow "S".

ADJUSTING VIEWFINDER. The viewfinder can swivel 360°, thus allowing for framing from any position, which is often a great convenience. This finder is removed by loosening the ring (13). It swivels on an axis which is parallel to the sides of the frame, and button (14) regulates the friction on the swivelling action. The

219

thumbscrew (15) fixes the finder firmly in any desired position. The eyepiece is provided with an automatic closing device, which opens up when the eye is pressed to the eyepiece, and closes down again when pressure is released. The eyepiece can also swivel so that the operator can use either his right or left eye. Thumbscrew (16) adjusts the eyepice diopter reading to suit individual eyesight.

STARTING. The motor is started by means of a built-in switch (17). A pilot light is lit when the motor is running at the right speed, thus allowing the operator to check the state of the battery charge.

HOLDING INSTRUCTIONS. The Eclair NPR has been designed for hand-held shooting, with the back of the magazine resting on the operator's shoulder. It weighs 18 lb complete with magazine and motor. If it should be necessary to mount the camera on a tripod, a special hi-hat adapter must be used.

SUNSHADE. The matte-box and extendible bellows sunshade are mounted on a rigid boom, along which they can slide. This is also useful for supporting zoom and telephoto lenses. Also provided is a rotating disc allowing for insertion of polarizing filters.

Operation of Auricon Sound cameras

The various Auricon models differ considerably from one another, and the following points are intended to bring out only the most important features for handling these instruments. A detailed description of their operation, as well as recommendations for sound recording techniques, will be found in the exhaustive manual supplied by the manufacturers.

CONNECTIONS. The camera operator may perhaps be baffled by the profusion of cables supplied with these instruments. But he should remember his camera works in combination with an amplifier and other electronic equipment, and the foolproof characteristics of all connectors, which ensure there will be no mix-up, should set his mind at rest. The cables are:

(i) from power source to camera, to provide the drive;
(ii) from galvanometer or magnetic recording head in the camera to the sound amplifier;

(iii) from microphone to amplifier;

(iv) from camera or amplifier (according to sound equipment or camera model being used) to earphones, to monitor the recorded sound quality.

THREADING. The Auricon Cine Voice is supplied with a threading chart engraved on the camera body; in the other Auricons, this chart is stuck on the camera access door. The instructions on these charts must be strictly adhered to. Threading models 600, 600 Special and Super 1200, requires prior loading of the magazine in darkroom or changing bag. The Cine Voice uses 100 ft. daylight loading spools.

These cameras take 16 mm film with perforations on one side only. If magnetic sound is to be recorded, the raw stock must be supplied with magnetic track already striped on the edge in accordance with ASA Standard PH 22.28–1958.

Before threading, it is advisable to clean the film gate; also check that loops are the proper size and shape, and that the film passes correctly over the compensating sprocket near the recording head.

In the Cine Voice model, the spools must be pushed right back onto the shaft, after the footage counter arm has been swung away. First complete threading and insert the film end into the slot on the hub of the take-up spool, and only then mount the take-up spool on the take-up shaft.

Fig. 27. Threading path for film in the Auricon Cine Voice.

Models 600 and 1200 are equipped with a safety device which cuts the power supply if anything goes wrong with the take-up belt; the camera will run only if the take-up belt is working properly. When threading the 1200 bear in mind that two sprockets are used in this camera to drive the extra large load of film.

After threading the 600 and 1200 models, make sure to slip the magazine belt drive into place. Before closing the camera access door, start up the camera for a few seconds to check that it runs properly.

FRAMING AND FOCUSING. Viewfinding is by a different method in each Auricon model. The Cine Voice is provided with a side viewfinder allowing for parallax correction. But if a zoom lens with built-in reflex viewfinder is used, the camera door with built-in side viewfinder must be replaced by a special tubeless door. The finder on the zoom lens will permit very accurate framing, and focusing will be by means of the attached rangefinder.

The same side viewfinder can be employed on the two 600 models, but these cameras are also equipped with two additional systems. One is a small eyepiece at one side of the camera, which makes direct focusing possible when the turret is rotated until the taking lens is placed in front of it. The other is an optical tube with

Fig. 28. Threading path for the film in the Auricon Pro 600 model camera.

Fig. 29. Rear view of Auricon Pro 600. (1) Warning
light, (2) footage counter,
(3) on-off push button,
(4) telefinder eyepiece.

2 3 4

ten times magnification, working through auxiliary lenses mounted
on the turret, which are equivalent to the taking ones. This latter
system is useful with telephoto lenses.

As explained previously, focusing and framing with the Super
1200 is effected by a rackover ground glass system which, before
shooting, inserts mirrors at 45° behind the taking lens. This
device is controlled from behind the camera by a rotating handle.
When this handle is in the "g.g. focus" position, framing can be
carried out through the taking lens and focus adjusted, but the
camera cannot be operated. When the control handle is in the
Telefinder position, the viewing system sights through the auxiliary
lens, the mirror system is retracted and the camera can be operated.
The control-handle can be rotated very easily and smoothly even
with gloved hands.

VARIABLE OPENING SHUTTER. The Super 1200 model is equipped with a shutter whose variable opening is adjusted by a control
at one side. This allows for fade-ins and fade-outs and for shutter
speed adjustments from 1/50 to 1/200 sec. The calibrations on the
control are: open, $\frac{3}{4}$ open, $\frac{1}{2}$ open, $\frac{1}{4}$ open, closed.

223

STARTING. The Cine Voice is started by means of a lever switch and a neon lamp beneath it lights up when the motor is running. The two 600 models are provided with two push-buttons, one above the other, for starting and stopping, respectively. Two lamps on the camera front and one at the back go on when the motor is running. At the right-hand side there is another lamp which lights up to indicate that the camera is connected to the power source and that the "electromatic" take-up is running at $\frac{1}{3}$ of its power rating; when power is connected, this lamp comes on even if the motor is not running.

The model 1200 camera is started by means of a push-button placed on the rotating handle of the rackover framing device. Thus the start-up system will operate only when the bar is in the telefinder position for taking, and the framing device has been withdrawn from the viewing system. When the control-handle is in the "g.g. focus" position, the instrument cannot be started, thus avoiding mishaps. Should it be necessary to look through the taking lens when the camera is running (e.g. when checking shutter synchronization for back projection), the handle must be rotated to "g.g. focus" after the camera has been started, but it must be remembered that no image is being recorded on the film while the rackover system is in the viewing position. The instrument is stopped by pressing the red button above the rotating handle.

Fig. 30. Threading path for Auricon Super 1200 model sound camera.

(i) No means of correcting parallax is provided in the telefinder supplied for the Pro 600 and Pro 600 Special when using telephoto lenses, since the error is negligible.

Fig. 31. Rear view of Auricon Super 1200. (1) Footage counter, (2) cameraman's headphone plug, connection (3) telefinder eyepiece, (4) power line indicator light, (5) shift-over device with on-off push button.

(ii) In the Cine Voice, the footage counter is on the left-hand side of the camera, while on the other models it is at the back and is illuminated.

(iii) When working under very low temperatures, it is advisable to connect the camera to the power source some 30 minutes before shooting, so that the heater will be turned on. It will then gradually build up to a temperature adequate to free the lubricant. When the camera motor is started, the heater is automatically switched off. The heater is controlled by a thermostat working at a minimum of 65°F and a maximum of 70°F.

(iv) When rolls of film larger than 400 ft. are employed, the makers recommend the use of the 3 in. Auricon centres.

OPERATION OF AMPLIFIERS. This varies considerably according to type and model, as well as to choice of magnetic or optical recording. The Auricon company publishes a manual with precise instructions on the steps to follow in each case. A summary of the main points is given here so that the reader may get a general idea of how to proceed.

(i) Check the charge of the batteries feeding the amplifier, by means of the controls provided for this purpose (optical or magnetic amplifier).

(ii) Check that the frequency reading of the "record bias" is correct (61 kc/s) (magnetic sound amplifier).

(iii) Turn on the amplifier and adjust the intensity of the exciter lamp in the galvanometer according to the sensitivity of the film to be used (optical sound amplifier).

(iv) Establish a sound quality control channel, either directly from the microphone, or from the recording on the film's magnetic track (magnetic sound amplifier).

(v) Check volume by means of the volume indicator meter or by the volume control knob scale (sound amplifier for optical and/or magnetic recording).

(vi) Adjust amplifier according to the quality and/or characteristics of the sound to be recorded (sound amplifier for optical and/or magnetic recording).

REFERENCES

[1] Mitchell Camera Corporation, *Handbook M-202* (Calif. Jan. 1957); U.S. Navy Department, *Navy Training Courses: Photography*, Vol. 1 (1951);
U.S. Navy Department, *Navy Training Courses: Photographers Mate 1 & C* (1962).
[2] Pittaro, E. M., *TV and Film Production Data Book*, Morgan & Morgan, New York, pp. 249–253 (September 1959).
[3] Couthant, A., Mathot, J., A Reflex 35 mm Magazine Motion Picture Camera, *Journal of The Society of Motion Picture and Television Engineers*, pp. 173–179 (Aug. 1950).
[4] British Broadcasting Corporation, Eng. Div., *Arriflex 35 mm Camera Technical Instructions*, London (May 1960).
Arnold & Richter, K.G., *Handbook of the Arriflex 35 System*, Part 1, Instruction Manual, Munich (Dec. 1961).
Cinepress, *Repair and Parts Manual for Arriflex 35 mm Cameras*, Vol. 1, Hollywood (June 1966).
See also: Cameraflex Corp., *Instruction Book for Camera PH-330-K*, New York.
[5] U.S. Air Forces, *Handbook of Instructions with Parts Catalogue for the Type (A-3. 35 mm) Aircraft Camera*, Washington (Sept. 1942).
[6] British Broadcasting Corporation, Eng. Div., *Arriflex 16 mm Camera Technical Instructions*, London (May 1960).
[7] Bach Auricon, *How to use your Auricon 16 mm sound-on-film equipment: recording equipment*, Hollywood (Nov. 1960).

6

CHOICE MAINTENANCE AND INSPECTION OF CAMERAS

Very often the choice of a motion picture camera, whether for buying or renting, is the responsibility of the professional cinematographer. Film companies and independent producers usually consult the photography director on the advantages of certain equipment as against others, or on which is the most adequate instrument for a specific task. Correct advice can only be given after analysing various factors in their corresponding scale of value.

Normally, film companies either use their own instruments or rent them from camera and equipment rental firms. In the former case the company must be economically very solvent, usually with studios and laboratories, in order to afford investing a large capital in equipment; this must therefore be made to work continuously, either producing, or even sometimes renting equipment to others. On the other hand, cameras and accessory equipment are normally rented only by independent producers, who tackle films one at a time, each being an individual business transaction, and the rental fees are included in each film's budget; such independent producers generally avoid being tied up with long-term actors' contracts, maintenance of premises, or permanent personnel salaries.

A company will invest capital in costly equipment, especially cameras, only when they can programme a continuous output, when they want to be free from third parties for the material they shall use, and when their administration policy tends towards capitalization through such equipment. The absence of specific equipment for rental, and others, may sometimes be complementary factors.

For example, few TV newsreel companies rent cameras. The continuous use of the instruments would make rental too expensive and unpractical. The same occurs with institutions specialized in scientific films, who are continuously using instruments which are difficult to obtain for rental.

Choosing a camera

Before selecting a camera it is essential to determine the specific task in view. This brings us back to the subject of film production. Throughout the world there are four basic types of film: the feature film, the short (documentary or scientific) film, the news coverage film and the theatrical or TV commercial. Each of such main classifications is broken down into a series of sub-groups which define precisely each type of production.

Shooting methods

According to technical requirements or shooting methods, the above classified films can be shot as follows:
(i) direct sound recording on the film's own track (single system);
(ii) direct sound recording on a separate strip (double system);
(iii) silent printing of the image to add the sound track later (dubbing).

The first system is used for newsreels, especially for TV and has been mentioned before (see p. 118). The second system is used for feature films or for newsreels by means of special devices. The soundless image recording for adding sound later is mostly used for "shorts", publicity films, or low-cost feature films where fast shooting and low-cost media are essential.

Studio cameras

When using the double system, a silent camera must be used, which must work synchronized with the sound recorder. Such instruments are used for shooting feature films or publicity film with a dialogue, and are called "studio cameras", which are noted for the following characteristics:

BULK AND WEIGHT. The body of the camera is designed to dampen the noise made by the movements and to house a large synchronous motor. Therefore the instrument needs a rolling pedestal or dolly for displacements round the studio and it must be dismantled and reassembled each time the scene is changed when shooting outdoors.

228

PRECISION INTERMITTENT. Being provided with register pins, these instruments provide rock steady images, thus producing better quality photography with improved relief and definition. They also allow for special effects such as multiple exposures, travelling mattes, background projections, etc. which cannot be effected by other means.

EFFICIENT FOCUS CONTROL. Focus regulation by means of external controls or by cable connected remote control is essential when shooting scenes with continuous displacements of actors or combined actors and cameras. Studio cameras are generally the only instruments with facilities for such scenes.

SPECIAL POWER PLANT. Studio cameras are driven by AC fed synchronous motors to facilitate camera and sound recorder synchronization. When shooting away from public sources, AC converters must be used.

HANDLING AND OPERATION. Studio cameras are very complete and complex instruments which require more than one operator to work them.

HIGH COST. Instruments for studio work are very expensive: international prices range from US $5,000–30,000, according to make, model, and accessories wanted. The daily rent varies from one country to the other, but it will usually be found in the order of US $40 for the simplest models to US $80 for the most complex items.

It will be appreciated that studio cameras must be used when shooting by the double system; but on the other hand they necessitate complex accessories, shooting time per day is reduced by delays in readying for shooting, they require a larger number of technicians and consequently increase daily shooting costs in addition to rental or capital amortization costs.

Therefore, when planning a production, the excellent efficiency of direct sound recording must be weighed against its higher cost and slowness, in comparison to soundless shooting for a later dubbing.

Lightweight cameras

Shooting for postsynchronization is usually effected with lightweight cameras, whose characteristics are as follows:

SIMPLE INTERMITTENT MECHANISM. The intermittent movements

229

of most lightweight cameras do not include register pins and in some models the shuttles work with only one claw on only one side. Such mechanisms provide acceptable images, but they are not sufficiently steady for special effects.

NOISY OPERATION. The running noise of this type of camera sometimes disturbs non-professional actors, who feel camera-shy as soon as they hear it, especially when shooting "cinéma-verité" films.

NORMAL POWER PLANT. Their variable speed motors can be fed from batteries, and consequently they do not require heavy alternators.

MOBILE AND PORTABLE. This type of camera is easy to move assembled from one point to another of the set or location. It can even be kept in a carrying case, completely ready for immediate use. This avoids a great loss of time in assembling, etc.

RESTRICTED FOCUSING FACILITIES. Few lightweight cameras are provided with devices for following focus continuously. Focus adjustment by camera assistant is difficult as the scales are not easily visible. Sometimes this work must be carried out by the camera operator himself. This is a point to consider when planning to shoot scenes with continuous displacements of camera and actors.

MINIMUM CREW. Since these instruments lack elaborate refinements and are simple to operate and easy to carry, they can be operated by a minimum camera crew.

LOW COST. The international price of these cameras is from approximately US $2,000–3,000, according to make and model, and they are rented for about US $15 a day.

From the production point of view, therefore, though lightweight cameras have certain technical shortcomings, they bring about appreciable savings which can be summarized as follows: large number of takes during each working day, lower salary costs and lower rental or capital amortization costs.

Summary of factors

The above considerations on the advantages and shortcomings of equipment as applied to different types of shooting are only intended as a guide for selecting the best suited item, whether for purchasing or renting. Care must also be taken with the individual

230

technical characteristics of each instrument, with its working conditions and state of conservation.

If the purchase of a camera is contemplated, besides the above considerations, attention should be paid to the following:

(i) uniformity of make(s) used by the production company or group;
(ii) availability of spare parts;
(iii) experience of the company's operators and servicing technicians with the chosen instrument;
(iv) range of available accessories allowing for future improvements;
(v) suitability for use with the latest techniques.
(vi) possibilities of re-sale in the market where the purchaser works.

Maintenance and lubrication

One of the main chores of the camera operator is to check that his camera and its accessories are at all times working properly. In a studio this check is normally the responsibility of servicing personnel from the camera department, who are in charge of cleaning, inspecting and making ready all the cameras in the studio.

When shooting on location, far from the facilities provided by organized servicing, the task of inspecting, cleaning and lubricating the cameras is sometimes the responsibility of the camera assistant, who must carry out all this work with available facilities, and must report any difficulty to the camera operator.

General cleaning

To avoid breakdown and delay when shooting, it is highly desirable to clean out the camera and its accessories at the end of each day's work. The external parts of the camera most liable to get dirty are the camera body, the sunshade, the magazine and the front surfaces of the lenses.

Except for glass surfaces, all these items can be very easily cleaned. The dust should first be removed with a long-haired brush, and the component then wiped with a cloth soaked in petrol or cigarette lighter fluid.

Cleaning lenses and viewfinder optical surfaces

Before cleaning, lenses should be dismounted from the camera. Dust is the first thing to eliminate, and this is best done with a rubber-bulb blower, a fine camel-hair brush or a high pressure air supply. Dust tends to build up at the rim formed by the glass and the metal mount. If removal proves difficult, try an orange stick with its point protected by a soft linen cloth folded seferal times.

Should there be spots on the glass, clean by rubbing lightly, but only with special optical cleaning paper. If the spots resist this treatment rub with a very soft (preferably linen) lintless cloth soaked in a special fluid for optical surfaces. However, do not rub hard or long, as this may affect the antireflective coating.

After cleaning the external lens surfaces (never even try to clean the internal surfaces), replace the lens caps, and put the lenses in their cases or mount them on the camera. The optical surfaces of viewfinders or reflex shutters are to be treated in the same way as lens surfaces.

Cleaning inside the camera

The inside of the camera must be cleaned out daily. The dirt that must be eliminated is generally emulsion deposit, dust and dried up lubricating oil. The implements needed are: camel-hair brush, long-hair brush, rubber bulb blower, high pressure air and soft cloth. Cleaning procedures can be classified thus:

INTERNAL SURFACES OF CAMERA BODY. The internal walls of the camera are exposed to dust each time the camera is opened for threading. This causes an accumulation of dust in areas near the film path. Every trace of dust must be removed by means of the long-hair brush and the rubber bulb blower. The operation can be completed with a petrol soaked cloth, provided the walls are not lined with corduroy.

APERTURE AND PRESSURE PLATES. In most cameras these two plates can be removed or at least opened up to afford easy access. In either case the maker's instructions must be strictly observed. Before removing a plate from its mounting, care must be taken that the shuttle claws and the register pin are fully withdrawn, i.e. that they are away from the plates. The dirt collected by these parts is mostly emulsion deposit, and therefore must be removed at short intervals to avoid scratching the film. Normally a check is made after each take, while a thorough cleaning is made each time film is threaded into the camera, or after each 1000 ft. has been exposed.

This cleaning can be done with the camel-hair brush, or with an orange stick if too much emulsion has accumulated. Never use

232

hard materials for this purpose. Some makers recommend spreading paraffin thinly on the edges of the film track, others advise a light film of oil. In all cases the operator or assistant should follow closely the manufacturers' instructions for every camera he is handling, since each model is built of different materials and with different structural characteristics.

SPROCKETS AND FILM TRAVEL GUIDE ROLLERS AND GROOVES. All these parts, like the aperture and pressure plates, suffer from a build-up of emulsion deposits. However, cleaning may be rendered difficult by emulsion sticking in inaccessible recesses, as between sprocket teeth, on the curves of the rollers, and in the edges of grooves. These must be cleaned with the same devices as for the film gate, but it is advisable to finish off the operation with a soft cloth wiped over the cleaned parts. Take care, however, that no thread or particle of the cloth remains in the camera.

Cleaning the magazine

In Arriflex and Cameflex cameras, the continuous film drive mechanism is housed inside the magazine. Other magazines, such as those for the Mitchell, the Newall, the Debrie and the Vinten, have different characteristics which require special care for each chamber or compartment.

The points which must be carefully checked for cleanliness are the inlet and outlet slots (light traps), internal rollers and surfaces which may come in contact with the film, such as magazine walls. These zones must be inspected and cleaned each time the magazine is loaded, using the following procedure:

(i)   removal of dust by means of an air squirt and long-hair brush, especially from chinks, crevices, and light traps;
(ii) removal of emulsion deposits on rollers;
(iii) general cleaning of the whole magazine with a soft cloth.

Lubrication

Here the operator is advised to follow closely the manufacturer's instructions. The following information has been compiled for easy reference but may not be exhaustive.

LUBRICATION OF MITCHELL & NEWALL CAMERAS.
Type of oil:
      Mitchell camera oil;

233

Grease:
   light neutral bearing grease;
Lubricating points:
   movement: every 2000 ft.;
   eccentric arm bearing, timing clock unit, register pin bearings,
   eccentric arm bearing, eccentric shaft sliding-block bearing,
   top and lower sides of sliding block, rear bearing, pull-down
   claw arm, rear bearing of register pin arm, rear pivot arm
   bearing, front bearing of toggle arm, rear bearing of toggle arm;
Every 5000 ft:
   swivel block on register pin arm;
Every 10,000 ft.:
   pressure plate (two rollers);
Every 50,000 ft.:
   pressure plate retainer arm. Film rollers must be oiled according to manufacturer's instructions.

Fig. I. Lubrication points of Mitchell intermittent mechanism. Lubrication of all points shown after every 2,000 ft, except point 9, which should be lubricated after every 5,000 ft.

LUBRICATION OF DEBRIE SUPER PARVO REFLEX CAMERAS.
Type of oil:
   Huilfrigor or Mobiloil Arctic in case of aerial shooting,
   in the mountains or in polar regions. Huiltropic for cameras
   working in tropical regions;

234

Lubrication points:
two oil holes in front part of camera and in the shutter oil housing. Bearing housing situated inside camera, between magazines. Oil must be poured in until it reaches the mark on a special indicator.

LUBRICATION OF ECLAIR CAMEFLEX CM3 CAMERAS.
Type of oil:
high quality watch oil or Huilfrigor or Huiltropic as above;
Lubricating points:
oil holes are marked in red. All moving parts must be oiled when necessary. In the magazine the red screws must be removed and no more than two drops of oil introduced.

LUBRICATION OF ARRIFLEX CAMERAS.
Type of oil:
Esso Clock Oil 8119;
Grease:
Arriflex Spezialfett;

Lubricating points:
(i) grease hole on the right-hand side, next to the plate indicating the length of the loop;
(ii) claw shaft and guide (use oil);
(iii) bearing of the single-frame shaft situated behind the inching knob. Never lubricate in excess. The few lubricating points should be lubricated after 15,000 to 20,000 feet.

LUBRICATION OF EYEMO CAMERAS.
Type of oil:
Bell & Howell camera oil;
Lubricating points:
six oil holes in the front of the mechanism plate (two of them on the sprocket shaft). One drop every 3500 feet will be sufficient. A seventh oil hole is situated in the centre of the camera head Two drops each 1000 feet of film run.

LUBRICATION OF AURICON CAMERAS.
Type of oil:
Singer sewing machine oil;
Lubricating points:
oil holes marked in red in all models;
Rate:
one drop in each hole every five days of use.

Maintenance of Mitchell NC, BNC and Newall cameras

As the Mitchells, and their British counterparts, the Newalls, are the most widely-used cameras in large-scale studios, a few more details about their maintenance may prove helpful.

CLEANING THE APERTURE PLATE. The aperture and pressure plates (the film gate) should be cleaned each time before threading as follows:

(i)   prepare the camera as for threading (see page 153);
(ii) introduce a length of film between aperture and pressure plates to check that shuttle claws and register pin are completely away from the plates; perform the operation carefully since even slight mishandling may cause serious damage;
(iii) turn the two aperture latches at top and bottom of the film gate upwards, then draw the aperture plate very carefully out of the camera;
(iv) clean it with a camel-hair brush, and then reinstall it; great care must be taken in all these operations to avoid scratching, since this will damage the film and necessitate replacement of the damaged part.

CLEANING THE PRESSURE PLATE. Each time the aperture plate is cleaned, the pressure plate should also be inspected and cleaned. The latter is removed by swinging away the retaining frame behind it. Clean out all deposits of emulsion or gelatine with a camel-hair brush; check that the pressure rollers rotate freely; if they tend to stick, immerse the part in a highly refined thinner and rotate the rollers until they turn freely; remove from liquid and wait till it evaporates. Next apply a little of the special oil supplied by the makers and clean off the excess. Finally, reinstall pressure plate.

WARMING UP THE CAMERA. The operator should never forget to run the motor for a few minutes before threading the film. This warming will ensure steady running at the proper speed.

AFTER-THREADING CHECKS. Make sure that all guide rollers have been returned to position, and have not been left open after threading film round the sprocket. Also verify that the shuttle and register pin are in the correct position. If any of these parts are out of place, the camera access door cannot be secured.

Check the threading visually, and test that the movements run properly, by turning the motor flywheel. The upper loop should comprise about 22 visible perforations, from the sprocket to the film gate inlet, and the lower loop from the film gate outlet to the sprocket, 30 perforations.

CHECKS BEFORE SHOOTING. Never forget to remove the protective caps from the lenses. Check the position of the adjustable mattes by looking through the focusing tube. Verify that the shutter is either fully open, or in the setting fixed by the operator. Also make sure that the focusing of the side monitoring viewfinder corresponds with that of the lens to be used, and that the proper parallax correction has been set.

Just before shooting set the frame and footage counters to zero, and check that the camera is properly levelled. Make sure that the power supply for the motor is correct.

Operation and maintenance of batteries

Batteries are a common source of power for driving cameras when working out of reach of mains supply lines. There are three types of batteries used by the motion picture industry; the non-rechargeable, dry-cell battery; the rechargeable wet-cell battery; the nickel-cadmium battery (see end of chapter).

Dry-cell batteries are used only as highly portable equipment or on expeditions to places remote from mains supplies. They cannot be charged and their life is limited by internal chemical action, and also depending on the motor's power rating and the use made of the camera, Many specialized firms manufacture units for up to 12 v. and for 4, 7, 9·5 and 50 Amps/hour.

Accumulators can be either of the wet-cell type, with cells of 2 v. each, or of the solid electrolyte type, with cells of slightly lower voltage. The former are normally used in the industry; their plates are made of lead peroxide and the electrolyte is diluted sulphuric acid. The materials employed make them heavy items of equipment; their load is measured by the density of the electrolyte.

Solid electrolyte batteries are based on a principle of alkaline solution developed by Thomas A. Edison. Though the voltage of each cell is smaller than those of wet-cell batteries, they have other advantages making them very practical and are now increasingly used in the motion picture industry.

Choice of battery

The battery must be chosen according to the type of camera to be used, the characteristics of its motor, and the footage to be shot.

The nature of the job on hand: news coverage, documentary, feature film, etc. must also be considered.

The power consumption of large cameras like the Mitchell, Newall, Vinten or Super Parvo is considerable, and they therefore require batteries of a high amp rating. Generally motorcar batteries are used on such occasions; their power provides drive for many thousand feet of film. However they are excessively heavy, which is an important consideration when planning shots demanding frequent moving about.

Lightweight cameras are driven by small-consumption motors which therefore need smaller sized wet-cell accumulators or dry-cell batteries. Besides those made specifically for this purpose, motorcycle batteries or electronic flash wet-cell batteries can also be used. The important factor in such cases is small bulk and light weight, since they will be usually strapped to the operator's shoulder. Solid electrolyte batteries show these qualities best. The amp rating of batteries for lightweight cameras is never more than 7·5 amp/hr, which allow for shooting up to 5,000 ft. of 35 mm film and 8,000 ft. of 16 mm.

Checking battery charge

Normally the electricians on the production unit are responsible for maintaining and checking batteries, but it is just as well for all the camera crew to know about their care and maintenance.

At the end of each working day, the batteries used during the day's operations must be recharged. It is a good idea to number the units so as to determine at a glance which batteries have been used and so must be recharged, and which are ready for service. Battery charge may be checked as follows:

(i) unscrew the stoppers from the cells and observe whether the electrolyte covers the plates; if the latter show up above the surface of the liquid, top up with distilled water until the plates are immersed to a depth of $\frac{1}{4}$ in.

(ii) clean the terminals with a wire brush, and apply a voltmeter under load to the poles of each cell; the reading for each under full load should be 2 v.;

(iii) use a hydrometer to measure the density of the acid solution in each cell; when fully charged the reading should be 1·25–1·30; portable batteries are generally provided with floats painted in different colours to indicate at a glance the state of the charge.

Recharging the battery

Before recharging, make sure that the charge can be adjusted to the voltage of the battery, and so adjust it; then verify the

Fig. 2. Typical battery and charger connection.

ampere-hour rating of the battery, which will probably be given on the name or rating plate. The time required for recharging can be roughly estimated from this information. For example, if the battery is rated at 180 amp/hr. and it is to be connected to a charger supplying 18 amps. it will be recharged in about 10 hrs.

From the operator's point of view, the three most important elements of a battery charger are: the ammeter to indicate the rate of charge, the selector switch to regulate the current rating, and the two connecting cables, the red one of which corresponds to the positive pole, and the black one to the negative pole. These two cables are connected to the respective battery terminals and must be securely clamped on to make a resistance-free contact. The stoppers must be removed from the cells before charging begins, and naked lights must never be brought near a battery under charge.

The end of the recharging period is indicated by hydrogen bubbling from the cells. The density of the electrolyte should now be measured again; a faulty cell will be revealed by a low reading on the hydrometer. Batteries not in use should be given a topping-up charge every week or so.

Nickel–cadmium batteries

Solid electrolyte batteries of the nickel–cadmium type have a practically unlimited life; they have been tested over more than five

239

thousand recharging cycles without loss of capacity. Moreover, they retain 70 % of their charge after being laid up for more than a year, and the maintenance they require is negligible.

In the nickel–cadmium battery the positive plates are small diameter steel cells, finely perforated, where nickel hydroxide is introduced, and the negative plates are similar cells filled with cadmium hydroxide. The electrolyte consists of a 30 % solution of potassium hydroxide. Each cell has a rated voltage of 1·25 and a capacity of 6 to 10 amp/hrs. They can stand temperatures from -20 to more than 140°F; no gases are produced, and they can, moreover, be stored completely discharged without harm. The only maintenance required by some models is topping-up with a few drops of distilled water once a year.

Several manufacturers produce various models for 6, 7, 8, 9, 10, 12, 15, 16, 16·8 and 24 volts. The best known makes are Volta-Block, Dinamax and Power-Mite.

Checking the camera

In the vast and complex, technical-economic organization for producing motion pictures, one of the most crucial elements is undoubtedly the instrument for carrying out the plans and efforts of countless men. Should this instrument fail costly shooting will have to be repeated or, in the case of newsreels, will be irreparably lost.

It is vital that the camera should work efficiently, free from technical accidents which might spoil the filmed material. Consequently it is essential that production companies or teams should check carefully all cameras they use and schedule periodic inspections and overhauls.

This section sets out to describe concepts and methods to trace different mishaps and control performance of all camera types. Such checks have been simplified as much as possible, for the benefit of those who may not have available all recommended technical means. However, it is highly advisable to carry out this work with great care, so that faulty appreciation should not lead to distorted results, nor cause misadjustments of the checked instrument.

The checks hereunder are a summary of the tests normally carried out by the manufacturer before delivering equipment. The checks should be scheduled according to how much the instrument has been used, the conditions undergone, and the task to be carried out.

240

Complementary to the explanations hereunder, a "trouble shooting chart" is given at the end of the section, with the more typical difficulties that may arise while operating a camera. From a careful study of both, the newly initiated operator will know what to expect while working with his instrument, the reasons for any failures, and the possible immediate solutions.

Checking for film damage

One of the main functions of a cine camera is to allow film to pass through its mechanism and compartments without damaging it physically in the least. That is to say that after shooting the film must not show the least scratch on base or emulsion, nor any breakage, deformation, etc. of the perforations.

The first step of the check is to thread 15–20 ft. of raw stock and run it from one magazine to the other. Remove the film and place it on a table with a strong side lighting and examine it by reflection and very carefully, first the base and then the emulsion side. If no faults are found, the perforations must then be examined with a 10 × magnifying glass to check their physical conditions. If the shuttle of the camera being checked works on only one side of the film, bear this in mind and examine the perforations that were acted upon.

LOCATING CAUSES

Should a fault appear, proceed to locate it in the part of the camera producing it. Effect this by threading the camera again, but before making it run, remove the lens from its socket and mark the aperture frame on the film with a crayon. Run the camera until the crayon mark reaches the inlet slot of the take-up magazine chamber. Make another crayon mark at the outlet slot of the raw-stock chamber, and withdraw the filmlength from the camera for a very close examination. Locate the fault again and its distance from the crayon marks will determine the exact point on the mechanism which produces it.

Damages on the film surface are generally due to emulsion built-up on some parts of the mechanism, specially on the film gate. This is frequently the only part directly in contact with the film; the faces of other parts are machined so that contact with the film is effected only at the edges. Therefore, when scratches etc, appear on the emulsion or the film base, the first places to inspect should be the aperture and pressure plates. A small build-up of emulsion or celluloid dust from the film base will gradually adhere

241

firmly to the parts by the pressure of the film's constant passage. Besides the film gate, build-up may occur on the sprockets or on the guide rollers.

If no defect is found inside the camera, the damage may be produced inside the magazines. They must therefore be carefully inspected, specially at the sections where the film issues from the raw-stock chamber and enters into the take-up chamber. Emulsion or celluloid build-up may also occur at the guide or plush rollers that are found there. Such inspection must be made on all magazines used with the camera being inspected.

DAMAGE TO PERFORATIONS. Perforation breakage or deformation may occur in certain cameras, due to alterations of the film itself or to faulty operation of the shuttle and/or register pins. Sometimes, after long and heavy use, shuttle claws wear and, among other impairments, may cause perforation breakage or deformation. Some camera manufacturers have allowed for easy exchange of damaged claws; in other cameras the shuttle complete must be removed for repairing or replacing with a spare part.

Shuttle claws may also damage the perforations if they are misaligned. This may occur if the main shaft of a lightweight camera should be accidentally knocked. Under such conditions, the shuttle claws would not work into their correct position and, besides scraping the film edges, they would also slightly miss the perforation. If this misalignment is very slight, it may be remedied with slight pressure on the centre of the intermittent mechanism, to return the shuttle to its correct position, but if it is serious it should be repaired by an expert mechanic at a workshop.

Register pins may also produce perforation injury, as they are designed to work to very close tolerances. When affected by atmospheric conditions a film contracts or expands and the perforation position varies in relation to the action of the register pin. The pin meets resistance in locating the film firmly and steadily, thus producing injury.

The action of shuttle and register pins must be minutely inspected, first at the camera's normal speed, then at slow speed and then, if possible, in reverse motion.

Image steadiness control

Another essential condition of a cine camera is to provide a high degree of steadiness of the images printed on the film. The quality of the image obtained on projection depends on this

242

steadiness. The image printed on the film frame is magnified about 500× when projected on the screen.

Image steadiness is a quality depending closely on the camera's intermittent drive mechanism. We have already seen that there are simple mechanisms, in which only the shuttle acts on the film, and more complex movements using register pins to place the frame exactly behind the aperture. With the naked eye it is difficult to tell the difference between images printed by one system or the other, but when the register pin system is used there is better definition and multiple exposures can be effected without blurred edges

According to existing standards, limit values by which one frame may differ from another is 0·015 to 0·02 mm for material shot with instruments without register pins, and 0·008 to 0·012 mm for films taken with cameras having register pins. Therefore, when there are doubts that an instrument does not meet such requirements image steadiness checks must be made on the basis of such values.

Procedures for checking the steadiness of images produced by a camera are generally based on effecting takes with double exposures of a special test chart. However, there is a very simple method providing excellent results without recurring to the

Fig. 3. Method of aligning a camera to an unsteadiness test chart.

double exposure system. In both systems, the main difficulty lies not on how the test is carried out, but on the correct evaluation of the readings obtained.

DOUBLE EXPOSURE METHOD. For this method there are several procedures which differ only in the design of the test charts. The way to shoot these charts and the evaluation of results are very similar. In all of them the camera must be firmly installed on a rigid support so that the unit is completely motionless. The chart is then seated on a firmly placed board and correctly lit. Whichever the type of chart, it is fundamental to present its surface squarely to the optical axis of the taking lens, in order to avoid deformations at the ends. Therefore it is advisable to use medium focal length lenses for this check.

The technical characteristics of the film to be used in the test are also important. The raw stock must be carefully controlled so that all its values comply with world established standards for motion picture negatives. The film must be in a perfectly normal condition, since any contraction or expansion due to atmospheric conditions might impair the correctness of subsequent readings.

The test take is fairly simple. After complying with the above requirements, half of the chart is screened off with an opaque black cover. The uncovered half of the chart is shot with about 15 ft. of film, taking care that the starting point is clearly identified. The lens is then covered and the film is wound to the starting point. The black cover on the chart is changed to the opposite side, the lens is uncovered and the same length of film is shot again taking the other sector of the test chart.

There are various types of test chart with special designs to obtain very precise readings. They use a combination of geometrical figures in a cross-formation to study horizontal and vertical displacements of the frame. The figures are rectangular or trapezium-shaped with black patches opposite white patches. All these charts are based on the vernier principle in order to facilitate the subsequent evaluation from their position in relation to each other. In some cases these figures are composed of the separately exposed halves, so that when the two halves are combined, a white wedge is obtained against a black background, and the length of the base of this triangle-shaped wedge will vary in direct ratio to the registration unsteadiness.

When such charts are not available, some manufacturers propose a very simple check. A large cross is made with $\frac{1}{4}$ inch white

244

masking tape on a surface of approx. 35 × 50 inch, black solid background. The camera is placed so as to cover the complete figure exactly and two exposures are made with the same film. Any differences existing between the superimposed images would show the unsteadiness values produced by the camera's mechanism. The vertical arm of the cross will show image steadiness in one direction and the horizontal arm will show unsteadiness in the other direction.

All these tests can be evaluated by studying each frame through a microscope. A displacement measurement is established for each frame and the sum of the maximum values in each direction will determine the unsteadiness value. Generally these processes are not more exact than 0·004 to 0·005 mm. But this is sufficient to comply with requirements of most cameras. If image unsteadiness do not exceed $\frac{1}{4}$ of one per-cent of the dimensions (length and height) of frame, image steadiness may be considered acceptable.

SINGLE EXPOSURE METHOD. The double exposure method demands that the camera should be reversed, which motion not all instruments are capable of effecting. In such cases the single exposure method may be used, with a fixed matte. By this method, instead of measuring misadjustments of two exposures, the position of the ends of the matte are compared. This is effected by placing a matte in the filter slot of the film gate, with indentations on one horizontal and one vertical side of the frame.

Fig. 4. Characteristics of a mask for measuring image unsteadiness in a camera.

The test is made as follows: remove lens from its socket, place a lamp at a certain distance from and directed towards the camera; start the camera. After developing the film thus exposed, frames are obtained with clear cut shadows which duplicate the dimensions and outlines of the matte. This film length is then installed on a bench with special registrations; each frame is viewed through a microscope and the positions of such indentations, both horizontal and vertical, are measured to a fraction of an inch. The maximum differences should be those allowed by the unsteadiness standards.

Checking the shuttle/shutter synchronization.

The function of the shutter is to blank out from the sensitive film the light rays coming through the lens, while the former is driven by the shuttle claws to place a new frame behind the aperture. The shutter's work is synchronized with the shuttle travel, to allow light through only when the film is rock-steady. If such synchronization should become misadjusted, the image would be printed with a number of evident faults, such as: incorrectly exposed frames, uneven spacing, vertical displacements (ghost images), etc.

Generally, shutter and shuttle may become unsynchronized due to incorrect assembly after an overhaul, or to breakage or loosening of some part of the mechanism. When this occurs, perfect synchronization must be achieved again in order to eliminate such unacceptable defects. Procedures vary according to each camera's mechanical characteristics. After re-adjusting the mechanism, a critical synchronization check must be made.

When the lack of synchronization is very slight, it shows up by an evident blurring at the printed frame corners. Consequently this specific point must be checked on inspecting an unsynchronized camera. There are several methods for effecting this: the simplest is to take shots of a special test chart for lenses; an open filament lamp is placed at each corner and in the centre of this chart, facing the camera and fed at a low voltage.

After estimating the type of emulsion to print the filament without overexposing or blurring, the camera must be firmly seated on a rigid base and framed so that each of the lamps is very near each of the corners of the frame. Shoot about twelve to fifteen feet of film taking the chart and the lamp filaments.

Study the processed negative with a $10\times$ magnifying glass to check the definition of the filaments in the corners, and verify if there are blurred or ghost images there. The central lamp serves as a comparison standard. This test must be effected with maximum shutter opening and then repeated with smaller openings to establish rendition in each case.

Checking coincidence of aperture and reflex viewfinder fields.

Work requiring critical framing often demands that the operator should check if the camera complies with the fundamental condition that the frame on the reflex viewfinder should cover exactly the same field that is included by the aperture.

Present day wide-screen systems with different sized apertures often need the use of masks on the reflex viewfinder to reproduce the dimensions of the frame being printed. But a slight misplacing of the mask or a slight mistake in its dimensions may cause very serious framing errors, especially when effecting takes for multiple exposure and other special effects.

Therefore, cameras without direct-through-the-film viewing must be checked that their viewfinder and aperture fields coincide. This is verified by determining the aperture outline (perimeter) on a test chart and then adjusting the viewfinder mask to this outline.

Place a test chart with a ground-glass light bulb at each corner on a firm board. The position of each lamp should be easily adjusted and each should have a clearly visible black cross on its front surface, made with a vertical and a horizontal line. The camera is placed before the chart so that the inner angle of the cross on each lamp coincides with the edges of the corresponding corner on the aperture. This coincidence must be made through the aperture itself, with the camera stopped, the shutter open, and the lens diaphragm at full opening.

After effecting this critical framing, view through the reflex finder and check that the crosses are in identical position. Should there be any differences, the mask must be adjusted or changed for another one with the correct dimensions. This method can also be applied to monitor viewfinders, fixed side-viewfinders and other viewing systems.

Checking that the camera is light-tight

Light leaks into the camera may be due to dropped-off screws, cracks in the walls, door misadjustment, dents due to wear and tear, etc. But they may also be caused by carelessness in closing doors or cover-plates, and in installing the magazine, shooting while the direct or reflex viewfinder eyepiece is exposed to direct sunlight, or forgetting to fit protection lids on empty lens sockets in a turret. Checks must also be made to determine whether film fogging is due to causes other than the camera: light leaks in the darkroom, changing bag or faulty seals in film can.

Some manufacturers recommend a light-tightness test consisting of threading highly sensitive film in the camera and after carefully closing all doors and covers, exposing it for about fifteen minutes to direct sunlight, moving it about different positions. A more methodical control is effected by individual tests of the most critical parts, threading each time a different film length, removing lenses from the turret, opening viewfinder eyepiece, etc. and then processing each film length separately.

Checking exactness of lens focus and values on scale ring

The markings on the lens focus ring occasionally do not correspond to the real values, due to the harsh treatment and extreme temperatures that cameras must sometimes undergo.

This correspondence can be checked by a careful analysis of focus definition of the image produced on the plane of the film when the lens is set at infinity. But this study is very difficult due to the grain of the ground glass, the small size of subjects in an image produced by a short focal length lens, and other optical factors.

Focus exactness of a lens and its correspondence with markings

Fig. 5. Method for checking the rendition of a lens by means of an autocollimator.

24

on the focus ring is nowadays controlled by a device known as an autocollimator. It consists of an optical tube coupled to a special projection system called a collimator, which emits a light beam from a small lamp inside it. The beam goes through a mask and produces an image on a reflecting surface in the optical tube; the image is of similar conditions as if it comes from infinity. When the camera is adequately aligned with the autocollimator, the image from the optical tube reaches the plane of the film, where it is reflected, either by the film's bright surface or by a mirror placed at the aperture, back to the checking instrument where it can be precisely measured in the exact form it was produced by the camera lens.

Autocollimators are light, portable instruments, usually with their own battery power source which can be used for fast checks that the infinity setting of a lens is exact. But when installed on test benches they allow for complex studies in optics, and with a special test chart several optical problems can be analysed, such as: aberrations of lenses, transmission quality of filters, photographic resolution of the optical unit, contrast, and various others.

These instruments are built both in Europe and in America. Those made by von der Gonna in Munich (Friedrich), Kinoptik in France and Zoomar or Richter Cine Equipment in USA, are among the best known.

REFERENCES

[1] Brosio, V. *Manuale del Productore di film*. Edizione dell'Ateneo, Roma (1956).
[2] Gordichuk, I. S., *Sovietscaia kinosiomochnaia apparatyra*, Iskusstvo Ed. Moscow, (1966).

7

SHOOTING TECHNIQUES

Focusing

To focus an object on the plane of the film, the distance from the camera to the object is measured and the lens is adjusted to the corresponding figure. This simple method ensures that the image obtained is sharp—or at least sufficiently so to satisfy the spectator in the cinema. But present day styles of shooting based on editing within the frame and dynamic movement of the actors, frequently combined with dollying or travelling shots, have necessitated the development of more sophisticated focusing techniques.

For many years past, however, quite elaborate methods of following focus have been commonplace in the studios, and this in turn has been reflected in the evolution of camera design. The Mitchell camera, and types based on it, provide knobs and dials for both side and rear operation, with white scales on which focusing distances can be temporarily marked. The Technicolor Corporation pioneered the use of interlocked electric motors for remote operation of focus controls, so that the operator was able to change focus when physically distant from the camera itself, which might be perched on a high crane while he was on the ground. Vinten of England, in their Everest camera, tried to popularize a built-in rangefinder which freed the operator from the need to use mental estimations or external markings, but this innovation did not meet with success.

Focus puller

The importance of follow-focus techniques meant that a special place in the camera crew was assigned to the focus puller, whose job it became to measure the distance to significant points in a travelling shot—wherever, in fact, alterations of focus were required—and so mark these that during the actual take, the lens focus could be smoothly altered or "pulled" as changes in the relative position of camera, actors and scene demanded it.

To make matters more difficult, movement of the focus control is not simply proportionate to change of distance, but becomes much greater as the distance lessens. Thus the angular rotation of the focus knob is the same from 4 to 5 ft. as it is from 10 to 20 ft., and from 20 ft. to infinity. This sort of variable movement requires a good deal of practice on the part of the focus puller.

Some camera techniques, however, tend to mitigate these difficulties. Among these are the use of extreme wide-angle lenses with their inherently large depth of field; faster emulsions and higher studio lighting intensities, which permit the use of greater stopping down and zone focusing in which the plane of sharp focus is suddenly shifted from one part of a scene to another.

Fig. I. Newman Sinclair follow-focus device. Can be fitted to many professional cine-cameras as well as Newman Sinclair models. Dials can be engraved for lenses of various focal lengths.

But the normal practice is still to use reference marks on the studio floor, which the actors must sense if they cannot look directly at them, and which the focus puller must follow as the camera moves past them. Often many rehearsals are needed until all the relative speeds of movement have been synchronized and firmly established. For instance, if the actor moves too fast and arrives at one of his marks too quickly, the crane or dolly pusher will have to accelerate unexpectedly to keep the right distance relationship. This will throw the focus puller off balance, since he will not be able to twirl his knob fast enough, and a long take will have to be done again.

Modern conditions

But the latest shooting techniques make this sort of careful rehearsal impossible; and in television it is often uneconomic. The modern free-swinging use of the camera has, however, made critically sharp focusing less essential. The public has now grown accustomed to large out-of-focus areas in a scene, especially when the movement is rapid or violent, and will even tolerate it when the cameraman shifts onto the blurred features of an actor and then sharpens focus on him.

It would be quite wrong to imply, however, that focusing techniques have become slovenly in recent years. The need for extreme speed in shooting, especially for TV, and the modern emphasis on mobility, have put a premium on rapid focusing. The reflex shutter has made this possible by enabling the operator to see exactly what is on his film. But only long practice and the development of a sort of sixth sense allow him to anticipate where his subject will move to next, so that he can alter his focus to match this movement precisely. In this kind of situation, where movements must be spontaneous, the one-man camera crew is much more effective than a team which must rehearse and repeat the action.

Composition

In motion pictures, composition is the art of correctly placing the various moving or static elements of an image within the frame. The quality of composition or framing determines the aesthetic values of the picture and constitutes the visual balance.

Although the gift of good composition is an intangible quality, there are certain elastic rules to such factors as balance, harmony, discord, symmetry and pace. Among the guides to good composition are the following:

Avoid symmetry and try to balance the masses within the frame.

252

Elements which should be seen complete, must never be partially within and partially outside the frame.

The subject should always be framed with adequate space; it should not be so small as to be lost in the frame, nor so large that vital parts of it must be cut off and lost.

Dispose your subjects over the various field depths so that they neither conceal one another, or produce a confused composition.

253

When the main subject is in the background or in medium shot try to frame some secondary subject in the foreground to accentuate depth.

Paintings, tapestry, and similar subjects with no relief should never be shot from one side, as this will produce a deceptive perspective.

Landscapes will be more dramatically rendered by avoiding straight lines and by enhancing curves.

Never place an important subject behind an essential element in the scene, as this will diminish the value of both.

Avoid horizontal symmetry; in particular, place the horizon above or below the horizontal mid-line of the frame.

The masses in a frame should never be equidistant from each other.

Try to avoid straight parallel lines when they attenuate perspective and reduce depth of field.

Composition for reverse shots

Dialogue scenes are usually covered from reverse camera positions, either in close shots or a pair of medium shots.

The subject facing the camera gets two thirds of the screen space. The one with his back to the camera gets only one third of the space. This distribution is also applied to wide screen compositions.

Medium shots on a wide screen get a slightly different treatment.

256

The screen is divided into three equal parts and the subject facing the camera is placed in the centre of both main and reverse shots.

Different cutting heights for framing the human figure

In professional cinematography there are standard cutting lines applied to the human body when different types of shot are desired. These lines are shown on the illustration below.

ECU   Extreme close-up

MCU   Medium close-up

Waist shot

MS   Medium shot

Knee shot

Film Language

In the course of his professional career, the camera operator is sometimes faced with the complex task of personally directing a film. This occurs when the cinematographer must act as operator-director in films such as newsreels, shorts, documentaries, etc. For such events it is essential that, besides sound technical know-how, he should also know the basic rules of cinematographic language in order to make the resultant product smooth flowing.

Effective cinematographic language is based on two main factors: control of movement on the screen and the previous preparation of material to be filmed bearing in mind its subsequent editing. With this in mind and applying some of the narrative techniques created during motion picture's 70-year history, a highly professional level will be attained in line with highest world-accepted motion picture standards.

From the point of view of filmed narrative, there are two typical techniques used nowadays: one is sometimes known as "editing within the frame" and the other is "cut-editing".

Editing within the frame

This method consists of long-sustained takes with the actors moving continuously and being followed by a mobile camera. It requires professional actors who are accustomed to making exact movements, who know the correct position to stop, and can memorize long dialogues. These takes must be planned in detail beforehand, to determine the best positions, stopping points, and how the camera should follow. To maintain fluidity, directors use several arrangements, according to requirements of the script, of the specific actors and of the set. These allow for background variation of the scene, for alternating characters in the frame, for variations of planes and of zones of interest.

The most characteristic of these arrangements are:

COMBINED MOVEMENTS BY THE ACTORS. When two characters face each other in a long dialogue, the scene would be too static if it was not broken by the actors moving in the scene one at a time and meeting again at different points. For example: A and B face each other in a conversation. Suddenly, without interrupting the dialogue, B moves away to another part of the scene, and the camera, which at first covered both, now follows B with a pan.

From the new position B continues his conversation with A who is now outside the frame. After a predetermined time, B returns to A's position and the camera frames both of them again. Quite often this is repeated by the other character.

This simple resource affords pictorial variation in the image:

Fig. 2. Editing within the frame. A player who moves from zone to zone on the set and is followed by a panning camera will present successive and different pictorial arrangements on the screen. This method is smoother than a cut editing pattern, where the player moves in and out of each shot to obtain the same effect. Long takes using this technique of combined camera and performers' movement allows a more realistic approach to dialogued scenes.

the pan and the change of plane of action when the characters move from and return to the original position, as well as the modification of the number of characters in the frame.

DISPLACEMENTS FROM ZONE TO ZONE. This device is also very much used on the stage and it consists of the displacement of actors during a dialogue, one in front of the other, to modify their position in the scene. This change is repeated by the various actors and produces a constant change of framing and a gradual movement to another zone.

The change from zone to zone is normally effected by panning or by travelling takes. Sometimes an actor moves away from a group towards another group in a distant zone of the scene. This changes the zone of interest, and the character links the two areas without need for cutting. For example, when a large scene must be shown at the beginning of a sequence and an important area therein must be pinpointed, a character moves within such scene and the camera follows him until he passes in front of or through the zone of

259

*I

interest; there the camera stops and the "decoy" moves out of the frame.

Combined actors' movements and changes of zones are basic principles of editing within the frame; many variatons afford efficient filmed narrative. The above cases are the simplest. Analysing the possibilities carefully, we realise that the character's displacement can be either depthwise (from or towards the camera) or from side to side, that the moving actor's body position can be changed to emphasize or neutralize a character, that there are innumerable combinations of displacements of actors with a mobile or a fixed camera, etc. Thus, we have an infinite variety of resources for each specific requirement.

Editing within the frame tends to help filmed narrative to flow smoothly, due to the absence of cutting and the combination of continuous displacements of actors and camera within established premises.

Cut-editing

This technique is diametrically opposite to the above described method. Takes are short, the characters move less and the camera displacements are smaller. From the production point of view, this type is of much lower cost, because expensive rehearsals are not needed to prepare the combination of movements of cameras and actors. Furthermore, the actors do not need to remember long lines, or effect very precise movements. However, this technique demands extreme care in conceiving each individual take, because its efficiency depends on how it links with the next take. It is based on the principle of shooting in order to edit afterwards. This requires that the director should continuously observe several rules which ensure continuity.

CUTTING ON THE MOVEMENT. If two static shots of a subject are joined the result is a jerk, caused by the sudden change in the dimensions of the elements in the image. It has long been realised that this jerky effect is decreased by effecting the change while the subject is moving within the frame. At the critical moment, the attention of the audience is centered on the movement and does not notice the change of shot so much, thus achieving smooth flow.

The cutting technique requires that in each take the subject should effect the movement complete and at the same speed. Later, on editing, $\frac{1}{3}$ of the movement of the first take is used,

260

together with $\frac{2}{3}$ of the second take. Another requirement to make this method of cutting work is to place the subject in the same sector of the frame, but to shoot from a different angle in each take.

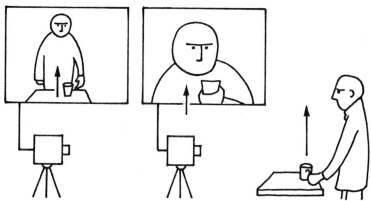

Fig. 3. Cutting on movement. The best way to join two takes featuring the same players is to have them repeat the last motion of the first take at the beginning of the second shot. Thus, part of the action ending the first take is matched with its completion on the second take. Smooth pictorial transition is then obtained.

Cuts on movement are very much used nowadays in all sorts of films. The director should plan such cuts beforehand every time he intends editing that way, specially when shooting dialogue scenes. If extreme focal length lenses are used in each take (for example: wide angle and telephoto), a careful watch must be kept on the speed at which such movements are made, because these extreme lenses modify the real speed on the screen.

ENTRANCES INTO AND EXITS FROM THE FRAME. Cut editing necessitates entrances of subjects into the frame and exists therefrom. If this is applied adequately, dynamic effects are produced. It also covers zone to zone displacements, and characters alternating in the frame. In usual practice, screen entrances and exits are used to shorten the movement of subjects across the frame, in combination with a change of shot. Continuity is attained by cutting during the subject's movement.

Entrances and exits must be shot so that the subject moves at the same speed and in the same direction. Among the different variations the following are usual:

(i) exit from the screen on one shot and entrance on another shot;

(ii) entrance into the screen and immediate exit, to re-enter on another take;

(iii) entrance into frame up to half way across, then cut and re-entrance again on another shot up to mid-frame.

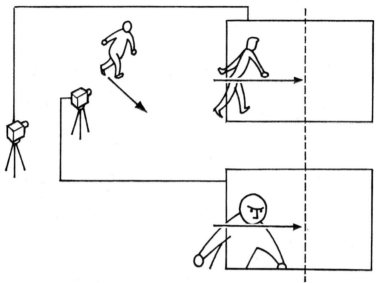

Fig. 4. Another form of cutting on the movement. A player's movement to a pre-determined end position can be planned to cover the travelling distance in two different takes. The first one will show most of his movement along the path, while on the second, the final part of his movement is recorded by the camera as he re-enters the screen and stops at his destination. This solution features the repetition of the screen zone in the two parts into which the movement is broken down.

Entrances and exits of subjects are always combined with a change of shot. Usually, in the case of entrances into a zone, a long or medium shot is first shown, and then a close shot. Exits are shown the other way round.

PLACING CHARACTERS ON THE FILM FRAME. Cinematographic continuity necessitates that the characters maintain their geographic position in the frame. This is attained by the camera's location in relation to the actors, so that they keep their position in the correct sector of the frame. For example, "B" faces the camera on the right hand side of the frame, while "A" is on the left hand side with his back to the camera; on effecting the reverse shot the camera must be placed so that the characters maintain the same position, i.e.: "A" must still be on the left hand side but facing the camera, and "B" still on the right hand side, but with his back to the camera. Thus the audience will appreciate the situation correctly, otherwise a jerk would be produced, confusing the audience and reducing continuity.

It is therefore essential to study the camera position for each take in order not to break this premise. Generally, the camera's point of view is determined on the basis of eyesight direction of the main characters, and the projections thereof; the camera should always be placed on the same side of such imaginary line.

Fig. 5. Direction of gaze. The direction of the gaze exchanged between two players forms a line between both performers. One side of this line must be chosen to locate the camera sites that will cover the scene. Constant screen position of the players is then ensured. If a camera site is placed on the other side of this line the positions of the players on the screen will be reversed, and the take will not cut properly with the others.

A careful camera positioning in relation to actors is also fundamental for a proper direction of sight, because on the shots near to the camera, the direction of eyesight on closeups is always along separate half-planes, which must always be in opposite directions, in order to facilitate cutting.

Hand-held camera

Shooting while holding the camera in the hands is standard procedure for newsreel and combat area reporters, but is now increasingly employed in making documentary films, and even in feature films under extreme conditions when the camera cannot be put on a tripod or when special effects of movement are sought.

The main factors to take into account for hand-held shooting are the stability of the instrument and of the operator, and the latter's ease of action; all three require that the operator should have a steady hand, should know how to hold the camera firmly, and be able to control his body balance.

Position of the camera

The design of modern hand-held cameras is such as to provide conveniently shaped curves combined with proper arrangements for secure gripping. With minor differences, three basic holding positions can be distinguished, depending on the shape of the camera:

   (i)   holding by hand from underneath the camera;
   (ii) holding the camera from above or from the side, while supporting part of its weight on the shoulder;
   (iii) supporting all the weight on the shoulder.

Fig. 6. Correct position for holding the Arriflex 35 camera with shoulder attachment.

CAMERAS HELD ONLY BY THE HAND. These cameras are provided with a hand grip situated beneath the instrument: among them are the Bell & Howell Filmo and Eyemo, the Arriflex 35, the Cameraflex and the Sputnik. The operator's wrists and forearms bear the weight of the camera. Additional support can be supplied by a shoulder attachment (Fig. 6).

HAND-AND-SHOULDER HELD CAMERAS. The idea was evolved after research by the U.S. Government on a combat camera during World War II; and the resulting instrument, the Cunningham, showed the advantages of using the shoulder as a main support. This is facilitated by the shape of some cameras, in

Fig. 7. Holding the Cameflex.

Fig. 8. On-the-shoulder position applicable to several newsreel cameras.

265

which the magazines are attached at the rear and are rested on the front part of the shoulder, which thus acts as a support. This takes some of the weight off the wrists and forearms and distributes it over the shoulder and the full length of the arm, thus affording greater steadiness. This type includes the Cameflex, the Sinclair Model P/400, and the Kohbac Automat.

SHOULDER SUPPORTED CAMERAS. This is the latest development, based on the principle adopted in 1935 by Askania Werke for their lightweight Askania Schulter by which most of the weight is borne by the shoulder, while the arms only act as a complementary steadying element, by gripping either beneath or at a side of the camera. The Mitchell Mark II, the Panaflex, the new Eclair 16 mm, and other instruments conceived for TV news coverage, have applied and improved on this method.

When describing the original concepts which led to the design of the Askania Schulter, one of the designers, Dr. Ing. P. Heinish, chief engineer of the well-known Berlin manufacturers, pointed out that many hand-held cameras demanded operators to be athletes when having to run with a heavy instrument to effect a take which should be free of unsteadiness due to gasped breathing.

This led to adopting the shoulder as support for the magazine and thus the whole instrument, freeing it of throbbing off the chest and pulse. It was also verified that the major portion of a camera's weight is its film load and the magazine housing it. The Askania Schulter has a body at right angles, with one side resting on the operator's shoulder and the other covering half of the operator's face. This allows for easy holding and handling.

Position of operator's body

From the point of view of a steady take, there is another factor just as important as holding the camera: the positioning and balance of the operator's body. Unless these techniques are learned the full potentialities of the camera will not be realized.

When shooting, the operator's body must be perfectly balanced so as to produce a minimum of sway. Although specific circumstances may sometimes require the operator to shoot while sitting or lying down, the normal position for hand-held takes is standing up, since this has been proved to afford greater ease of operation and camera steadiness.

The way the operator stands is also important to his stability. Balance for this type of shooting is best obtained by standing with

266

the right foot some ten inches in front of the body's vertical line, and the left foot about four inches to one side. The weight of the body must be distributed on both feet but slightly more on the left foot. This not only affords great stability but also ease of action. An operator standing thus will be able to effect 100° angle pans without moving his feet; he will also be able to tilt 90° with ease while maintaining his stability.

When special shots or situations require the operator to shoot from a sitting or lying down position, there is little advice to give. If the operator is sitting, it would be well that he rest his back against, or his elbows upon, some prop. If he is lying down on his face he may rest his elbows or the camera on the ground. If on his back, he will evidently need a good prop to help support some of the weight of the camera.

Accessories for hand-held shooting

Since the lightweight camera for hand-held shooting is now extensively used in many types of film making, some manufacturers have set themselves to produce useful auxiliary supports.

S.O.S. BODY BRACE. Manufactured of aluminium alloy to afford a rigid and strong frame of light weight, it allows for installing the camera with a 200 or 400 ft magazine. The design of the frame distributes the weight of equipment over the shoulder and the waist.

ARRIFLEX SHOULDER-POD. This accessory, designed for use with the Arriflex camera, can also take the Eyemo, the Cameraflex and the Newman Sinclair. It consists of a chromed-metal frame which is fitted over the shoulder and under the armpit. The camera support can be adjusted in extension and inclination to give greater flexibility in use.

NEWMAN SINCLAIR UNIPOD. Consists of a telescopic adjustable tube with small circular plate at the end, about two inches in diameter. Its minimum length is about 2 ft. 10 in. and its maximum extension is 5 ft. 3 in. It is provided with a leather strap for easy handling.

KENYON GYROSCOPIC STABILIZER. This device was originally designed for use with high magnification binoculars, but has proved its efficiency in hand-held motion picture shooting. The high speed gyroscope it contains produces a very effective resistance to jerky camera movements, which makes possible the use of

267

telephoto lenses on hand-held cameras with minimum image oscillation. This accessory is very compact and is attached to the camera base by means of a threaded pin. There is a special

Fig. 9. Kenyon gyroscopic stabilizer.

model for heavier, medium-weight cameras. A nickel-cadmium battery and inverter unit provides the necessary power for the Kenyon Stabilizer for a minimum of three hours continuous running.

Anamorphic systems

Background and fundamentals of the anamorphic system

The visual characteristics of the higher animals are such that their field of view is much more extended horizontally than vertically. In man, the eyes are placed side by side in such a way that their fields of view complement each other and overlap. This leads to a strong emphasis on the horizontal.

The standard motion picture frame, with its four horizontal to three vertical units, is unanimously accepted in preference to square or circular forms which have sometimes been advocated.

When the motion picture industry felt the need for a change in the standard frame ratio to increase audience attention, it was a horizontal widening of the image frame which was proposed, changing the aspect ratio from 4:3 to 8:3 or thereabouts.

The process by which this was to be done was an old one: Fresnel had used cylindrical lenses as far back as 1825, and during the 1930s Professor Henri Chrétien used what he called an anamorphic lens to compress the image while filming and to expand it afterwards during projection.

The term "anamorphic" is applied to any optical system capable of compressing a normal image, and subsequently projecting it back in its original proportions without apparent distortion.

The first practical anamorphic lenses consisted of cylindrical adaptors mounted in front of a normal camera lens. A concave cylindrical lens with a vertical axis of curvature acts as a wide-angle attachment in the horizontal plane only (the image in the vertical plane being unaffected). The lens constants were set so that the anamorphic factor was 2. Thus, when used in combination with a standard camera lens, an anamorphic lens acts as an optical transformer, doubling the horizontal field of view of the standard lenses, and compressing the image within the standard 3:4 frame. A similar converter is used in the projector to return the image to its original 3:8 proportions.

The first really practical anamorphic lens was Professor Chrétien's Hypergonar. It comprised two achromatic systems, one convergent and the other divergent, and its elements were calculated to reduce aberrations to a minimum. Two forms of the lens were designed, one for use on the camera, one on the projector.

Fig. 10. Integral anamorphic lens.

In 1952 Twentieth Century Fox acquired the rights to the Hypergonar lens, and commissioned the American optical firm of Bausch & Lomb to manufacture improved lenses based on this design. This was no easy job, for intricate mechanical problems in connection with the focusing system had to be solved. After much research, improved anamorphic optical systems for coupling to standard lenses were produced, and these were followed by units combining the standard spherical lens and the anamorphic system in a single mounting.

Subsequent improvements attained a high degree of perfection in correcting distortion at the ends of the frame, where vertical lines tended to converge and horizontal lines to curve, thus lowering the quality of the image. The lenses commissioned by Twentieth Century Fox from Bausch & Lomb were made under the registered name Cinemascope which also designates the complete system developed by that studio. In recent years, many other anamorphic systems have been developed, and some of these are listed in a later section.

Modern anamorphics follow the original pattern: either an anamorphic adapter is fitted in front of the standard lens, in which case both elements require separate focusing; or the anamorphic and the basic spherical lens are fully integrated, when only a single focusing control is needed. When an adapter is employed with a standard lens, the focal length in a horizontal plane will effectively be halved. Thus for purposes of calculating the horizontal angle of field, a 35 mm lens will become an 18 mm, a 75 mm a 38 mm, and so on, while in the vertical plane the acceptance angle will remain unchanged.

Fig. 11. Totalvision anamorphic block unit mounted on Came 300 Reflex camera. Note the geared connection with the focusing ring.

Integral or block anamorphics have effective focal lengths of 15 up to 600 mm, and anamorphic zoom lenses are coming into use. Most of these lenses are available with mountings for Mitchell, Debrie, Arriflex, Eclair and other well known makes of camera.

Image quality of anamorphic lenses

There are various factors which determine the optical quality of the image formed by an anamorphic lens unit.

DEFINITION. The definition of an image taken through an anamorphic lens can be tested by checking that focus is maintained all along the horizontal and vertical lines. This can be carried out with acceptable accuracy by the help of the focusing chart provided by some makers which can be placed on the edges of the "lily" or colour chart shot at the start or end of each take.

When integral block anamorphic systems are used, focusing is adjusted with only one ring; but with coupled lenses, focus adjustments must be carried out simultaneously on the two rings corresponding to the primary and secondary lenses respectively. This requires either a high precision mechanical adjusting device, or the help of two camera assistants. In the latter case it is desirable that the scales on the rings of the primary and secondary lenses be calibrated identically. Finally, when focus is controlled visually, directly through the taking lens, it is better to view the squeezed image rather than the unsqueezed image seen through many viewfinders.

DISTORTION. A faulty proportioning and forming of shapes in the image is one of the most important factors to look for and correct when using anamorphic lenses. When checking distortion, the operator should concentrate on vertical and horizontal lines extending from side to side of the frame. Image distortion often results from lack of precision in mounting and centring the anamorphic lens on the camera. A practical method of checking consists of critical examination of the outline of an anamorphic image as seen through the camera's direct focusing tube through the taking lens. For this purpose a plumbline can provide a vertical line, while the long pan handle of a previously levelled tripod head may be used to set the horizontal line. For more critical tests, there is no alternative to setting up the lens and camera on an optical bench.

ANAMORPHIC COEFFICIENT. The anamorphic coefficient of a

system can be checked by the experienced eye, observing whether the subject going across the frame from side to side maintains the same compression factor throughout its travel. In older anamorphic systems, the compression factor tended to become less as the subject approached the camera, producing unpleasant distortions in close-up. If modern anamorphics give rise to distortion, it is probably due to incorrect setting up.

Techniscope

In mid 1963 Technicolor introduced a new shooting technique, which brings about a saving of 50 % in raw stock and film process-

Fig. 12. Techniscope format. *Above:* size of the two-perforation frame. *Below:* the 4-perforation frame with a 2:1 anamorphic compression applied during printing.

ing costs. This system, developed at Technicolor Italiana by Dr. Giulio Monteleoni and Mr. Giovanni Ventimiglia, uses a frame which is one half the height of the standard frame (two perforations instead of four). By a special printing process, this two-perforation-high frame is changed into a standard four-perforation frame with an anamorphic image of 2 to 1 squeeze ratio, ready for projection. To film, in Techniscope, the camera requires some modification.

272

(i) the aperture must be changed to the new frame size;

(ii) the intermittent drive must be modified to make the film travel the height of the reduced frame;

(iii) the viewfinder has to be adapted to the new image shape.

Arnold & Richter, German makers of the Arriflex, have produced a model for Techniscope shooting with 200° shutter opening and 9·5 × 22 mm. In the USA the Mitchell Camera Corp. and Birn & Sawyer Cine Equipment have specialized in adapting various cameras to the new system. Other manufacturers have followed suit, among which Eclair have introduced a Cameflex model (CM-3T) which can be easily and rapidly adapted by exchanging aperture plates and adjusting shuttle travel.

The advantages of the new technique mean that the shooting time per foot of film is doubled, so that a 1000 ft. magazine provides the same shooting time as 2000 ft. of film by the standard method. With the improvement in grain and resolution of modern integral tripack materials, Techniscope gives excellent picture quality on large screens. But the small size of the negative area does introduce some limitations when projecting onto the very largest screens.

Zoom or vari-focal lenses

General

When shooting a film, the camera operator must be able to vary the field of view without changing his position, and consequently must be equipped with several lenses covering an ample range of focal lengths. Well aware of the advantages there would be in combining a wide range of focal lengths in a single optical system, lens designers developed a lens with variable focal length, which came to be called a zoom lens. The new lens had to meet the most exacting optical and mechanical requirements, and many difficult technical problems could only be solved when advanced electronic computers became available.

However the success achieved by this new type of lens was not so much due to the fact that it could replace several others of different focal lengths, but that it opened up a new possibility to the camera operator of continuously changing the focal distance of his lens, thus obtaining the effect known as optical travelling or zooming. Zooming creates the illusion, at least in part, that the camera is moving towards or away from the scene. It is carried out by gradually changing the focal length and thus the magnifica-

273

tion of the lens, so that the subjects in the scene increase or decrease in size.

The principle of construction of zoom lenses is the controlled displacement along the optical axis of a set of elements in relation to another set which remains stationary. All the elements and movements must be calculated and constructed with such high precision that during the displacement of the mobile unit, the diaphragm and focus settings are maintained constant, while only the focal length changes.

Some zoom lenses are equipped with a beam-splitter reflex viewfinder with a prism and semi-reflecting glass at 45°, built into the lens, to afford exact framing throughout the range of focal lengths. As the beam-splitter is placed in front of the last set of elements, focusing cannot be checked by means of this viewfinder. To compensate for this, many models of zoom lens are provided with a rangefinder or telemeter.

Originally, variable focus devices were available only for substandard cameras, and they became increasingly popular. Subsequent improvements have put them on a level of quality which meets most of the exacting requirements of the professional motion picture industry. Among the latest models for 35 mm are the B3, B4 and C3 Pan Cinor models of the French firm Som & Berthiot, and the LA2, LB1, LB3, LB4, L5 and 10 × 25 of Pierre Angénieux. A survey of zoom lenses can be found in the table on page 302.

Recommendations for zooming

The widespread use of zoom lenses in professional motion picture production has highlighted the importance of the following:

(i) whenever a zoom lens is used on a camera with a lens turret, make sure that the lens is well seated and the turret lock works properly;

(ii) when working with a hand-held camera, mount the camera whenever possible on a tripod before shooting with a zoom lens, since the inevitable lack of rock steadiness in handheld shooting will show up unfavourably when the lens is in the telephoto position;

(iv) when focusing a scene before the take, adjust the lens focus to the telephoto position, where it can be accomplished more critically; the focus of shorter focal lengths will then be automatically correct;

274

(iv) when zooming with the hand wheel or lever, bear in mind:
    (a) to use the long control lever whenever possible;
    (b) move the lever by holding it lightly with forefinger and thumb;
    (c) allow for inertia at the beginning and momentum at the end of the run by respectively increasing and decreasing the speed gradually;
(v) when zooming towards a scene, frame it beforehand at the final zoom position, since the initial framing will not remain constant if not properly centred;
(vi) when effecting a slow zoom towards a static subject, the camera speed may be increased;
(vii) at the end of a zoom keep on with a static take of the scene, so that it can be adequately appreciated and will be long enough to allow for subsequent editing.

Special devices for zoom lenses

Servo controls for operating zoom lenses have now become available. Some years ago studios developed systems for remote control zooming, but the use of these was limited to the individual companies. More recently, manufacturers have introduced devices which can be attached to any lever-controlled zoom lens. Their main characteristics are:

(i) very smooth movement;
(ii) working speeds from $2\frac{1}{2}$–10 seconds for the total zoom range;
(iii) can be installed on the lens or in the tripod-head handle;
(iv) some work with dry-cell batteries as power source;
(v) different models for sound and silent cameras;
(vi) finger-tip starting and stopping control;
(vii) rheostat for adjusting working speed.

Some models have also been produced for applying to handwheel-controlled zoom lenses.

The photographic report

In all organized motion picture production there should be strict control of the work to be carried out each day. This allows for keeping a continuous, step-by-step watch on the film, so that cost fluctuations can be closely checked. The most efficient and complete method for carrying this out is the printed form. Usually the production department of a studio has forms printed

CAMERA REPORT

PATHE LABORATORIES, INC.
— NEW YORK

105 EAST 106TH STREET ·· TRAFALGAR 6·1120
NEW YORK 29 N Y

Date_____

Director_____ Cameraman_____

Company_____

No. or
Name of Picture_____

PRINT CIRCLED TAKES ONLY

Scene No.	Day or Night	TAKES					
		1	2	3	4	5	6

IMPORTANT
FILL OUT INFORMATION ON REVERSE SIDE OF ORIGINAL COPY

No. Cans to Lab._____ Bal. Neg. on Hand_____

Good Footage_____ Received_____

N. G. Footage_____ Exposed_____

Waste Footage_____ On Hand_____

Emul. No._____ Total Footage_____

Form L -7

Fig. 13. Photographic
or camera report.
(*Courtesy of the Pathe
Laboratories Inc.*)

276

for its own use in production, and for the sound recording crew, for the art staff and cast, and one for the camera crew, which is known as the photographic report. This form permits full control of shooting, and this is of great use not only for the camera crew itself but for the production unit as a whole. The photographic report will be carboned in triplicate and all the technical characteristics of each take must be noted, as well as the necessary indications for the processing laboratory. At the end of the day's shooting the three copies are distributed as follows:

Copy 1 to the laboratory with the film negatives,
Copy 2 for the production department,
Copy 3 for the files of the camera crew.

From the filled-in data, the production people can determine how many takes were made, which were repeated and how many times, which takes will be printed, as well as the daily and total amounts of raw stock used. The camera crew, on their side, will be able to determine all the technical conditions under which the takes were made, which cameras and other equipment were used for each take, in order to be able to go through the same takes again, or to trace the source of any fault.

The mobile camera

All professional and many amateur films make extensive use of the mobile camera, the basis of a technique sometimes called "editing within the frame". Though the travelling truck and dolly are the most commonly used devices for shooting with a mobile camera, there are occasions when travelling shots are required which cannot be taken in this way. This section describes the mounting of cameras on various vehicles, and suggests ways of obtaining an image free of jerkiness and unsteadiness, defects which often occur as a result of inexperience.

Mounting the camera on a motor car

Many silent films reveal that the camera was often mounted on a car to follow or lead other vehicles in motion, or for long sustained takes of moving subjects. The films of Mack Sennett, Buster Keaton and other comedians of the time are examples of perfection in this technique. The method used was very simple, the mere setting up of a tripod-mounted camera in an open car. With the advent of hand-held cameras, many cameramen resorted to shooting from inside a car, but the results are seldom satisfactory. In the first place, the human body is not well suited to absorb the vehicle's vibrations, which are thus transmitted to the operator's wrist; but worse than this, the operator, in trying to keep his eye constantly to the viewfinder, transmits the swaying and unsteadiness of his body to the camera. In the silent film era this did not happen as cameras were too heavy for hand-holding, and moreover were crankhandle driven, thus requiring a tripod mounting which produced excellent results.

In consequence, most professional operators nowadays mount their cameras rigidly when shooting from a car. Methods are:

  (i) the camera is mounted on a hi-hat securely fixed to a base mounted across the car's bonnet;

  (ii) the camera is mounted at the end of a long board passed under the seats and jutting out through the open door (this is for shooting a car in side view);

(iii) the camera may be installed behind the car's front seat, for taking the actors' backs, or for shots showing a car coming up from behind; "baby" tripods are very useful on these occasions.

Many Hollywood studios make use of specially designed cars provided with improved suspension and facilities for installing cameras and lighting equipment at different levels and positions.

Mounting the camera on aircraft

Air shots are frequent in professional film making. Besides the aeroplane, the helicopter is the favourite type of aircraft, because of the wide range of movements it allows. In both types of aircraft, the camera is always rigidly mounted. For shooting from a helicopter experts advise that the aircraft should be flying at speeds between 15 and 25 knots, and that the flying manoeuvre known as autorotation should be used if possible. During the autorotation, power to the rotor is cut off so that the blades turn freely and the aircraft descends gradually with a slight forward motion towards the target. Other factors for obtaining good footage are: sufficient forward speed to provide lift to the craft, and an adequate wind blowing with force against it.

New anti-vibration devices

We have seen that a rigid mounting is recommended in all cases when shooting from a vehicle in motion. The following factors are also a help:

278

(i)   use of wide-angle lenses to reduce the effect of vibration;
(ii) increase of camera speed up to 32 frames per second if allowed by the character of the shot;
(iii) the camera should be mounted away from the vibration centre.

More recent devices intended to subdue vibrations include a camera stabilizer designed by French engineers for use in a helicopter, called Helivision, which was first used in the film "Voyage en Ballon" by Albert Lamorisse. This achieved sensational results, as it made steady shooting possible with telephoto lenses from a helicopter, together with zooming as the aircraft moved towards or away from the subject.

Another device of similar characteristics, Ceco's Aero-Vision, has appeared on the American market, working on the same principles as Helivision. Its main characteristics are:

(i)   weighs only 120 lbs.;
(ii) allows for quick mounting on helicopter or other vehicle with only four bolts;
(iii) permits the use of 10:1 25/250 mm zoom lenses;
(v)   provides a seat for the operator.

Fig. I4. Aero-Vision anti-vibration mount installed in a helicopter.

A small mount developed some time ago by Danelan Ltd. of England, is of a shape similar to a triangle, which allows for placing a tripod in it, and thus eliminates vibrations. This useful accessory weighs no more than 22 lb. and is very practical for takes from unsteady travelling trucks, or indeed from any sort of vehicle of the kind described above.

Finally, Tyler Camera Systems Company have produced an automatically controlled portable unit with seat for operator, power source and other facilities, devised specially for installing on aircraft, helicopters, motorcars, boats, wheelchairs, and all types of vehicle.

Another device conceived for compensating vibrations is the *Dynalens*, from Dynasciences Corp., making use of a complex optical system on the taking lens and a steadying gyroscopic unit. This instrument is mounted on the camera lens and has a range of angular compensation of about 4°. The latest model, the S-038, has an elliptical shape, weighs 5·5 lb. and is operated by a DC source of 28–32 v. or an AC source of 115 v.

On the spot coverage

The shooting of news items where they occur is the most characteristic task of the newsreel cameraman. It calls for a wide range of shooting techniques, both to help the operator and to turn out a more vivid final product.

These technical rules range from the correct way of holding the camera to how the story must be told. Adherence to these rules is indeed the hallmark of professionalism.

Hand-held operation

Though it is advisable to use a tripod whenever possible, there are many situations which can only be covered with a hand-held camera. In these cases it is obvious that the framing will not be as steady as if the operator were shooting from a tripod; the human body is not a rigid support and its stability depends on its positioning (both natural and with artificial aids), on its balance system, and on the normal functioning of the operator's breathing and blood circulation.

After a run, the faster heart beats will produce an abnormal throbbing of the pulse and consequent unsteadiness. Therefore, avoid physical exertion before hand-held shooting. If this is unavoidable, make the first takes with wide-angle lenses, so as to give the pulse time to return to normal. After this has slowed down, change to other lenses with a longer focal distance better suited to the shot in question. The use of telephoto lenses with hand-held shooting should be avoided whenever possible, and when essential should be confined to the 50 mm on 16 mm cameras for close-ups.

Framing

This is the cameraman's most important preoccupation when shooting an item of news interest or telling a story in images. Among the many points of view from which a scene can be shot, he alone has the responsibility of choosing that angle that will be seen by the audience. His choice should be based on sound technical reasoning and never (or very rarely) on instinct.

The rectangle of the standard motion picture frame, longer than it is high, is an excellent medium for producing good composition. The operator will be constantly placing subjects at all distances from his camera: background, medium shot, close-ups, so that they show up and help to describe the action as vividly as possible.

Panning and tilting

Panning is swivelling the camera in a horizontal plane, while swivelling in the vertical plane is known as tilting. Both are an aid to filmed narrative and give freedom in four important respects:

(i)   following the movements of a subject over any depth range;

(ii) viewing a scene too wide to embrace with the field of view of the lens, and covering it with a movement very similar to that of the head when observing the same scene;

(iii) allowing for a smooth change in subject distances, if the camera movement is combined with the displacements of the subject in a determined direction;

(iv) smoothing the passage from one scene to the next one, or bringing out an important detail in one of the scenes.

However, panning is the Achilles heel of many camera operators, who do it either inaccurately or too often. In view of the fast pace and short duration of TV newsreels, panning should be on a strictly functional basis. This is because panning slows down the pace and panned shots cannot be shortened. Many of the panned

281

shots rejected in the cutting room reach the waste bin because they are inaccurate or unplanned. The commonest mistakes are listed in the panning trouble chart on page 295.

Zooming

The zoom lens is undoubtedly one of the most important innovations in modern motion picture technique. It affords a new and valuable aid to imaginative film narrative. It makes reflex viewing possible when using cameras without this built-in. But, most important, it combines in a single lens all focal lengths necessary to cover a story, and furthermore adds the dramatic effects of drawing near the subject or moving away from it, by the mere action of a small lever. But these remarkable powers lend themselves readily to misuse, and exaggeration will turn the advantages of the zoom lens against the cameraman and spoil his story rather than improve it.

A wide range of zoom lenses is available for 16 mm cameras. Some cover a 10:1 span of focal lengths, while others range only from a medium wide-angle lens to a medium telephoto lens. In practice it is advisable not to use the full range, unless the scene specifically requires this.

How to tell the story

When time is short, as in TV coverage, there is only one way to tell a story: as directly and effectively as possible. The image on the TV set must portray action fast and vividly, in order to keep audience attention centered on the small screen. In the newsreel, responsibility is shared between the editor and the camera operator. No matter how expert the editor, the final product will lack the quality and interest demanded by the audience if the cameraman's coverage is not good enough.

Very often there will not be time to edit the story in such a way as to bring out the necessary qualities of fluidity and pace. Consequently it is essential that the operator should as far as possible edit in his camera, so that his footage is almost ready for going on the air.

Every day of our lives all of us tell some story or other. But only the cameraman has the responsibility of telling the story with realistic images, from a specific point of view and for a vast audience. For this task he must combine technical discipline with sound journalistic know-how and intuition. The cameraman should be working out the structure of the news item in his mind from the moment he receives the assignment; and it is essential for him to know as much as possible about the event in question so that his coverage is fully adequate and, if possible, in its proper sequence. Moreover he will need to be nimble-minded enough to foresee the development of events he is covering, and thus be ready to shoot them as they occur.

Continuity

When telling a story, the narrator must go through three successive stages: in the first the audience is placed in the setting where the event occurred; next the characters or elements which make up the story are introduced, and last the images should unfold the event or action or conflict on which the whole news story is centered. These stages must be shot in this specific sequence, and each may comprise one or more shots as may be needed to portray the event fully. The takes should be long shot or medium shot, to include the most significant components of the scene and of the participating characters or elements. Once the main theme is reached, its details should be covered with medium shots and close-ups. If the action being taken is long, it may sometimes be advisable to re-identify the characters or elements with quick establishing shots, and then return at once to the main points of interest. It may also be helpful to insert cut-away shots showing the reactions of non-participants, to accentuate the importance of a scene and avoid any feeling of monotony.

Pace

The main factor determining the pace of a news story is the length of each take. A minimum time is required to depict an event which varies according to the distance from the camera at which it occurs. For close-ups, a take should last about two seconds. For medium shots, each take should last some three to four seconds. Long shots should be held longer, as they generally include several elements which claim audience attention; four to five seconds is a reasonable length. Of course, the length of a take will vary according to the elements included in it and the time taken by the action being covered, but the above figures are values which may be used as a guide.

Another point to take into account is the climax of each shot; for example, when shooting a plane about to take off, the camera must continue until the undercarriage effectively leaves the ground, as the footage up to this point shows action which is merely

283

passive. It is also important to remember that each take must have action within the borders of the frame to hold audience attention; two consecutive takes with internal action of this kind are more effective and fluid from the editing point of view than two passive takes.

The golden rule of the newsreel cameraman—constant change of field depth and continual change of angle—gives the narrator that forward impetus and momentum which is needed for TV news.

REFERENCES

[1] Marcelli, J. V., The Technique of Follow-Focus, *American Cinematographer Magazine*, p. 34 (Jan. 1961).
[2] Nilsen, V., *The Cinema as a Graphic Art*, Hill & Wang, New York.
    Kraszna-Krausz, A. *La Composicion*, Foto Bibliotecta. Ed. Omega, Barcelona.
    Faveau, P., *La Perspective*, Ciné Memo Prisma, Prisma Ed., Paris.
[3] Chretien, H., La Cinematographie Panoramique par le procedé Hirégonar, *Bulletin de l'Association Française des Ingenieurs et Techniciens du Cinema*, No. 11, pp. 13–23 (1952).
[4] Bendford, J. R., The Cinemascope Optical System, *Journal of Society of Motion Pictures and Television Engineers*, pp. 64–70 (January 1954).
[5] Pohl, W. E., Techniscope, *Journal of the Society of Motion Picture and Television Engineers*, Vol. 74, No. 2, p. 121 (Feb. 1965).
[6] Shappert, V. Gli Obiettivi da ripresa a distanza focale variabile. Differenti principi ed evoluzione delle forme, *Bullettino Tecnico della Associazione Italiana Cineoperatori*, No. 5 (Aug. 1960).
    Shappert, V., Progres de L'Optique Francaise, *La Technique Cinematographique*, No. 160. Dic. (1955).
    Kingslake, R., What makes the zoom zoom, *Modern Photography*, p. 76 (June 1961).

Trouble Shooting Chart

Camera operation mechanical trouble chart

TROUBLE: *The motor will not run*

PROBABLE CAUSES		REMEDIES	
(i)	internal safety switch in "off" position;	(i)	open camera and check that safety switch is in "on" position;
(ii)	insufficient power from source;	(ii)	check line voltage under load;
(iii)	faulty contact in connections;	(iii)	check that plug is pushed home into socket;
(iv)	damaged power feed cable;	(iv)	examine motor and power feed cable all along its length; check that cable feeds power continuously;
(v)	damaged switch;	(v)	check continuity with tester;
(vi)	excessively low temperature;	(vi)	check that motor runs adequately when detached from camera and at normal temperatures;
(vii)	damaged part jamming drive mechanism;	(vii)	rotate the motor flywheel by hand and verify whether intermittent drive works properly or is jammed; if motor flywheel does not rotate, detach motor from camera and check that coupling is not faulty;

Camera operation mechanical trouble chart—continued

TROUBLE: The motor will not run

PROBABLE CAUSE		REMEDIES
(viii)	damaged motor;	(viii)	send motor to specialist workshop;
(ix)	piece of broken film jamming the mechanism;	(ix)	examine intermittent drive mechanism, shuttle, register pins, and sprocket; also check aperture plate and pressure plate seat;
(x)	in spring-driven cameras, breakage of the spring or jamming of winding mechanism.	(x)	in spring motor, check tension of springs, and verify that the winding key works properly.

TROUBLE: Faulty image framing

PROBABLE CAUSES		REMEDIES
(i)	monitor viewfinder not corrected for parallax;	(i)	adjust monitor viewfinder for parallax according to distance from camera to subject;
(ii)	incorrect viewfinder field in relation to type of lens being used.	(ii)	check the focal length and lens field and place proper mask in viewfinder.

TROUBLE: Obstruction in lens field

PROBABLE CAUSES	REMEDIES
(i) sunshade not mounted correctly or too small for the lens;	(i) check mounting of sunshade by direct viewing through taking lens;
(ii) faulty insertion of mask or filter;	(ii) push mask and filters home when inserting them;
(iii) telephoto lens in field, when using wide-angle lens.	(iii) remove telephoto lens when using wide-angle lens.

TROUBLE: No image on film

PROBABLE CAUSES	REMEDIES
(i) shutter fully closed;	(i) check shutter opening before shooting;
(ii) lens cap left in place;	(ii) remove lens cap before shooting;
(iii) camera in focusing position.	(iii) when using rackover type camera, always return to taking position after framing.

287

TROUBLE: *No image through reflex viewfinder*

PROBABLE CAUSES	REMEDIES
(i) shutter in image recording position;	(i) rotate inching knob until the image appears;
(ii) viewfinder protector in closed position;	(ii) open viewfinder protecting device.

TROUBLE: *Blurred or jerky images*

PROBABLE CAUSES	REMEDIES
(i) tripod unsteadiness;	(i) make sure the tripod is steady before shooting;
(ii) damaged intermittent drive mechanism;	(ii) send camera to repair workshop;
(iii) film shrinkage due to working under excessively hot ambient conditions;	(iii) protect camera from direct sunrays; store film in cool place or refrigerator, when shooting in tropics; keep magazines under shade and protected by white bag; if possible use adjustable register pin cameras and adjust the pin to maximum steadiness value, which will also produce minimum camera noise;
(iv) use of telephoto lens on hand-held camera;	(iv) when using telephoto lens, mount hand-held camera on tripod;
(v) camera used on vibrating vehicle for travelling shot.	(v) on unsteady vehicles, fix camera very firmly, use wide-angle lenses and/or vibration absorbing devices.

TROUBLE: Camera runs too slow

PROBABLE CAUSES	REMEDIES
(i) power system terminals make faulty contact, or are worn or dirty;	(i) clean and/or tighten the terminals;
(ii) the battery charge is too low;	(ii) check voltage of power source; change batteries; if there is no spare battery, the charge may be momentarily raised by exposing run-down battery to sun; under extreme conditions use motor-car battery by connecting camera terminal to cigarette-lighter plug, but check beforehand that car battery voltage and that of camera motor are the same;
(iii) very cold weather affects mechanism lubrication.	(iii) use grease or oil supplied for the purpose.

TROUBLE: Camera runs too fast

PROBABLE CAUSES	REMEDIES
(i) voltage greater than it should be;	(i) use adequate voltage for camera motor;
(ii) speed control not in correct position;	(ii) check tachometer for proper speed;
(iii) wrongly adjusted speed control;	(iii) rotate speed control to proper value;
(iv) damaged motor rheostat;	(iv) send camera to repair shop;
(v) damaged camera mechanism.	(v) send camera to repair shop.

TROUBLE: Excessive camera noise

PROBABLE CAUSES		REMEDIES
(i)	lack of adequate lubrication;	(i) makers instructions regarding lubrication schedule should be strictly followed;
(ii)	wrongly adjusted pressure plate;	(ii) check whether shuttle or register pins graze or scrape film track between pressure and aperture plates;
(iii)	shutter running off-centre;	(iii) send camera to specialist workshop;
(iv)	damaged mechanism.	(iv) rotate motor flywheel by hand and check if noise comes from drive mechanism; send camera to specialist workshop.

TROUBLE: Loops are lost

PROBABLE CAUSES		REMEDIES
(i)	loops too short;	(i) check threading in camera; adjust film loops to correct size;
(ii)	damaged shuttle claws or register pins;	(ii) verify that there is no damage to any of the faces of the shuttle claws and/or register pins;
(iii)	faulty perforation in raw stock.	(iii) check perforation of raw stock, if necessary by return to supplier.

TROUBLE: Film damaged while travelling through camera

PROBABLE CAUSES		REMEDIES
(i)	dirty or scratched aperture plate;	(i) remove aperture plate and clean it carefully; if its surface is scratched it must be replaced by a new one;
(ii)	dirty or scratched pressure plate;	(ii) remove pressure plate, clean rollers and edges as well as front face;
(iii)	faulty threading;	(iii) check that threading has been effected correctly;
(iv)	film scratched in magazine or in its travel through camera.	(iv) check that magazine is clean and verify the state of rollers.

TROUBLE: Fogged film

PROBABLE CAUSES		REMEDIES
(i)	wrongly adjusted magazine light-traprollers;	(i) check seat of light-trap rollers on magazines; after loading magazine keep film inlet and outlet slots from direct light;
(ii)	faulty sealing of magazine lids;	(ii) after loading magazine check that lids seal effectively and that they fit properly into their flange seats;
(iii)	camera access door not correctly sealed or misadjusted;	(iii) check that camera access door seals correctly;

PROBABLE CAUSES	REMEDIES
(iv) faulty attachment of magazine to camera top;	(iv) check that magazine is correctly seated on camera;
(v) reflex viewfinder with open eyepiece while taking;	(v) while shooting, always keep reflex viewfinder eyecup covered by the eye; when shooting with both eyes away from finder, close the tube with the protection device;
(vi) light leaking in through faulty mountings on lens turret;	(vi) when using only one lens on a turret, cover the other lens housings with their protection caps;
(vii) shutter remains open for too long at the end of a take.	(vii) when working with reflex camera, at the end of each take close the shutter to the viewing position to avoid bright light filtering through to the film, thus fogging the first few frames of the next take.

TROUBLE: Unsteady images or uneven running

PROBABLE CAUSES	REMEDIES
(i) loops are too small;	(i) adust loops to dimensions specified by makers;
(ii) line voltage drops (fluctuations);	(ii) check voltage with voltmeter when camera is running under full load; verify AC frequency with a frequency meter;

TROUBLE: Unsteady image or uneven running

PROBABLE CAUSES	REMEDIES
(iii) damaged motor;	(iii) before shooting, run motor separately from camera to make sure that it is working properly;
(iv) camera running in cold conditions;	(iv) run camera for a few minutes without film since many cameras need warming up before shooting;
(v) film roll wound too tightly;	(v) check that film roll in magazine is neither too tightly nor too loosely wound on core;
(vi) magazine take-up belt too tight;	(vi) loosen or change belt;
(vii) faulty loading of magazine;	(vii) check the loading of raw stock into magazine; check that roll seats properly on core; check that length of film roll is not greater than magazine capacity as this may cause grazing against magazine walls;
(viii) film roll edges grazing magazine walls.	(viii) if film has to be rewound in darkroom before loading, take special care that the side faces of the roll are perfectly flat and smooth, as any ridges are likely to graze against magazine walls.

K

293

TROUBLE: *Image intermittently out of focus*

PROBABLE CAUSES		REMEDIES
(i)	some fault in the exposure mechanism;	(i) send camera to a specialized workshop to check that the aperture and pressure plates, and the intermittent drive, are properly adjusted;
(ii)	film base has shrunk;	(ii) check camera with another type of film;
(iii)	faulty lens mounting or seating;	(iii) examine lens mountings and seats carefully.

TROUBLE: *Film intermittently fogged*

PROBABLE CAUSES		REMEDIES
(i)	magazine not loaded in complete darkness;	(i) check light seal of darkroom or changing bag;
(ii)	light allowed in through reflex viewfinder;	(ii) take care to close reflex viewfinder tube after each take; when shooting with the sun behind the camera, be extremely careful that light does not penetrate through eyecup;
(iii)	camera lets light in when stopping.	(iii) at the end of a take, many cameras overexpose and fog the last few frames as the motor freewheels to a stop; to avoid this effect spoiling a take, wait a few seconds after the order to cut before switching off the camera.

TROUBLE: Ghost images

PROBABLE CAUSE	REMEDY
(i) shutter is out of synchronism with intermittent movement.	(i) send camera to specialist workshop.

Panning trouble chart

FAULT: Pan travel jerky throughout

PROBABLE CAUSES	REMEDIES
(i) inadequate or faulty tripod head;	(i) check working condition of head, if possible use gyro or gear head;
(ii) unsteadiness of operator during pans.	(ii) maintain body stability throughout pan, balance turning of body with camera rotation.

FAULT: Pan travel jerky at the beginning or end

PROBABLE CAUSE	REMEDY
(i) inertia is overcome jerkily.	(i) start panning slowly and increase speed gradually; at the end of pan reduce panning speed gradually; to overcome inertia effects, use a gyro head.

FAULT: Frame out of level at end of pan

PROBABLE CAUSE	REMEDY
(i) tripod out of level.	(i) when setting up the tripod, rotate the camera 180° and check levelling of head throughout rotation.

FAULT: Stroboscopic effects during panning

PROBABLE CAUSE	REMEDY
(i) exposure time incorrect in relation to panning and to position of elements in scene; excessively narrow taking angle.	(i) shoot the same take from a wider angle.

FAULT: Pan stops short

PROBABLE CAUSE	REMEDY
(i) static scene at end of pan not shot.	(i) before and after a pan, shoot a static scene to allow the spectator's eyes a rest; this also facilitates editing.

FAULT: Image distortion at edge of frame

PROBABLE CAUSE	REMEDY
(i) use of extreme wide-angle lens.	(i) avoid panning with very wide-angle lenses.

FAULT: Blurred pans

PROBABLE CAUSE	REMEDY
(i) camera was panned too fast.	(i) when panning on a static scene, e.g. a landscape, rehearse the shot beforehand to obtain the most natural panning speed; if a poor tripod head makes slow smooth pans impossible, raise camera speed to 32 f.p.s.

FAULT: Subject goes out of frame during pan

PROBABLE CAUSES	REMEDIES
(i) faulty framing;	(i) when panning on a fast moving subject, keep it framed so that half of the screen area remains empty ahead of it;
(ii) incorrect panning speed in relation to the speed of the subject;	(ii) keep panning speed proportional to the movement of the subject;
(iii) panning action not previously planned.	(iii) if the subject zigzags or moves in a complicated pattern, establish reference points and rehearse the scene before shooting.

FAULT: Unrealistic displacements of subject in frame

PROBABLE CAUSE	REMEDY
(i) excessive panning in following a subject over a uniform background.	(i) when panning on a subject moving over a uniform background (e.g. planes in cloudless sky), do not attempt to pan abruptly so as to keep the subject in frame, as this will only tend to produce an apparent unrealistic movement of the subject itself.

8

TABLES

FORMULAE

Weights and Measures

Millimetres $\times$ 0·03937 = Inches
Inches $\times$ 25·40 = Millimetres
Feet $\times$ 0·3048 = Metres
Kilograms $\times$ 2·2046 = Pounds
Pounds $\times$ 0·4536 = Kilograms
Grams $\times$ 0·03527 = Ounces
Ounces $\times$ 28·3495 = Grams

Ohm's Law

$$\text{Watts} = \text{Volts} \times \text{Amperes}$$

$$\text{Watts} = \frac{\text{Volts}^2}{\text{Ohms}}$$

$$\text{Volts} = \text{Amperes}^2 \times \text{Ohms}$$

$$\text{Volts} = \text{Watts} \times \text{Ohms}$$

$$\text{Amperes} = \frac{\text{Volts}}{\text{Ohms}}$$

$$\text{Amperes} = \frac{\sqrt{\text{Watts}}}{\text{Ohms}}$$

$$\text{Ohms} = \frac{\text{Volts}}{\text{Amperes}}$$

$$\text{Ohms} = \frac{\text{Volts}^2}{\text{Watts}}$$

Exposure and lens formulae

$$\text{Shutter Opening} = \frac{\text{Frames per second} \times 360°}{\text{Exposure Time}}$$

$$\text{Exposure Time} = \frac{\text{Frames per second} \times 360°}{\text{Shutter Opening}}$$

Depth of field

$$\text{Nearest Distance in focus} = \frac{H \times D}{H + (D - F)}$$

$$\text{Farthest Distance in focus} = \frac{H \times D}{H - (D - F)}$$

H = Hyperfocal Distance
D = Object-camera distance
F = Focal length

CHARACTERISTICS OF CERTAIN ANAMORPHIC SYSTEMS
(*Note*. All focal lengths require division by 2 to give the effective horizontal angle.)

Trade name	*Country of origin*	*Characteristics*
Alexcope	Argentine	Uses aspect ratio of 2·55 to 1 with magnetic sound track and 2·33 to 1 with optical sound track. The system comprises 2 sets of Bausch & Lomb primary lenses coupled to anamorphic Cinepanoramic. Focusing is effected mechanically on both lenses.
Cinemascope	U.S.A.	2·55 to 1 and 2·33 to 1 aspect ratios. Optical system designed by Bausch & Lomb comprising integral block lenses with 35, 40, 50, 75, 100 and 152 mm focal length. Focusing is effected by a ring on the mounting.
Cinepanoramic	France	2·33 to 1 aspect ratio. Anamorphic lens for coupling to standard primary lens. The focusing ring admits the insertion of a lever for hand adjustment. Employed in Europe under different patent names.
Dyaliscope	France	2·33 to 1 aspect ratio. Anamorphic coefficient: 2. Integral block anamorphic optical system with focal lengths of 40, 50, 75 and 100 mm. There are also anamorphic models for coupling to primary lenses. Block systems are focused with only one lever. Coupled systems must be focused individually at primary and anamorphic. The makers of this lens have recently introduced a variable focus (zoom) anamorphic system with focal lengths from 35 to 140 mm, at f3·5.
Naturama	U.S.A.	2·33 to 1 aspect ratio. Standard primary lenses coupled to anamorphic "Cinepanoramic". Single control synchronized focus adjustment.
Panavision	U.S.A.	Anamorphic coefficient: 2. Aspect ratio of 2·35 to 1. Fairly recently developed anamorphic lenses with a high resolution, and distortions completely corrected. Block mounted for focal lengths of 35, 40, 50 75, 100, 150 and 210 mm. Aperture f/2·3 except for 100 mm (f/3) 150 mm (f/3·2), and 210 mm (f/5·6). Supplied with mountings for NC and BNC Mitchells.

300

Trade name	Country of origin	Characterisics
Pictoscope	U.S.A.	Optical system made up with normal primary lenses and anamorphic "Pictoscope" lens for coupling, supplied in three models: N° 600, 630 and 670. Each anamorphic model covers a certain range of primary lenses.
Scanascope	U.S.A.	Anamorphic system for coupling by means of special mount. Works with primary lenses from 40 to 100 mm.
Ultrascope	Germany	Anamorphic coefficient: 2. Block system for 50, 85, 135, 300, 400 and 600 mm focal lengths. Two focus adjusting rings calibrated in meters and in feet. There is also a 40 mm wide angle Ultrascope and a 300 m lens of 76–300 mm at f/5·6.
Totalscope	Italy	2·33 to 1. Anamorphic coefficient: 2. This system consists of Taylor & Hobson primaries to which a Cinepanoramic anamorphic system is coupled. Either with individual focus adjusting, or equipped with special mechanical device for synchronizing focus adjustment.
Vistarama	U.S.A.	2·66 to 1 aspect ratio. Anamorphic coefficient: 2. Optical system comprising standard primaries and Vistarama anamorphic system for coupling.
Iscomorphot	Germany	Block unit with focal lengths of 50, 75 and 100 mm. Focus adjusted with only one lever, and with minimum focusing distance of one metre (3 ft.) with use of attachments.
Totalvision	France	Anamorphic coupling lens. To be used with 40, 50, 75 and 100 mm primaries. Includes sunshade. Standard specifications.
Agascope	Sweden	Anamorphic factor: 2. Block unit, with focal length of 46, 75 and 105 mm. Focus and iris controls can be readily connected to control knobs. Excellent resolving power.

WINDINGS AND TYPES OF CORES USED IN SOME 35 mm CAMERAS

Make	Capacity	Type of core	Winding
Arriflex 35	200–400 ft.	2 inch	emulsion in
Akeley Sound	400–1000 ft.	2 inch	emulsion out
Bell & Howell Eyemo	100–400 ft.	93 mm spool 2 inch	emulsion in
Cameflex	100–200–400 ft.	2 inch	emulsion out
Came '300 Reflex Eclair	1000 ft.	2 inch	emulsion out

WINDINGS AND TYPES OF CORES (*continued*)

Make	*Capacity*	*Type of core*	*Winding*
Mitchell BNCR, BNC, NC, Standard and Mark II	400–1000 ft.	2 inch	emulsion in
Newall	400–1000 ft.	2 inch	emulsion in
Newman Sinclair	200 ft.	Special core (25 mm)	emulsion in
Parvo Debrie Mod. L.	400 ft.	Special core (50 mm)	emulsion out
Super Parvo Debrie	1000 ft.	Special core (78 mm)	emulsion out
Technirama	1000–2000 ft.	2 inch	emulsion in (1000 ft. magazine) emulsion out (2000 ft. magazine)
Twentieth Century Fox	1000 ft.	2 inch	emulsion in
Vinten Windsor	400–1000 ft.	2 inch	emulsion in

SURVEY OF ZOOM LENSES
FOR 16 MM MOTION PICTURE CAMERAS

Make	*Zoom range*	*Focal length*	*Maximum aperture*
Angénieux	1:4	17–68 mm	F/2·2
Angénieux	1:4	17½–70 mm	F/2·2
Angénieux	1:4	12–50 mm	F/2·5
Angénieux	1:4	20–80 mm	F/2·5
Angénieux	1:10	12–120 mm	F/2·2
Angénieux	1:20	12–240 mm	F/4·8
Som Berthiot Pan Cinor	1:4	17½–70 mm	F/2·4
Som Berthiot Pan Cinor	1:4	25–100 mm	F/3·5
Som Berthiot Pan Cinor	1:5	17–85 mm	F/2
Som Berthiot Pan Cinor	1:5	17–85 mm	F/3·8
Canon	1:4	25–100 mm	F/1·8
Canon	1:8	15–120 mm	F/1·3
Canon Zolomatic	1:10	15–150 mm	F/2·4
Canon	1:11½	15–170 mm	F/2·5
Elgeet Zoom Navitar	1:4	20–80 mm	F/1·8
Schneider Variogon	1:5	16–80 mm	F/2
Traid Twenty-Eighty	1:4	20–80 mm	F/2·5
Vario-Switar	1:4	18–86 mm	F/2·5
Wollensak	1:3	20–60 mm	F/1·8
Zeiss Vario Sonnar	1:6	12·5–75 mm	F/2

SURVEY OF ZOOM LENSES
FOR 35 MM MOTION PICTURE CAMERAS

Make	Zoom range	Full length	Maximum aperture
Angénieux	1:4	35–140 mm	F/2·2
Angénieux	1:4	35–140 mm	F/3·5
Angénieux	1:4	25–100 mm	F/3·5
Angénieux	1:10	25–250 mm	F/3·2
Angénieux	1:10	24–240 mm	F/2·6
Canon	1:4	45–200 mm	F/2·8
Voigtlander	1:2·5	36–82 mm	F/2·8
Som Berthiot Pan Cinor	1:4	38·5–154 mm	F/3·8
Som Berthiot Pan Cinor	1:4	38·5–154 mm	F/2·4

RECOMMENDED PRACTICE FOR TELEVISION SAFE TITLE AND SAFE ACTION AREAS IN 16 & 35 MM MOTION PICTURE FILMS

	Width in.	Height in.
16 mm Safe Title Area	0·294	0·221
35 mm Safe Title Area	0·633	0·475
16 mm Safe Action Area	0·331	0·248
35 mm Safe Action Area	0·713	0·535
16 mm TV Station Projector Aperture	0·379	0·284
(16 mm TV Transmitted Image Area	0·368	0·276

APPROXIMATE WEIGHT OF SOME 16 MM CAMERAS (BASIC UNIT)

Camera	lbs.
Arriflex Mod. ST	6½
Arriflex Mod. 16 M	12
Arriflex Mod. BL	18
Auricon Cine Voice	12
Auricon Pro 600	21
Auricon Pro 600 Special	15
Auricon Super 1200	32
Beckman & Whitley R-16.E	11
Bell & Howell Filmo	7¼
Beaulieu	4
Paillard Bolex	6½
Debrie CX-16	16½
Eastman Kodak Reflex Special	24
Eclair N.P.R.	18
Eclair Cameflex 16/35	13
Mitchell SSR-16	18
Pathe Webo	4½

APPROXIMATE WEIGHT OF SOME 35 MM CAMERAS

Camera	Weight lbs
Mitchell and Newall	
Camera, lenses and case	50
Accessory case with contents	50
Two 1000 ft. magazines and case	49
Synchronous motor in case	37
Standard tripod with friction head and pan handle	39
Newall Blimp, complete	95
Arriflex IIC	
Camera, lenses and accessories in large camera case	50
Camera with variable speed motor for forward and reverse drive, lenses, matte box and 400 ft. magazine	13
400 model Blimp	47
1000 model Blimp with camera, motor and 1000 ft magazine	129
Eclair Cameflex CM3	
Camera, lenses, accessories and 400 ft. magazine in carrying case	45
Camera with motor, magazine and three lenses in turret	13
Cameblimp	110
Eclair Came 300 Reflex	
Camera case with camera and viewfinder	193
Camera ready for shooting	177
Bell and Howell Eyemo	
Model Q (less motor and magazine)	12
Model K (with one lens)	11

35 MM CAMERA APERTURE SIZES

Aperture	Width ins.	Height ins.
Academy Aperture	0·868	0·631
Full Aperture	0·980	0·735
Cinemascope Aperture	0·868	0·735
Panoramic Aperture	0·868	0·447
Techniscope Aperture	0·868	0·373
Vistavision Aperture	1·485	0·991
Technirama Aperture	1·496	0·992

SHUTTER OPENING AND EXPOSURE TIME FOR VARIOUS 16 MM
MOTION PICTURE CAMERAS RUNNING AT 24 FRAMES PER SECOND

Make	Shutter opening	Time
Arriflex Mod. ST	180°	1/48
Arriflex Mod. 16 M	180°	1/48
Arriflex Mod. BL	180°	1/48
Auricon Cine Voice	173°	1/50
Auricon Pro-600	173°	1/50
Auricon S. 1200	173°	1/50
Beckman & Whitley R-16E	180°	1/48
Bell & Howell Filmo	204°	1/44
Paillard Bolex H-16 Reflex	130°	1/65
Eastman Kodak Cine Kodak Special	165°	1/52
Eastman Kodak Reflex Special	170°	1/51
Eclair N.P.R.	180°	1/48
Eclair Cameflex 16/35	200°	1/44
Maurer Mod. 150	235°	1/37
Mitchell 16	235°	1/37
Pathe Webo & 16-AT/BLT	180°	1/48
Tolana Sincroflex	200°	1/44
Tolana Sonoflex	200°	1/44
Traid 805 Fototracer	204°	1/44

SHUTTER OPENING AND EXPOSURE TIME FOR VARIOUS
35 MM MOTION PICTURE CAMERAS RUNNING AT 24
FRAMES PER SECOND

Make	Shutter Opening	Time
Arriflex IIB & IIC	180°	1/48
Arriflex Techniscope	200°	1/44
Bell & Howell M. 2709	170°	1/51
Bell & Howell Eyemo	160°	1/54
Cameflex CM3	200°	1/44
Came 300 Reflex	180°	1/48
Mitchell Standard & H.S.	170°	1/51
Mitchell NC & BNC	175°	1/50
Mitchell Mark II	180°	1/48
Newall	175°	1/50
Newman Sinclair A.K.	160°	1/54
Technicolor Technirama	175°	1/50
Vinten Everest II	170°	1/51
Wall	170–190°	1/51–46

Features	Beaulieu R-16E	Beckman & Whitley CM.16	Debrie CS 16	Debrie CX 16	Eastman Cine-Kodak Special II	Kodak Reflex Special
100 ft. daylight leading spools.	×	×	×	×	×	×
200 or 400 ft. external magazines.	×	×	×	×		×
200 ft. film chamber					×	
1200 ft. external magazines		×				×
Single system optical sound						
Single system magnetic sound		×	×			
Reflex shutter viewing	×		×			×
Beam-splitter reflex viewing		×			×	
Spring drive motor.					×	
Electric motor	×	×	×	×	×	×
Pilot-pin registration		×				
Fixed shutter	×	×	×	×		
Variable shutter					×	×
Continuous drive movement		×				
Built-in light meter	×					
C Mount lenses	×	×	×	×		×
Turret	×		×		×	×
Monitoring viewfinder						
Tachometer						
Noiseless running	×	×	×	×		
100 ft. daylight loading spools	×	×	×	×	×	×
200 or 400 ft. external magazines	×	×		×		
200 ft. film chamber			×			
1200 ft. external magazines	×	×				
Single system optical sound			×			
Single system magnetic sound					×	×
Reflex shutter viewing					×	×
Beam-splitter reflex viewing					×	
Spring drive motor					×	
Electric motor	×	×	×	×	×	×
Pilot-pin registration	×	×				×
Fixed shutter					×	×
Variable shutter	×	×	×	×		
Continuous drive movement						
Built-in light meter					×	
C Mount lenses	×		×	×	×	×
Turret	×	×	×	×		×
Monitoring viewfinder	×	×				
Tachometer		×				
Noiseless running				×	×	×

SHUTTER EXPOSURE TIME AT 24 FRAMES PER SECOND FOR DEBRIE PARVO L AND 58, AND SUPER PARVO CAMERAS

Shutter Opening Calibration	Angle	Exposure Time
Parvo L and 58		
1	20°	1/432
2	41°	1/220
3	62°	1/141
4	83°	1/106
5	104°	1/84
6	125°	1/69
7	150°	1/57
Super Parvo V and AN		
1	25°	1/345
2	46°	1/187
3	66°	1/130
4	87°	1/97
5	112°	1/77
6	140°	1/61
7	180°	1/48

INTERMEDIATE AND HIGH SPEED CAMERAS

Make	Film mm	Max. Speed f.p.s.	Capacities ft.	Features
Eclair GV 16	16	200	100	Pilot pin, variable shutter, numbering device, designed for research and industrial purposes.
Fairchild H.S. 108	16	14,000	100	Rotary prism camera, eight side prism, two timing marker lamps, adjustable aperture (8 or 16 mm format), high speed motor, several speed ranges according to voltage applied.
Fairchild H.S. 401	16	8000	400	Rotary prism camera, magnetic brake, complete auxiliary equipment.
Fastair H.S.	16	600	200	Built to withstand acceleration forces. Choice of 3 film magazines: 50, 100 and 200 ft.
Fastax WF1.	16	16,000	100	Rotary prism camera, two motors, neon timing light, automatic switch, direct viewing and focusing.
Fastax WF2.	16	18,000	400	Same as above.

Make	Film mm	Max. Speed f.p.s.	Capaci- ties ft.	Features
Fastax WF3.	16	8000	100	Same as above.
Fastax WF3.T.	16	6000	100	Same as above.
Fastax WF4.	16	9000	400	Same as above.
Fastax WF4T.	16	6000	400	Same as above.
Fotomatic Traid 560	16	200	200	Governor-controlled 24 v. motor, built-in radio interference filters and heaters.
Fotoscorer Traid 200	16	200	400	28 v. DC or 115 v. AC. Rotary disc shutter, exposure 1/1000 sec.
Fototracer Traid 805	16	64	1200	Designed for observing rocket test or long-run applications. Trip switch, four speeds, "C" type mounting, 200° shutter, 28 v. motor.
Hy-Cam	16	6000	100	Rotating prism camera with disc shutter, "C" mount lenses, interchangeable film magazines, very portable unit.
Nova	16	10,000	100	Rotating prism camera, seven configurations, interchangeable aperture, 1,200 ft. external magazines, interchangeable prism.
Pentazet	16	3000	100	Rotating prism camera, direct viewing, 35 mm, f. 2·8 standard lens, 125 mm f. 2·8 complementary lens, 220/380 V. special motor, 300 f.p.s. minimum speeds.
Photo-Sonics 16 mm 1a	16	300	100	Pilot-pin movement, 24 v. DC motor, very rugged design.
Photo-Sonics Mod. 1.D.	16	3000	1200	Rotating prism camera, reflex viewing, safety switch, timing lights, interchangeable shutter.
S.D.S. 6050	16	200	200	110° f/1·5 periphoto lens, two 12,000 rpm camera drive motors, rotary disc 36° shutter, GSAP lens mount.
Wadell, H.S.	16	3000	400	Rotating prism camera, viewfinder with parallax correction, relay operated cut-off switch, supplementary gear trains for special motors, electronic flash synchronization, double timing lights, external magazines.

Make	Film mm	Max. Speed f.p.s.	Capacities ft.	Features
Traid Fotopak/15	16	100	50	Developed especially for cramped spaces, 28 v. DC governor-controlled motor, variable shutter, weighs 2¾ lbs.
Bell & Howell 2709	35	200	1000	See Chapter II, Sect. B.2.
Bourdereau U.R.	35	1000	1000	Disc shutter-rotating prism combination, two main sprockets, magnetic tachometer, removable aperture plate, 110 v. 2-phase, 4 H.P. AC drive motor.
Bourdereau GV	35	300	1000	140° variable shutter, three lens turret, registration pin movement, 400 and 1000 ft. interchangeable magazines, 110 or 220 v. AC motors.
Cinerama Mod. H-35	35	300	1000	Pin registration, reflex viewing, intermittent movement, variable speed transmission, modular design, remote control receptacles, timing lights, trouble free interlock system.
Debrie Cine Theodolite	35	100	400	Incorporated in a theodolite, with a very long focal lens, marking device, frame size of 24 × 36 mm, horizontal film travel.
Debrie Gux	35	300	1000	Special design mechanism, top mounted magazine with meter counter, very compact construction.
Debrie Speedex	35	240	1000	16–240 f.p.s., 24 v. DC motor or 100 and 220 AC, registration pin movement, 132° interchangeable shutter.
Debrie Speedo	35	240	1000	Very similar features.
Debrie G.V.	35	240	400	Electric motor or hand-crank option, interchangeable shutter, registration pins, direct focusing.
D.M.N. Milliken	35	250	1000	Dual film movement, pilot pins, rackover viewing system, 120° adjustable shutter, electrical brake, 24 f.p.s. minimum speed, antivibration film transport system.

Make	Film mm.	Max. Speed f.p.s.	Capacities ft.	Features
Eclair GV. 35	35	120	400	Shutter adjustable between 0 and 160°, 24 to 120 f.p.s., viewing on detachable viewfinder, 2 double feeding claws movement, with 2 double pilot claws. 27 v. or 220 v. AC motor, neon marking device.
Fastax WF5	35	6000	100	Rotary prism camera, reflex viewing, two motors, double timing lights, bayonet lens mount, variable aperture.
Fototracker Traid 75A	35	80	400	Designed for airborne recorder, quick speed change gears, variable shutter, 28 v.DC motor, 100 ft. daylight spools.
Mitchell High Speed	35	128	1000	Two-claw pulldown with two register pins, rising and falling front, rackover focusing system, viewfinder with parallax correction, etc.
Newman Sinclair H.S.	35	120	200	Electric motor drive, lens accommodation from 9·8 mm, approximate size 20 in. × 8 in. × 12½ in.
Photo-Sonics 2A	35	200	100	Very rugged design, pilot pin movement, 24 v. DC motor.
Pentazet 35	35	40,000	50	Rotating mirror camera, variable apeture, 45 mm. f.2 standard lens, 350 mm, f.2.8 complimentary lens very compact size.
Vinten H.S. 300	35	275	1000	Adjustable shutter between 0° and 170°, pilot pin registration, parallax-corrected viewing, two-speed gearbox to cover range from 50 to 275 f.p.s.
Photo-Sonics 1A	70	400	80	Pin-registered movement, 24 v. DC or 110 v. AC motor, frame height 0·218 in.
Photo-Sonics 1B	70	400	1000	Pin registered movement, 24 v. DC or 110 v. AC motor, frame height 0·218 in. top mounted magazine.

35 mm MOTION PICTURE CAMERAS EMPLOYED IN SOME COUNTRIES

	Mitchell Reflex	Mitchell Mod. NC	Mitchell Mod. BNC	Super Parvo Debrie	Came 300 Eclair	Arriflex	Cameflex	Vinten	Other makes
Argentine	X	X		X		X	X		
Brazil		X		X		X	X		
Chile		X				X			
England	X	X	X			X	X	X	X
France	X	X	X	X	X	X	X		X
Germany	X	X	X			X	X		X
Italy	X	X	X	X		X	X	X	X
Japan	X	X		X		X	X		X
Mexico	X	X				X	X		
Poland		X		X	X	X	X		X
Spain	X	X	X	X		X	X		X
Sweden		X		X		X	X	X	X
Uruguay		X				X	X		X
U.S.S.R.		X	X			X	X		X
U.S.A.	X	X	X			X	X		X

CAMERA OPERATOR'S CHECKING LIST BEFORE SHOOTING

1. Camera firmly installed and levelled.
2. Enough raw stock for the programmed take.
3. Connections effectively made and correct voltage.
4. Film correctly threaded.
5. Clean aperture plate.
6. Safety switch in *on* position.
7. Footage counters set to zero.
8. Selected lens properly mounted and adjusted.
9. Filter (if needed) in correct position.
10. Camera in taking (not focusing) position.
11. Monitor viewfinder corrected for parallax and adjusted to lens to be used.
12. Sunshade correctly selected for the lens to be used, and equipped with its proper masks.
13. Tripod head controls in position.
14. Shutter opening properly set (variable shutter models).
15. Motor selected for the required speed.
16. Motor and camera must have been warmed up.
17. Magazine belt adjusted.
18. Camera movement should have already been tested.

Cameras	Available motors
Mitchell BNC Model	Synchronous, 3-phase, 220 v. AC. Interlock, 3-phase, 220 v. AC. Multi-duty 220 v. AC or 96 v. DC. Variable Speed (8 to 24 f.p.s.) 110 v. AC or DC.
Mitchell NC Model Standard and High Speed	Synchronous, 3-phase, 202 v. AC. Variable Speed 12 v. DC. Variable Speed 110 v. AC. High Speed with rheostat control (24–120 f.p.s.) 110 v. AC, 96 v. DC, 220 v. AC. 3-phase M.D.
Bell & Howell Standard	Westinghouse interlock, 32 v. DC. 12 v. DC. 24 v. DC. 110 v. AC or DC. H.S. 110 v. AC. Richardson (Animation) 115 v. AC.
Bell & Howell Eyemo	Synchronous, 110 v. AC–60 c/s Universal Var. Speed. 100 v. AC. Field 12 v. DC. Field 24 v. DC.
Cameflex CM3	Synchronous, single phase 110 v. AC. Synchronous, 3-phase, 220 v. AC. Non-synchronous 3-phase 220 v. AC. Non-synchronous 110 v. DC. Transistor controlled. Constant speed (8 to 40 f.p.s.), 8 to 12 v. DC, and 24 v. DC. Manufactured by Kinotechnique, Paris 220 v. AC. Model with magnetic circuit breaking. 24 v. DC. Field. 12 v. DC. Field. 6/8 v. DC. Standard (55 W).
Arriflex IIB, IIC	Standard Model, 18/16 v. DC. 20/24 Synchronous 115 v. AC 60 c/s. Animation 24 v. with special unit to adapt it to 110 v. AC. Cinekad synchronous 220 v. AC. N.C.E. Animation 115, v. AC. Reverse Mod. 16. v. DC.
Debrie Super Parvo	Synchronous, 220 v. 3-phase AC. Interlock, 220 v. AC. Synchronous, 110 v. AC. Field 24 v. DC.
Camé 300 Reflex Eclair	Synchronous, 3-phase, 220 v. AC 50 c/s (24 f.p.s.) Synchronous, 3-phase, 220 v. AC 60 c/s (24 f.p.s.) Field (variable speed) (22 to 26 f.p.s.) 25 v. DC.

ARRIFLEX FITTING CHART GUIDE FOR TAYLOR HOBSON LENSES SERIES III COOKE SPEED PANCHRO

This chart guide indicates any interference of the taking lens by the other lenses on the turret.

Lens in taking position	Fitting
18 mm with filter holder	Must be used single mounting
18 mm without filter holder	Ditto
25 mm with filter holder	Ditto
25 mm without filter holder	75 mm must be used without filter holder and sunshade. 100 mm must be removed.
32 mm	Ditto
40 mm	Ditto
50 mm	Ditto
75 mm	100 mm must be used without filter holder and sunshade.
100 mm	75 mm must be used without filter holder and sunshade.

35 MM MITCHELL & NEWALL CAMERAS

FITTING CHART GUIDE FOR TAYLOR HOBSON LENSES SERIES III COOKE SPEED PANCHRO IN TURRET

This chart guide indicates any interference of the taking lens by other lenses on the turret

Lens in taking position	Fitting
18 mm with filter holder	25 mm with filter holder and 100 mm can only be mounted in the opposite (not adjacent) position.
18 mm without filter holder	100 mm can only be mounted in the opposite position.
25 mm with filter holder	18 mm and 100 mm with filter holder can only be mounted in the opposite position.
25 mm without filter holder	Ditto
32 mm	Ditto
40 mm	No interference occurs at either the adjacent or opposite mounting positions.
50 and 75 mm	Ditto
100 mm	At the shorter focusing distances the gear of the 100 mm lens, if mounted in the position adjacent the 18 mm lens, will foul the filter holder of the 18 mm lens.

313

CAMERA EQUIPMENT RENTAL DIRECTORY

West Coast
Birns & Sawyer Cine Equipment Company, 6424 Santa Monica Boulevard, Hollywood 38, Calif.
F & B/Ceco Inc., 6446 Santa Monica Boulevard, Hollywood 38, Calif.
Gordon Enterprises, 5362 North Cahuenga Boulevard, North Hollywood, Calif.
Hollywood Camera Company, 6838 Sunset Boulevard, Hollywood 28, Calif.
Hollywood Camera Exchange Ltd., 1607 Cosmo Street, Hollywood 28, Calif.
Lloyds Camera Exchange , 1612 North Cahuenga Boulevard, Hollywood 28, Calif.
Mark Armistead Incorporated, 1041 North Formose, Hollywood 46, Calif.
Masterlites Cine Rentals Inc., 7277 Santa Monica Boulevard, Hollywood, Calif.
Tech-Camera Rentals Inc., 6450 Santa Monica Boulevard, Hollywood 38, Calif.
S.O.S. Photo/Cine Optics Inc., 6331 Hollywood Boulevard, Hollywood 28, Calif.
Traid Corporation, 17136 Ventura Boulevard, Encino, Calif.

Mid-West
Behrend's Rental Corporation, 161 E. Grand Ave., Chicago 1. 111.
Masterlite Rentals of Arizona, 834 N. Seventh St., Phoenix, Ariz.
Producers Services Incorporated, 2519 Maple Avenue, Dallas, Texas.
Jack Frost, 234 Piquette, Detroit, Mich.
Victor Duncan & Company, 234 Piquette, Detroit 2, Michigan.
Syncron Corporation, Wallingford, Connecticut.

East
Camera Service Centre, 333 West 52nd St., New York, N.Y.
F & B/Ceco Inc., 315 West 43 St., New York, 36, N.Y.
F & B/Ceco Inc., 51 East 10th Ave., Hialeah, Florida.
General Camera Corporation, 321 W. 44th St., N.Y.
General Camera Corporation, 2945 N.E. 2nd Ave., Miami, Florida.
National Cine Equipment, 209 W. 48th Street, New York 36, N.Y.
The Camera Mart Inc., 1845 Broadway, New York 23, N.Y.
S.O.S. Cine Optics Inc., 602 West 52nd Street, New York.

Jack A. Frost, 6 Shawbridge, Toronto, Canada.
Toronto Camera Exchange Limited, 293 Church Street, Toronto 2, Ontario.

Don Long (Cinematography) Ltd., 11 Moxon Street, London W.1.
Samuelson Film Service Ltd., 303 Cricklewood Broadway, London N.W.2.
Mole-Richardson (lighting equipment only), Chase Road, London N.W.10.

Chevereau, 20 Rue de La Chine, Paris 20.
Mole-Richardson, 28–28 bis. Rue Marcelin-Berthelot, Paris.
Caliop, 12 Rue St-Fiacre, Paris 2.

Mole-Richardson, Vía del Velodromo 68–74, Roma; Vía Pestalozzi 18, Milano.
Vicenzo Mariani, Via Baldo degli Ubaldi 226, Roma.

Mole-Richardson, Gustavo Fernandez Balbuena 13, Madrid (2)
Albiñana, Encarnacion 24, Barcelona.
Arturo Gonzalez P.C., José Antonio 66–2° Izq. Madrid 13.
General Organizacion, José Antonio 464, Barcelona (15)
Eduardo Perez Climent, Breton de los Herreros, 56, Madrid (3).
Felix Duran Aparicio, Pinos Alta, 3, Madrid (20).

Samuelson International N.V., Building 67, Schiphol Airport, Amsterdam.

GERMANY
Mole-Richardson, Hofangerstrasse 78, Munchen 8.

GREECE
Mole-Richardson, 60 Vasilissis Sofias Ave., Athens.

PUERTO RICO
Wialliam Moraski, Film Center Bldg., San Juan.

ARGENTINE
Alex Film Laboratories, Dragones 2250, Buenos Aires
Delta, S.C.A., Bernardo de Irigoyen 745, Buenos Aires.
Estudios Lumiton, Bme Mitre 2349, Buenos Aires.

URUGUAY
Carrillon Films, Justicia 2106 Ap. 1. Montevideo.
E.P.C. Bartolome Mitre 1356 Piso 3, Montevideo.
Cinema, Andes 1382 2do Piso, Montevideo.
Tecnocine, Colonia 1171, Montevideo.

HAWAII
Motion Picture Service Center, 2424 Kalakaua, Honolulu.

MANUFACTURER'S DIRECTORY OF PROFESSIONAL MOTION PICTURE CAMERAS

Acmade X-Ray Cameras: Acmade, The Rank Organization, Woodger Road, Shepherds Bush, London, England.
Acme Process Camera: Producers Services Co. 1145 NO. McCaddin, Hollywood 38, Calif., U.S.A.
Arriflex 35, Arricord, Arriflex 16ST, Arriflex 16M, Arriflex BL, etc.: Arnold & Richter, A.G. Munchen, Turkenstrasse 89, W. Germany.
Auricon Cine Voice, Pro-600, Super 1200, etc.: Bach Auricon Inc., 6950 Romaine Street, Hollywood 38, California, U.S.A.
Askania Z, Askania Schulter, Askania H, Speed, etc.: Askania Werke, A.K. Berlin, Fridenau-Dundesalles 86–89, W. Germany.
Bourdereau High Speed Cameras: Ets. A. Bourdereau, 262 Rue de Belleville, Paris, France.
Beckman & Whitley Model 339, 357, etc. High Speed Cameras, CM-16, Newsreel: Beckman & Whitley, San Carles 3, California, U.S.A.
Beaulieu R-16 camera: 8 Quai du Marché Neuf, Paris 4, France.
Bolex Paillard 16 mm cameras: Paillard S.A. 1401 Yverdon, Suisse.
Bell & Howell Filmo 16 mm cameras and Eyemo 35 mm cameras: Bell & Howell Company, 7100 McCormick Road, Chicago 45, Ill., U.S.A.
Cameflex 16/35, 35 mm, Came 300 Reflex, Aquaflex, Camematic, Cameraeclair, Cameraflex, Reflex Radar Boresight, Data recording cameras, etc.: Federal Manufacturing & Engineering Corp., 1055 Stewart Ave., Garden City, New York, U.S.A.
Canon Scoopic 16: Canon Camera Co. Inc. 3,5 Chome Ginza, Chuoku-Tokyo, Japan.
Cinerama High Speed Cameras: Cinerama Camera Corporation, 11930 W. Olimpic Blvd., Los Angeles, California, U.S.A.
Eastman Kodak Special II and Kodak Reflex Special 16 mm cameras: Eastman Kodak Company, 343 State Street, Rochester 4, New York, U.S.A.
Eclair 16 mm (N.P.R.), etc.: Eclair International Diffusion, 12 Rue Gaillon, Paris, France.
E.T.M. 16 mm camera: Electro-Technique-Mecanique, 27 Rue de Constantinople, Paris, France.
Fairchild High Speed Cameras: Fairchild Camera & Instruments Corp., Robbins Lane, Syosset, L.I. New York, U.S.A.
Fastax WF5, WF7, WF8, WF9, WF10, WF18, etc. High Speed Cameras: Wollensak Optical Company, 850 Hudson Ave., Rochester 21, N.Y., U.S.A.

Mitchell BNC, NC, Standard, H. Speed, Mitchell 16, SSR-16, BFC, FC, Mark II, E: Mitchell Camera Corporation, 666 West Harvard St., Glendale 4, Calf., U.S.A.
Milliken High Speed Cameras, Underwater cameras, etc.: D. B. Milliken, 131 North Fifth Avenue, Arcadia, California, U.S.A.

Newall cameras and studio equipment: G. B. Kalee Limited, Rank Precision Industries Ltd., Mortimer House, 37–41 Mortimer Street, London, England.
Newman & Sinclair P.400, Auto-Kine Mod. G, N.G.: James A. Sinclair Co. Ltd., 3 Whitehall, London, England.
Oxberry Process Camera: Oxberry Corp., 25-15, 50th Street, Woodside, N.Y., U.S.A.
Pathé Webo & Model AT/BLT: Consortium Pathé, 14 Av. de la Place, Joinville-Le-Pont-Seine, Paris.
Photomechanism Cinefluorographic cameras: Photomechanism Inc. 15 Stepar Place, Huntingdon Station, New York, U.S.A.
Red Lake High Speed Cameras: Red Lake Labs. Inc., 271 Corvin Drive, Santa Clara, California, U.S.A.
Rodina, Moskva, Mir, Druzhba, Convas Avtomat, Panorama, Era, Rossiya, etc.: Mashpriberingtorg, Smolenskaia Sennaia 32–34, Moscow G-200, U.S.S.R.
Strobodrum Ultra-High-Speed Cameras: Impulsphysik, GmbH, 2000 Hamburg 56, Sülldorfer Landstrasse 400, Germany.
Super Parvo Color, Mod, V, Parvo L & 58, High Speed cameras, Simmer, Debrie CS16, Debrie CX16, etc.: Etablissements André Debrie, 111–113 Rue St., Maur, Paris, France.
S.D.S. Instrumentation & Special works cameras: Scientific Data Systems Aerospace Systems, 600 East Bonita Ave., Pemena, California, U.S.A.
Twentieth Century Fox Cameras: Twentieth Century Fox Studio, Camera Department, 10201 Pico Blvd., Los Angeles, California, U.S.A.
Technirama Technicolor Camera: Technicolor Corporation, 1033 N. Cahuenga Blvd., Hollywood, 38, Calif., U.S.A.
Vinten Windsor, Vinten Everest II, Vinten H.S. 300, etc.: W. Vinten Limited, Western Way, Bury St. Edmunds, Suffolk, England.
Waddel High Speed Cameras, John H. Waddel Inc. Syosset, New York, U.S.A.

GLOSSARY

A   ABERRATION. Defect in the rendition of a lens due to non-convergence of light rays in the focus and producing in the image a loss of definition and of likeness to original subject.

APERTURE. (i) Opening in the aperture plate in contact with which the film runs through the film gate. Thus the aperture frames the image produced by the lens on the film. (ii) Effective size of the lens opening through which light passes to the film. (also stop, f-stop, f-number, or T-stop.)

APOCHROMATIC. Lens designed for colour photography, in which the light rays of the three basic colours converge at the same focus,

AUTOCOLLIMATOR. Instrument for checking visually the rendition of a lens.

B   BARNEY. Flexible cover thrown over the camera as a substitute for a blimp. when sound filming. It reduces camera noise.

BEAM-SPLITTER PRISM. Used in some viewfinding systems to conduct a portion of the light away to the viewfinder while the remainder passes through to the film.

BIPACK SYSTEM. Method by which two films in contact run through the intermittent movement of a camera.

BLIMP. Rigid soundproof cover for a camera used when sound filming. Although camera noise is eliminated it allows full control from the outside.

C   CAMERA SLATE. Board, used at the beginning of takes, showing the shot number, number of take, and other details about the film.

CLAW. Metal tooth in the intermittent movement of a camera which engages with the perforation and pulls down the film frame by frame.

CRANE. A camera support of large size which carries the camera on a pivoted arm.

D   DIAPHRAGM. Variable control regulating light passing through the lens.

DISSOLVE. Where the end of one shot gradually merges into the beginning of another. A dissolve control is fitted to some cameras, but normally the effect is produced by optical printing in the laboratory.

DITTY BAG. Small bag hanging between tripod legs used for keeping accessories.

DOLLY, CRAB DOLLY. A wheeled vehicle for carrying the camera in tracking shots. Crab dolly allows oblique or sideways movements.

E   EMULSION. Light sensitive coating on one side of the film, identifiable as the dull side, which when inserted in the camera gate should face the lens.

EXPOSURE. Amount of light permitted to reach each frame while filming.

F   FILM PLANE. Position of the film in the gate indicated by the symbol $\ominus$ on the outside of the camera body.

FOCAL LENGTH. The distance from the centre of a lens to the surface of the film when the lens is focused on a distant object. This distance governs the angle of view of the lens—a short focal length lens has a wide angle of view, a long focal length lens has a narrow angle of view.

FOOTAGE COUNTER. Indicator showing footage run through camera while filming.

F.P.S. Frames Per Second. The number of pictures produced every second, as the film passes through the camera.

317

FRAME. A single picture on a length of cinematograph film. The frame line is the narrow line dividing frames.

FRAMING. Arranging the subject within the picture area.

G GATE. The part of the camera mechanism in which the film is held while each frame is exposed.

GIMBAL TRIPOD. Camera support providing stabilization of the camera independently of the support itself. It allows horizontally steady shots to be taken from a moving platform such as a ship at sea.

GRATICULE LINES. Lines engraved in the viewfinder to give a perimeter of the area covered by the camera lens, or measurements of screen proportions etc.

H HIGH SPEED CAMERA. Camera specially designed to film at shutter speeds much higher than normal.

HI-HAT. A small metal platform for mounting the camera a few inches above floor level.

I INTERCHANGEABLE LENSES. Lenses of fixed focal length which are dismounted and interchanged for those of other focal lengths.

INTERLOCKED MOTORS. Interlocking between two motors so that their rotors and stators are similarly positioned, thus providing constant synchronism of the intermittent movements of two cameras or one camera and a projector for rear projection work.

INTERMITTENT MOVEMENT. That part of the film drive mechanism which stops, positions, and advances the film frame by frame when the camera is running. It is the primary feature governing picture quality and steadiness, and must be of the very highest precision.

L LOOP. The film is formed into two loops, one either side of the intermittent movement to allow freedom of activity between that mechanism and the continuous film feed.

M MAGAZINE. Lightproof housing containing the film, usually detachable and holding 400 ft. (16 mm) or 1000 ft. of film (35 mm).

MATTE-BOX. Box shaped or bellows attachment fitted in front of the camera lens. It holds mattes (opaque cards) which mask off part of the image, and it also serves as a filter holder.

MONITOR TV VIEWFINDER. An externally mounted TV monitor attached to the viewfinder of a camera so that the image may be viewed by several persons simultaneoulsy. A recording device may be employed to play back the take immediately after shooting so that the scene may be checked before processing and printing.

O ORTHOCHROMATIC. Film sensitive to all colours of the visible spectrum except red.

P PANCHROMATIC. Film sensitive to all colours of the visible spectrum.

PARALLAX ERROR. An error from displacement of a viewfinder above or to one side of the taking lens in certain camera designs. The view through the finder differs slightly from that on the film, but the difference is only apparent when working at short range.

PERFORATIONS. Holes in cinematographic film by which sprockets and claw mechanism drive it through the camera.

PAN. An abbreviation of 'panoraming', swivelling the camera in a horizontal plane.

PAN AND TILT HEAD. Fitting on tripod for making pan and tilt movements. (*TILT*). Swivelling the camera in a vertical plane.

PILOT PIN. See REGISTER PIN.

PRESSURE PLATE. A plate behind the aperture which applies back pressure to hold the film accurately in the focal plane. The pressure plate incorporates rollers to minimize frictional contract with the film.

R RAW STOCK. Unexposed cinematograph film.

RACKOVER. Method used on some cameras whereby the entire film mechanism is displaced to one side so that a viewfinder can come into position behind the lens. The lens is racked back before shooting begins.

REFLEX VIEWFINDER. Optical system allowing viewfinding through the actual taking lens of the camera while filming.

REGISTER PIN. A precision pin in the film gate which engages with a perforation while each frame is being exposed, and withdraws when the film moves on. With the fixed pin (Bell & Howell system) the film seats itself on the pins for each frame. With the other system (Mitchell), the pins are inserted and withdrawn mechanically.

REGISTRATION. Ability to position each frame correctly and hold it steady while being exposed.

RHEOSTAT. An adjustable control used on 'wild' motors to vary the current and so the filming speed, over a continuous scale.

S SHUTTER. A device for obscuring light from the film while it moves on from one frame to the next. A variable shutter is one whose opening may be adjusted to let in more or less light.

SHUTTER ANGLE. A rotating shutter with an adjustable opening lets light through to the film according to any setting up to half its total area i.e. 180°. The shutter angle is the size of that opening, e.g. 90° (half open), 45° etc.

SHUTTLE. The moving part which carries the claws and gives them their reciprocating motion.

SIXTEEN MILLIMETRE. Smallest gauge of cine film used in professional film production.

SPROCKETS. Toothed wheels inside the camera which drive the film by engaging with the film perforations.

STARTING SWITCH. Switch for starting the camera motor.

START-UP. Inertia of the film at the beginning of a shot.

STOP-FRAME EXPOSURES. Single frames exposed at longer intervals than in normal continuous running.

SYNCHRONOUS MOTOR. Motor deriving its constant speed from a 50 or 60 cycle alternating current.

T TACHOMETER. Film speed indicator calibrated in f.p.s.

TELEMETER. Rangefinder.

TRIANGLE. Metal plate with slots for tripod legs, placed beneath a tripod to prevent the legs from spreading.

TRIPOD HEAD. Fitting on a tripod to accommodate the camera. It may be of friction, fluid or gyroscopic type.

TURRET (*Lens*). Rotating plate on the front of a camera holding two or more lenses which may be interchanged without removing them from the camera.

V VARIABLE SPEED MOTOR (or 'WILD MOTOR'). Motor that can be operated over a range of speeds by adjustment of a built-in rheostat. It is only used for shooting silent sequences which will be post-synchronized.

VERNIER (OR NONIUS). Device for obtaining fractional subdivisions of a normal scale.

VIEWFINDER. Any viewing system which gives a framed representation of the image as it will appear on the film.

W WEAVING AND BREATHING. Faults in film movement. Weaving is a shift of the film up and down or side to side. Breathing is a movement of the film back and forth in and out of the image plane.

Z ZOOM LENS or VARI-FOCAL LENS. Lens which varies its focal length over a continuous range by operating a control, so giving a greater or less magnified image.

INDEX